# Many People, Many Ways

# Many People,
# Many Ways

## Understanding Cultures
## around the World

Compiled by Chris Brewer and Linda Grinde

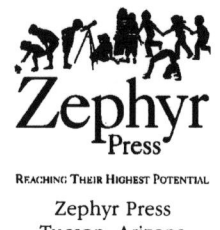

REACHING THEIR HIGHEST POTENTIAL

Zephyr Press
Tucson, Arizona

Many People, Many Ways
Understanding Cultures around the World

Grades 4–8
1995 by Zephyr Press
Printed in the United States of America

ISBN 1–56976–017–9
Cover design: David Fischer
Design and production: Dan Miedaner

Zephyr Press
P.O. Box 66006
Tucson, Arizona 85728–6006

---

Library of Congress Cataloging-in-Publication Data

Many people, many ways : understanding cultures around the world /
   edited by Chris Brewer.
        p.   cm.
     Includes bibliographical references (p. )
     ISBN 1-56976-017-9
     1. Ethnology.  2. Culture.  3. Multiculturalism.  I. Brewer,
Chris, 1953-    .
     GN316.M36  1995                                    94-47390
     306--dc20

---

# Dedication

## Jeanne R. Hamilton
### 1919–1992

Jeanne Reunauver Hamilton was born in Plains, Montana, to a pioneer family. Her aunt was the first white woman born in Montana Territory. Jeanne was an artist and teacher for nearly forty years. Her painting *Montana Landscape on the Line* is well known throughout Montana and more than 400 of her portraits hang in homes across the United States.

Throughout her life, Jeanne's goal in teaching art was to help people release their creativity. For many years children in the Flathead Valley looked forward to the summer art classes Jeanne traditionally held in her backyard. In 1981 she established the Creativity Center in Kalispell to further this aim and it continues today as a monument to the creative genius of Jeanne R. Hamilton.

C
O
N
T
E
N
T
S

# Acknowledgments

I would like to thank the following people, who
supported this Creativity Center project:

Milt and B. J. Carlson, Vern Wyman, Betty and Fred Bryant,
Shining Mountains Church, Bob Dombroski,
Alice Sowerwine, and Myrle Hoster.

The following people contributed ideas for the illustrations in this book:
Cas Still, Laurie Herron, and Emi Gregg.

## Creativity Center, Inc.

The Creativity Center, Inc., is a nonprofit arts education organization founded in 1981 by artist
Jeanne Hamilton. The center is dedicated to nurturing creativity in children and adults through
classes and workshops. Programs presented by the center promote visual arts, music, drama,
poetry, writing, video production, movement, and learning strategies. The Creativity Center
provides educational programs for public and private schools, businesses, service organizations, and medical institutions. Facilitators at the center are talented artists, educators, and
therapists. *Many People, Many Ways* was written and illustrated by nine of the center's
facilitators. Royalties from the sale of this book support The Creativity Center and help fund
projects in creative fields. Please feel free to contact us at the following address:

P.O. Box 227
Kalispell, MT 59903
(406) 755–4875

*M*any *People, Many Ways* is designed to help students and teachers explore the concept of culture and to appreciate the diversity of cultures in the world. Information about specific cultures is provided to facilitate thinking about why groups of people live in the ways they do. The nine cultures that are the focus of this book represent a variety of races and environments. We rely on you to bring in additional resources, perspectives, and information to fill out the picture. Our inclusion of information about religious beliefs and cultural conflicts is intended not to promote certain values or lifestyles but to encourage understanding and cooperation among people of the world.

Because we believe that people learn best through experience, each chapter offers ideas for activities that will help students experience aspects of various cultures. Activities in "What Is Culture" help students and teachers explore elements of culture. Activities in "The Global Community" emphasize common human experiences while acknowledging the creative and diverse approaches to life that people in various cultures have developed. These activities also promote effective intercultural communication skills. The posters that accompany this book are designed to inspire curiosity about the cultures and to provide images that project a meaningful aspect of each culture.

The chapters have been divided into categories that will help you access general information about particular groups of people and the land in which they live. The comprehensive range of curriculum topics will help facilitate an integrated curriculum (including language arts, history, science, social studies, mathematics, and the arts), and the activities are designed to include Howard Gardner's multiple intelligences. Using activities that reflect each intelligence will allow your students to express themselves in their most natural modes and will increase students' abilities in the areas they may need to develop.

P
R
E
F
A
C
E

# Contributors

CHRIS BREWER is an international teacher/trainer, author of five books, and a musician. She teaches cultural music appreciation at a community college and has great interest in multicultural education. She is president of the Creativity Center and compiler for *Many People, Many Ways*.

JOHANNA BANGEMAN—teacher, writer, artist, and mountaineer—has a Christian and Zen Buddhist background. She lives with her two teenagers in western Montana. She is currently working on her master's degree in interdisciplinary studies.

EMI GREGG is a Shoshone artist whose reproductions and wearable art grace museums and galleries throughout America, Europe, and Australia. She also teaches crafts. Emi learned her basic skills from her mother and grandmother at an early age. She strives to share her culture through her art and her teaching, nourishing the strength, beauty, and courage of Mother Earth and all her inhabitants.

B. J. CARLSON is active as a community volunteer, organizer, and fund raiser in several nonprofit agencies in the Flathead Valley of Montana. She and her husband have developed Earth Son, a center that focuses on Creation Spirituality.

CAS STILL is an artist and writer who lived and traveled for 20 years in Mexico and the Caribbean. Among her many island destinations was the Republic of Haiti.

LINDA GRINDE enjoyed three years on the big island of Hawai'i, where she told stories as an artist in the schools and directed plays at the Aloha Theater in Kona. Linda is an educational specialist with a master's degree in theater.

SUE MALLETTA taught primary school for 27 years in Montana. She especially enjoyed developing authentic cultural art projects for her students. Some of those projects are found in her chapter.

PAULA O'LESKA grew up in Poland, where she became an interpreter and a teacher of English. She is the founder and director of the Kinesiology Training Institute in New York City, where she teachers brain and body integration techniques.

# What Is Culture?

## Definitions and Elements of Culture

One of the definitions of culture in *Webster's Tenth Collegiate Dictionary* is the customary beliefs, social forms, and material traits of a racial, religious, or social group. If we were thinking about the people who belong to a cultural group, we might define them as a group of people facing similar challenges and a common environment who work together to create meaningful ways to survive and experience life.

People who share a culture develop a way of life that is passed from generation to generation through patterns of behavior. By "way of life" we mean farming and hunting techniques, food preparation, home-building techniques, courtship rituals, relationship patterns, modes of playing, community organization, religious practices, ethical systems, methods of education, systems of defense, and the myriad other everyday forms and beliefs that characterize people's lives.

A culture represents one viewpoint of the world that is shared among people. For example, depending on the cultural group you belong to, you might believe that

> *spirits inhabit objects in nature*
>
> *the soul returns in another form after death*
>
> *you are rewarded or punished according to the way in which you live your life*
>
> *people should share material wealth equally*
>
> *a social hierarchy is important*
>
> *accumulating wealth is important*
>
> *spiritual growth is important*

## Aspects of Culture

► Culture gives meaning to life. People with a common culture have established standards of right and wrong, explicit and implicit rules that help preserve values, social and political goals, means of recognition for accomplishments, explanations of the natural world and the human role in it, opportunities for relating to others, and roles in the community.

► Cultural values determine what is good, desirable, and worth retaining. These values delineate such things as personal honor, family and social structure, service to others, care of

*Only by addressing the need for a global perspective in their learning can we help students feel that they can make a difference, that they can face the future with confidence.*

*—Pamela Elder and Mary Ann Carr*

the land, provision for future generations, justice, attainment of wealth, and harmonious living.

▶ A cultural group develops traditions that teach children about the culture and that remind its members of the values held by the group. Examples of traditions are religious celebrations, festivals, national holidays, rituals, ceremonies, family activities, and social procedures.

▶ Culture includes the customs that support people's beliefs. We see evidence of our customs every day in the clothes we wear, the ways in which we prepare food, the ways in which we greet and treat one another, our family relationships, and our rites of passage.

▶ A cultural group establishes ways to govern itself, including developing procedures for determining leadership, establishing rules and laws, policing the community, adjudicating violations, and enforcing consequences.

▶ A cultural value might be a support system to care for its members. Most societies develop ways of providing for the needs of children and the elderly, caring for the ill, protecting members from harmful elements, and preserving established human rights.

▶ Culture includes the expression of a people's beliefs, values, feelings, and the meaning of life. Visual art, music, dance, drama, poetry, story, ceremony, and language are all modes for expressing meaning.

▶ Most cultural groups develop ways to play and bond. Play can involve sports, games, celebrations, and similar activities.

▶ Cultural groups develop ways to improve living conditions based on need, available resources, and their approach to and understanding of nature and science.

# *The Nature of Culture*

The culture of a particular group depends partly on the specific challenges facing that group and partly on its unique and creative responses to those challenges. Societies will change and adapt as their environment and needs change. Adaptations can occur through changes in genetics, social structure, or attitudes.

History shows that societies experience cycles that include periods of rapid change as well as long periods of slow change. Hunting and food-gathering peoples who have little contact with other groups change very slowly because of their isolation, small size, and the hard work necessary to survive.

Cultural diversity often causes confusion and even hostility among people of differing cultures. There may also be a positive exchange of perspectives, technology, and ideas when people with differing backgrounds meet. We are seeing more homogenization as industrialized cultures have become predominant. It is worth remembering, however, that not all individuals in a cultural group necessarily share all the beliefs of the culture. Sometimes people are intentionally excluded from or choose not to participate in cultural forms.

## Activities

1.  Look up several definitions of culture. Interview at least five people, asking them for their definitions of culture.

    ▶ Using the different elements found in your search and interviews, come up with your own definition of culture. Make a large poster that illustrates the elements of culture as you see them.

2.  Explore your own culture. Make a list of the traditions, customs, values, and beliefs your family practices. Find out the origin of each.

▶ Share one of your cultural traditions or customs with the class and have them participate in some way.

3. Make a list of six or more different forms of government in the world. Research the different forms and write a brief description of the structure and function of each.

   ▶ With your friends, develop and present a short skit that demonstrates how one of these forms of government functions.

4. Find out what indigenous means. Are there indigenous people living in the area where you live? If so, find out where they live and something about their culture. If there are no longer indigenous people in your area, find out how they used to live.

   ▶ Make a map showing the locations they inhabited and draw a picture showing something about their lifestyle. If you belong to an indigenous group, share with your friends some aspects of your culture.

5. Choose an indigenous culture somewhere in the world other than where you live and find out about the lifestyle of that group. How do they live? What things are important to them? How have "civilization" and "technology" made an impact on their lives?

   ▶ Make a documentary filmstrip about their lifestyle. Tape record or write out the narration for the filmstrip.

6. A folktale is a story about the lives of people of a particular area. Find a folktale from the culture of an indigenous group in your area. How is this folktale similar to and different from other folktales you have heard?

   ▶ With friends, dramatize the local folktale for the class.

*To survive, the human race must get along; it must solve its differences somehow as the stakes continue to rise. Today, every nation's security depends upon every nation.*

*—Pamela Elder and Mary Ann Carr*

5

*Exposing students to art from all over the world brings them the wonder of art in all its many forms, expands their knowledge of what art is, and shows them the variety of ways design problems can be solved.*

—*Jo Miles Schuman*

7.   After reading several folktales, think about the elements of a folktale.

   ▶   Make up a folktale about the people in your family, neighborhood, or city. Illustrate your folktale. Present your folktale in a book, or tape record your story.

8.   Choose one of the symbols of your culture. Find out what it means.

   ▶   Draw and color the symbol, making an attractive poster. In writing or in an oral presentation to your class, describe the symbol and explain how it originated, what it symbolizes, and why it is important to you and your culture.

9.   Get a copy of the latest census. What cultural group is the largest in your town, county, or state? Which group is the most powerful? What effects does this population have on other groups?

   ▶   Make a pie chart showing the various cultures in your town, county, or state as percentages of the whole population. Present your chart to the class.

10.   Find out if the various cultural groups in your area have activities, festivals, or celebrations that you can attend. If so, choose one to learn about and attend at least one of the activities.

   ▶   Present what you learned to the class. If possible, invite a member of the group to visit class and help you inform others about this cultural event.

11.   Explore the music of three cultural groups in your area. How does the sound of the music make you feel? Find out about one of the instruments used.

   ▶   Make one of the instruments. Play some music for the class and tell them about the music and the instrument you made.

12. Develop imaginary cultures. There will be two teams. Each team will decide what its culture believes about various aspects of life and will develop appropriate traditions and rituals. They will collect objects that they might use for their celebrations and other rituals.

    ▶ Bury the artifacts in sand or packing beads. Now each team becomes a team of archaeologists who find and identify the artifacts left by the other imaginary culture. As an archaeological team you must use the artifacts to decide what the culture you have discovered was like. See how closely your description of the culture matches what the other team had in mind. Prepare a display and an explanation of the artifacts you found.

13. Many people have had to leave their homeland or have been displaced within their own country. A few examples are Jews, American Indians, Aborigines, Tibetans, Haitians, and Puerto Ricans. Choose one group on which to become an expert. Learn about the old and new ways this group has of doing things. How have these people maintained (or not maintained) their culture?

    ▶ Write a story that an older person in this group might tell his or her grandchild about the old ways and the changes that have come about.

14. Use the last census records or do some research to find out how many cultures coexist in the United States. Discuss the contributions these cultures have made to the country as a whole.

    ▶ Make a list, mind map, or chart of celebrations, foods, music, and dance that people in the United States have adopted from various cultures.

15. When more than one cultural group live in the same area, they may have conflicts. Make a list of

*In an enlightened multicultural society, individuals would be able to choose to retain their original cultures as well as enrich their lives through exposure to other cultures. If Spaceship Earth is to survive, we will need to make real the vision of a multicultural society in which individuality is encouraged, a variety of cultures flourishes, and yet teamwork is demanded.*

*—Laurie King*

the cultural groups in your area. Learn about any conflicts that have arisen because of varying lifestyles. Choose one area of conflict.

▶ Write a proposal in which you offer some solutions to the problem. Share your proposal with the class through a dramatization, an oral report, or an editorial.

16. Watch a movie that makes a statement about cultural conflicts (see, for example, *West Side Story, Sarafina, The Emerald Forest,* or *Fern Gully*). Critique the problems and solutions in the movie, and support your critical observations.

▶ Write an essay that describes and explains your position.

17. Think about challenges to survival such as weather, isolation, food availability, predators, cultural conflicts, and potential natural crises (earthquakes, tornadoes, volcanic eruptions, tidal waves). Look at the environment in your area and think about the challenges your community faces.

▶ Make a mind map of these challenges. Then make a mind map of the challenges facing people who lived in your area five hundred years ago. Compare this map with the one of current challenges.

18. Make a list of the technological changes that have affected people's lives in a particular area or time. What are the advantages and disadvantages of these changes? Consider whether some of these changes occurred because of another culture's presence. Take a stand on whether the changes are beneficial or harmful.

▶ Prepare an oral presentation, with visuals, of your belief.

19. Find out about the landforms and ecosystems in your area.

▶ Using clay, such as polyform, make a model of your area. Show the shape of the land, major rivers or lakes, trees, plants, and animals. If you live in a city, include scale model buildings, parks, and natural features. Refer to the model as you discuss how your culture views nature and the care of natural resources.

20. Choose four items from the following list that you think your culture values: monetary wealth, physical health, spiritual health, education, entertainment, religion, sports, arts, relationships, material objects, nature, peace. Add other items you think have a high priority in your culture. Look at the advertisements in a popular magazine or local newspaper and categorize the ads according to the four items you selected. Which areas had the most advertisements? What does this say about your culture's priorities?

▶ Create a portfolio of the ads. Place them in the appropriate categories.

21. Learn a folksong commonly sung in your culture. What is the song about and why is it something your culture would sing about?

▶ Teach it to your class and discuss why it is important to your culture.

## Teacher-Directed Activities

1. As a class, make a list of environmental problems in your town, state, or country. In groups, select one issue per group and discuss what aspects of the culture have allowed the problem to exist. How has the problem affected the culture? How does the culture need to change to resolve the problem?

▶ Have each group present their findings in a report, a newscast, drawings or murals, mime, or a mode they choose.

*Students today need, above all, a sense of purpose, a belief in their personal future as well as the future of the world itself.*

*—Pamela Elder and Mary Ann Carr*

2. Make a list of the countries where students, their parents, or their grandparents grew up. Highlight a map to show the countries of origin. Discuss the movement of people around the globe and the blending of cultures.

   ▶ Have a culture day in which students bring food and wear clothes typical of their culture of origin.

## Activities for Exploring the Cultures in This Book

1. Imagine you have just been given passage to one of the countries or areas in this book and $5,000 to spend there. Where would you go and what would you see? What kinds of transportation would you take? What foods would you eat?

   ▶ Keep a diary of your trip, experiences, and reactions to what you experience.

2. Find three examples of manufactured products that use raw materials from one of the countries or areas in this book.

   ▶ Make a display of the items that require the raw material. Make a poster that explains how the raw materials are used.

3. Imagine you are an explorer about to go into one of the countries or areas in this book. Find the major geographical regions of the place you are going to explore. What are the climates of these regions? What geographical features separate these regions? What is the best way to travel in these areas?

   ▶ Make a map and a travel plan for your exploration. Include important survival items.

4. Write to an agency that helps students find pen pals and get the name of a pen pal from one of the cultures in this book.

▶ Write a letter to your pen pal. Tell about yourself, your life, and your culture. Ask questions about your pen pal's culture.

5. Choose one of the cultures in this book. Find out about the homes the people build.

   ▶ Choose a home and draw a floor plan of it. Use graph paper to make it easier. Draw a floor plan of a typical home in your culture. Compare the living areas in both floor plans. Based on the floor plans, draw some conclusions about the cultures.

6. Learn about the five Earth systems: heliosphere, atmosphere, hydrosphere, lithosphere, and biosphere. Select one of the countries or areas in this book.

   ▶ Write a descriptive analysis of each Earth system in that area.

7. Separate into two teams. Each team will make up several questions about cities or other geographical elements related to the cultures presented in this book.

   ▶ Do a map treasure hunt. The teams will exchange their lists of questions. Teams will find the answers, then find the cities or geographical elements on the map.

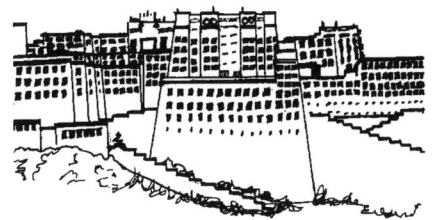

*It is our belief that the common survival of humanity in civility on this limited earth is going to require unprecedented levels of mutual understanding and tolerance and much higher levels of international and people-to-people cooperation than ever before. Our essential problem is how to develop an understanding of the commonality that we share in the problems of survival and stability. Like it or not, we have a common future. We will, all of us, have to work out our salvation in a moral context that encompasses the whole world.*

*—Soedjatmoko*

## The Global Community

As the world becomes more of a global community, its people must learn how to interact effectively with others from various cultural backgrounds. Our children must learn to communicate with people from diverse cultures in ways that honor the differences in culture while working toward common goals in a respectful manner.

The following activities build critical and creative thinking skills to help students and teaches explore various cultures. These activities can help students and teachers better understand global ecological interconnections, as well as develop more effective conflict-resolution techniques.

## *Activities – Geography*

1.  Select a latitude and list all the countries that touch that latitude, or choose a biome from the following list and find the countries that fall in those regions around the world.

    *tropical humid forest*
    *subtropical and temperate rain forest*
    *coniferous forest*
    *tropical dry forest*
    *temperate broadleaf forest*
    *evergreen forest and scrubland*
    *warm desert and semidesert*
    *cold winter desert and semidesert*
    *Arctic desert and tundra*
    *tropical grassland and savannah*
    *temperate grassland*
    *mountain and highland system*
    *island system*
    *lake system*

    Choose three of the countries and explore the lifestyles and cultures of the peoples that live in them. Do the similarities in climate create similarities in culture? How do the cultures differ?

    ▶ Make a mind map showing the common cultural elements, then create a mural or a collage based on the mind map. You may use any art materials to construct the mural or collage, but it may be interesting to use the materials that the people in the cultures you studied use to create their art.

2.  Find out more about the peoples presented in this book.

▶ Create a trivia game in which you and some friends each choose one of the cultures and make up twenty-five question cards about it.

## Activities – Ecology

1. Find out how much energy different countries around the world consume.

   ▶ After gathering your statistics, make a master chart or mind map of the results. The chart can be of any type, so be creative!

   ▶ Make a mural depicting the various forms of energy used and showing the different countries' consumption.

2. Select an animal species unique to one of the countries you have studied in this unit. Find out about it. How does it live? Does anything currently threaten its survival as a species? What?

   ▶ Make a mask of your animal. With others in your class, hold a life form forum. Each student will wear his or her mask and present the information learned as if the animal were speaking. Each animal will ask humans for what it needs to survive as a species.

*By helping children and families develop an appreciation for all cultures and backgrounds while retaining their own customs and ethnic identity, some progress toward harmony can be made.*

*—Judy Allen,*
*Earldene McNeill,*
*and Velma Schmidt*

## Activities – Heritage

1. Find an adult in the community who recently immigrated from another country.

   ▶ Write down at least ten interview questions about the person's culture of origin. Interview the person, and find an interesting way to present what you learn to your class.

2. Find out about different aspects of your cultural heritage.

   ▶ Put together a culture discovery box that includes implements used in your background

*In studying others, we study ourselves. There is much to be learned from all peoples; although there is a basis to human life common to all, it is our differences, subtle or marked, that make life interesting.*

*—Pamela Elder and Mary Ann Carr*

culture or cultures, books that might be read, items that represent the knowledge or intelligence that is important, and other objects you think represent the culture or cultures. Have some classmates go through the box and see if they can guess your cultural background. Have them tell what they think each object is used for.

3. Make a list of peoples that follow an agrarian or traditional lifestyle. Find out the details about how they live.

   ▶ Develop a project that shows others how they live. You may want to have a festival that celebrates a religious belief. You may want to put on a play, write and perform a song, write a short story—anything that imparts what you learned to your classmates without your merely telling them.

4. With other students, set up a committee to explore how the different groups presented in this unit maintain their cultural heritage. What religious rituals do they perform? How do they educate their children about cultural practices? What do they do in their day-to-day life? What obstacles to maintaining their heritage do they face, and how do they overcome those obstacles? Study your notes carefully to draw some general conclusions about how culture is maintained.

   ▶ Present to your class a lesson on how to maintain cultural heritage. Use examples from your studies.

5. Find out when and why people you have studied in this unit immigrated to the United States. What conditions existed that made them leave the countries of their birth? Where in the United States did they settle? What cultural contributions to their new country did they make? Then choose one of the cultures.

▶ Pretending that you are a person of your age immigrating with your family, keep a diary that details your family's decision to immigrate, the trip over, descriptions of the procedures you had to follow, where you lived, and any other entries you can think of.

## *Activities – Cultural Comparisons*

1. Find out what foods are eaten in each of the countries presented in this unit. Find out how the foods are grown, harvested, prepared, and served.

   ▶ With your class, hold a festival and serve a few dishes from each culture. Be sure you follow, as closely as possible, the traditional preparation and serving processes that each culture uses. You may want to invite another class or classes to share in your festival.

2. Explore the economies of the cultures studied in this unit. Find out from embassies, immigrants, and other sources how much certain household necessities cost and the average monthly wage for each culture. Find out the same information about the average mainstream household in the United States.

   ▶ By yourself or with some friends, draw up a household budget for a family from one of the cultures studied. Make a list of everything you need for the month, and decide how to spend the standard monthly wage. Draw up another budget that reflects a family in the mainstream U.S. culture. As a class, discuss the global division of wealth and the ways in which it affects the prevailing lifestyles in various countries.

3. When you have finished the unit, choose one of the children's stories.

► Alone or with some friends, choose one scene from the story you have chosen and create a charade of that scene. Present it to the rest of the class and see if the class can name the story and scene you are portraying.

4. Select one of the historical events you studied in this unit. Choose one of the participants in the event. For instance, you may choose to be one of the following:

*Lakota child being moved to the reservation*

*A U.S. soldier ordered to fire on the Lakota at Wounded Knee*

*A builder of King Tut's pyramid*

*Jewish child in Poland before World War II*

You may want to choose a person with whom you identify the least to understand a perspective that is quite different from your own.

► Keep a journal for one week from the vantage point of the historical figure you choose. Record the event as it happens, your feelings about the events, and your interactions with other people involved in the event.

5. Read about various aspects of the religions discussed in this unit. Think about the ways in which the beliefs you read about differ from and are similar to your own. Then pretend you are on a committee with one representative from each of three religions you have studied. The three groups have decided to share the rent for a building in which to worship. You are the facilitator in the negotiation process to decide who will use the building when and for what purposes.

► Work out a schedule that respects each group's needs to pray or meditate and hold other rituals and seasonal festivals.

6. Find songs from three different cultures represented in this unit. The songs should be on a

similar topic and should reflect the cultures' attitudes toward that topic: land, humanity, animals.

▶ Teach the songs to your class.

## Cultural Cooperation

1. Find out about the procedures the cultures presented in this book used to settle disputes and solve problems. Make an outline of one of the procedures.

    ▶ Choose a problem or a conflict that is occurring in your class now or one that keeps coming up. Choose two of the procedures you learned about and try to solve the problem or resolve the conflict using those procedures. Which worked better for you? Start a problem-solving file in which you keep the problems you solved and the techniques you used to solve them.

2. Alone or with some friends, explore a culture presented in this book in greater depth. Choose one aspect of the culture that you think would help other cultures.

    ▶ Write a proposal in which you suggest adopting that belief, practice, or attitude in your area of the world. How would people go about doing so? What would be the obstacles? What negative implications exist? How would you overcome them? After getting feedback from your teacher and classmates, try implementing your proposal in your classroom.

3. Select one of the environmental issues covered in this unit. With some classmates, review the issues.

    ▶ List the cultural practices that have contributed to the problem and how the problem affects the global environment. Share your lists with the rest of your class. Together hold

*The fate of the United States is inextricably bound up with the fate of the rest of the world. Despite the realities of interdependence, education is not keeping up with the new view of the world. Yet it may be the single most important task we face.*

*—Humphrey Tonkin and Jane Edwards*

a World Summit meeting with representatives from each culture represented in this book. They will create a master list of effects and solutions.

*Today's pluralistic world is rapidly becoming so complex, and the interaction among the world's peoples so entwined, that most major events require a broader view than was required in the past. Today a global perspective is needed to interpret the significance of events and the implications of decisions made by world leaders.*

*—Pamela Elder and*
*Mary Ann Carr*

## Overview

The South American coastal country of Brazil is largely covered with tropical rain forests, home to countless spectacular plants and animals. Here are more than 3,000 species of butterflies, piranha, 30-foot-long anacondas, 500 varieties of catfish, and the world's smallest deer. The Amazon River, which dominates not only Brazil but the entire

*Brazil was named for the triangular Brazil nut.*

*Brazil produces beef, sugarcane, cotton, and one-third of the world's coffee. Its forests provide prized hardwoods, latex from rubber trees, wax, and nuts. It has one-third of the world's iron ore reserves, bauxite, and manganese and is the world's largest producer of hydroelectric power.*

continent of South America, begins as a trickle in the high Andean mountains of Peru and empties into the Atlantic on the east coast of Brazil.

Brazil also includes hilly uplands, plateaus, and low mountains. One of the world's largest lava plateaus has created the dark purple soil that grows coffee so well. Along the eastern coast of Brazil, the highlands descend sharply to the sea in what is called the Great Escarpment. Brazil is also known for beautiful white sand beaches and excellent natural harbors.

## Historical Background

Lush and productive, Brazil was settled centuries ago by four groups of people that mixed to become the "Indians" Portuguese found there when they landed. The tribes often lived in isolation from one another and many developed their own languages. Today, two groups of native Brazilians may live next to one another but speak very different languages.

The history of Brazil's nonindigenous peoples begins in the 1500s, when Portuguese navigator Pedro Alvares Cabral landed on the South American coast and claimed the land for Portugal. Two weeks later he left, and thirty years later the first Portuguese settlement of Sao Vicente was founded. The Portuguese began to use the resource-rich land in ways new to the original inhabitants. They began to harvest and export large amounts of brazilwood, referring to the country as the land of Brazil in honor of this wood.

When the Portuguese discovered that sugar plantations would thrive on Brazil's northeast coast, they

began to export sugar. They enslaved the indigenous people and also imported West Africans as slave labor. The Portuguese and other Europeans developed additional industries, such as cattle ranching, rubber harvesting, and gold and diamond mining. Portuguese fortune hunters poured into the country. Recognizing the potential value of the land, other European countries sought to control Brazil. In 1630, the Dutch gained control of the sugar-growing regions for a brief time.

The advancement of French troops into Portugal in 1808 magnified Portuguese interest in Brazil. In fact, Portugal's royal court fled to Brazil and made it the seat of the Portuguese empire. Portuguese political influence was strong in Brazil for most of the century, though the reigning Dom Pedro declared Brazil independent of Portugal in 1822.

For 50 years Dom Pedro II, who took over leadership at age 14, ruled Brazil, and the nation prospered. War with Uruguay, Argentina, and Paraguay, however, was waged nearly constantly from 1850 to 1860. When a bloody five-year war with Paraguay began in 1865, Brazil expanded its military power. In the process of defeating Paraguay, Brazil became fragmented politically, and slavery was undermined. In 1889 the emperor was overthrown and a republic called the United States of Brazil was formed.

Ruled by governors who took turns as president, the new government, called the Old Republic, lasted until 1930 when the military took over the government, and Getúlio Vargas became president. Civil unrest forced him to declare a state of siege in 1937, and he was ousted by the military in 1945. Vargas was legally elected president in 1950, and the Second Republic began. Vargas remained Brazil's leader until 1954, when he committed suicide.

A series of new leaders ruled Brazil until the government was once again taken over by the military in 1964. For the next 20 years, various generals were elected head of state. In 1967 Brazil became the Federative Republic of Brazil. In 1985 Brazil elected a

*Brazilian rubber barons made great fortunes during the rubber boom. They used slaves to tap the rubber trees in the Amazon forests for the milky sap that produces latex, from which rubber is made.*

*The Amazon River system contains one-fifth of all fresh water on Earth. More water flows through the Amazon that through all the rivers of Europe added together. This major system has six times the volume of the Mississippi River. Athough it is not as long as the Nile, it is larger than the Nile in every other way. The Amazon is deep enough for ocean-going vessels to travel 995 miles upriver to Manaus in the heart of the Amazon Basin. These vessels could go another 1,000 miles with no danger of running aground.*

civilian leader, who cut the military budget, reduced the military's power, and turned some state companies over to private owners. President Itamar Franco gained the presidency in 1992.

## Activities

1. Research Pedro Alvares Cabral, the Portugese navigator who claimed the South American coast for Portugal in the 1500s. Who paid for his trip? What was its purpose? Was it successful or a failure?

   ▶ Make a map that shows Cabral's journey to and from the land that became Brazil.

2. Brazilwood was an early export from Brazil. Research brazilwood. What do the trees look like? How long is their natural life? What are the uses of brazilwood? Is it still an export of Brazil? What does the wood look like?

   ▶ After you learn about brazilwood, make a filmstrip illustrating what you learned. Write a script that you tape record or present when you show the class the filmstrip.

3. When the Portugese developed sugar plantations, they enslaved indigenous people as well as West Africans. Learn about growing sugar. Why is sugar grown on plantations? Why was slave labor used? Why is Brazil's northeast coast well suited for growing sugarcane? How is sugar refined?

   ▶ Write a story set on a Brazilian sugar plantation in the early years. Be sure to include slaves as well as other workers and the owners. People who read your story should learn about life on a Brazilian sugar plantation.

4. Research rubber trees. Learn about their life cycle and how the rubber comes from the tree. What is the process of making rubber? How was the process discovered?

▶ Make a large chart that shows the life cycle of rubber trees and how rubber is made.

5. Learn about Dom Pedro II. How did he become Brazil's ruler? What kind of person was he? What kind of leader was he? What important and interesting things occurred during his reign?

   ▶ With friends, develop skits that portray at least three important events in Dom Pedro's life. Be sure people watching learn about Dom Pedro from the skits.

6. Find out about Brazilian history. What do you think were the most significant events? What events changed the course of Brazilian history?

   ▶ Make a time line that shows the events and their effects. Illustrate your time line. Present it to your class.

7. Pretend you are a travel agent who has a client who wants to spend three weeks in Brazil. Learn about the cities, beaches, and special attractions a visitor should see. What foods should your client try? Avoid? What climate should she or he plan for?

   ▶ Plan the itinerary from the client's home to Brazil and back again. Find an attractive way to display the itinerary so you share what you learned with the rest of the class.

## *The People*

Fortune and misfortune have brought a variety of cultural groups together in Brazil. The native Indians were joined first by the Portuguese, who in turn imported three million Africans along with customs, music, and other cultural influences. Today Brazil is largely a blend of its Portuguese, African, and Indian heritages.

When slavery was abolished, European immigrants (mainly Italian) arrived to fill the work force. After the United States shut its doors to Asians in the 1920s, the

*Nine out of ten Brazilian cars run on alcool, a gasoline substitute made of fermented and distilled sugarcane.*

*Cowboys in Brazil are called* vaqueros *in the north and* gauchos *in the south.*

*Brazil has an educational TV channel, but most people watch the "Big Three" channels: Globo has variety shows, soap operas, and sports; Manchete features music and mini-series; and Record features talk shows and comedies.*

❖ ❖ ❖ ❖ ❖

*One of every ten Brazilians earns a living in the coffee industry.*

Japanese poured into Brazil. Sao Paulo today houses more than a million Japanese people, more than any other city in the world outside of Japan. Following World War II, Germans and Poles came in sizable groups and 50,000 more Portuguese arrived. Today Syrian and Lebanese immigrants are a major cultural addition.

The Portuguese first introduced Roman Catholicism to Brazil, and Catholicism is Brazil's official religion. But the Africans had their own religions, and voodoo practices were common to many of the native people. These spiritual beliefs have blended with Catholicism to form unique religions that weave the different belief systems together.

Brazil's large and still-growing population has generally been moving from impoverished rural areas to the cities, making these population centers swell. Slums, or *favelas,* also are growing and now surround the prosperous city areas. In Rio de Janeiro, one-quarter of the people live in favelas—most have no clean water or sanitation. Malnutrition and disease are major problems in Brazilian cities. Perhaps the saddest urban issue is the homeless children of Brazil: Of the country's 50 million children, 7 million have been abandoned by their families and live in the streets.

Throughout Brazil the people and their lifestyles vary greatly. Brazilians have names for the various attitudes of the groups of people. The bustling business *paulistas* of Sao Paulo are unlike the relaxed *cariocas* of the Rio de Janeiro beach areas and the romantic, imaginative *nordestinos* of the northeast contrast with the earthy *gauchos* of the southern plains. Despite their differences, Brazilians seem to accept one another and to appreciate the diversity in the same ways that they enjoy the array of plant and animal life found in their country.

## *The Amazon Indians*

Early Spanish explorers reported that the banks of the Amazon were densely populated. Though we may never know how many Brazilian natives there once

were, estimates are as high as five million. By the turn of the twentieth century, only 200 thousand Indians were left, and within another seventy-five years, barely half that figure remained.

The coming of European peoples presented the Amazon Indians with a critical challenge. The tribal people traditionally lived, as many still do, in a communal system, sharing land and resources. They cleared small plots of forest land for cultivation but moved to new areas before the soil was depleted, which allowed the forest to regenerate. The Europeans began dividing and selling the jungle land, often without taking into account the native peoples living there. Even today, the indigenous people are often given no notice that the rain forest they are living in will be cut down. Forced to leave their homes, some people move to other forest areas, while others go to the city. Neither choice ensures survival.

The Brazilian government has made attempts to provide protection for native peoples. The Service for Indian Protection was formed in 1910, and in 1961 the Xingu National Park was established as the first sanctuary for native peoples. Tribes from other areas were allowed to move into the reserve. Some tribes, such as the independent Xavante, spurned the government's efforts. Other peoples, such as the upper Xingu tribes, have accepted government assistance and moved into the protected reserve.

Native peoples have also begun to speak out for their rights. In 1989, the Kayapo discovered that the World Bank had funded a hydroelectric project that would flood vast areas of their land and destroy fishing. The Kayapo organized massive demonstrations and contacted the media. Their cry was heard, and the World Bank was forced to withdraw its support of the dam. The government arrested two Kayapo and an anthropologist, however, and charged them with violating Brazil's Foreign Sedition Act because they had appealed to the United States for assistance.

On the Xingu National Park, many families continue to live in oval huts made from palm branches and

*Most Amazon forest peoples can identify plants with useful purposes. Western medicine has adopted a number of rain forest plants for treatment of malaria, leukemia, and other diseases.*

*When the Portuguese arrived, Brazil had more than 700 distinct groups of Amazon Indians. By 1900 only 270 groups existed, and today as few as 180 remain.*

other local materials. The people's homes are simple but functional. Tribal activities are based on cooperation, sharing of resources, and sharing of work. An inherent part of the cultures has always been understanding and respecting natural systems. Many tribal children are taught to recognize hundreds of plant species and to know their uses as food, medicine, drugs, poisons, building materials, and others.

Amazon tribes are led by chiefs. The social system pays great attention to family relationships. The men of many tribes meet at night in the *maloca,* a community building and the focus of tribal life, to plan the next day, including the formal exchange of goods called *oolookee.*

Within the Xingu National Park are examples of ancient ways blending with modern technology to create new lifestyles. The Kraho tribe is seeking economic independence by raising a small herd of donated cattle. Other tribes, such as the Wauju, maintain their traditions of sustainable agriculture and trade crafts for steel axes, knives, scissors, matches, and aluminum pots. If you were to look at a map of Brazil, you would see that the small parcel of land set aside for native peoples is dwarfed by miles of land where the same people struggle to continue their traditional rhythm of life and survive the beat of the industrial drum.

## Activities

1. Learn as much as you can about the various groups who have immigrated to Brazil. Why did each group come to Brazil? What cultural artifacts did each group contribute to Brazilian culture?

   ▶ Make a very large map of Brazil on tagboard or poster board. Draw in landforms and geographical features. Show where in Brazil each group of immigrants settled, where they came from, and what they brought with them.

2. Within Brazil are unique religions that blend aspects of Roman Catholicism with native Indian and African religions. Learn as much as you can about Brazil's religions. What religious practices are unique, and where did they come from?

   ▶ With one or more friends, create and present a puppet show that showcases what you know about Brazilian religions.

3. Brazil has been called the Land of the Future because of its vast natural resources, yet many of its people are very poor. Research Brazil's economy and society. Why are so many people so poor? What might be done to change this situation? do you believe that Brazil is really the "land of the future"? Why or why not?

   ▶ Write an editorial that states and supports your belief about Brazil's future.

4. Learn about Brazil's slums, the favelas. What is life like for people who live in the slums? Can they improve their lives? Now learn about how wealthy Brazilians live. What effects, if any, do the lifestyles of each group have on the other group?

   ▶ Create a simulation based on what you learned about the Brazilian economy. Be sure that participants will learn about and experience important aspects related to Brazil's economic situation. Prepare a debriefing to follow the simulation. How did each group feel about their lives? About the other group? What do they predict might happen in Brazil in the future? Why do they predict that?

5. Brazilian native people may have numbered five million, but by the 1970s only 100,000 remained. Learn about these early Indians, how they lived, and why they died.

   ▶ Make an illustrated time line that shows significant events and estimated population numbers. Include your prediction of what the next 100 years holds for these people.

*There is a strong distinction in Brazil between rich and poor: two percent of the white population holds most of the country's wealth. African Brazilians and Indians suffer the most economically.*

*Brazil is paying a high price to harvest its natural resources: about 80 percent of the rain forest is now gone, and the soil cannot regenerate the great forests.*

❧ ❧ ❧ ❧ ❧

*The Atlantic coast rain forest once reached from Recife to Rio de Janeiro to Florianopolis, covering 400,000 square miles. This rain forest has been reduced to less than 5 percent of its original cover, and now exists mostly in steep mountainous regions. Every year a section of forest the size of Connecticut is destroyed.*

6. Become an expert on one of the Brazilian Indian tribes. Find out about how they live, where they live, and what is important to them.

   ▶ Create a board game that teaches players about the people.

7. Find out about Chico Mendes. What was he known for? How did he die? Why do you think he died in this way?

   ▶ Alone or with some friends, create a drama of the Chico Mendes story. Perform it for your class.

8. Find out about the Wauja land court case. What people were involved? What was the dispute about? What was the final decision? Do you think the decision was fair?

   ▶ Write a newspaper article or put on a television news show about the case.

## Wildlife and the Environment

If you were to take a walk through the wildlands of Brazil, you would find yourself surrounded by a spectacular abundance of plants and wildlife. Going for a swim in the Amazon River places you in the company of a vast variety of creatures—among them manatees, pink river dolphins, giant river otters, tiny water opossums called yapoks, dangerous electric eels, piranhas, sting rays, and millions of small tropical fish. If you were to swing through the forest canopy you would find 30 species of monkeys and hundreds of birds, from brightly colored parrots to the world's largest and smallest hummingbirds. But more than any other life form, you would find thousands of invertebrates—bugs! One scientist found more than fifty different species of ants on a rain forest tree.

To survive in the rain forest, animals have evolved unique methods of protection. For instance, the hoatzin bird's nickname is the stinkbird—it smells so

bad that potential predators don't even want to come near it. The beautiful red, yellow, and black coral snake manufactures poison that can kill an enemy in seconds. Other Amazon creatures work together for survival. The Azteca ant, for instance, lives on the swollen thorn acacia tree, which provides for all the ant's needs. The ants return the favor by protecting their host—whenever the ants feel something brushing against the tree, they fiercely repel the unwanted visitor, including vines and other plants.

Among the most biologically rich of all land on Earth is the Amazon Basin. Our understanding of the value of many Amazon species is not complete. We have not yet recorded all of the plant and animal organisms within this system, nor do we know their value to the ecosystem, to humans, or to our planet. We do know that the rain forest's vast plant life makes a major contribution to the maintenance of Earth's atmosphere.

Recent human use of Amazonian resources has resulted in extensive destruction to large tracts of the rain forest, including the plants and animals. It has been estimated that Brazil was losing 12.5 to 22.5 million acres of rain forest each year at the beginning of this decade. Many rain forest products such as Brazil nuts and rubber, can be harvested without harming the environment. Timber harvests, iron ore mining, gold mining, and beef production, however, result in total destruction of the rain forest and, in some cases, pollution to the waterways. Plant and animal species are losing their habitats and probably entire species face extinction.

Public awareness has increased protection of the spectacular Amazon rain forests, but this natural wonder, which has evolved over 70 to 100 million years, could be destroyed in a few years unless protection and management efforts increase.

Will the rain forests and the life within them survive? Perhaps only through human awareness and determination.

*Two-thirds of Brazil is covered by tropical rain forests. If you were to block off a four-square-mile patch of forest and inventory the life within it, you would find as many as 1,500 species of flowering plants, 750 tree species, 125 mammals, 400 birds, 100 reptiles, 60 amphibians, and 150 butterflies. About 500 varieties of catfish swim in Brazil's rivers, and more than two-thirds of the world's bird species live in Brazil, along with 200 kinds of snakes and perhaps two million species of insects.*

*A Brazilian legend
says that pink river
dolphins can take on
human form and
leave the water to
dance with women.
They wear hats to
cover their blowholes.*

❖ ❖ ❖ ❖ ❖

*Brazil's forests have
unusual creatures:
tapirs, hooved mam-
mals that are excellent
swimmers; piranha
fish, which can strip
the meat from a calf in
one minute; and birds
with eyelashes.*

❖ ❖ ❖ ❖ ❖

*Water lilies grow so
large in Brazil that
a child can lie down
on one.*

## Activities

1. Research the ways in which the rain forest contributes to the balance within the Earth's atmosphere.
   Then research the estimates of rain forest loss.
   Calculate the damages that might occur if the
   current rate of destruction continues. Find out
   what the greenhouse effect theory is.

   ▶ Make a large chart that shows your figures to
   your class. Explain the impact the destruction
   has on the planet as a whole; include the
   greenhouse effect theory as part of your
   explanation.

2. Learn about the multitude of wildlife in Brazil.

   ▶ Make a very large map of Brazil, and draw in
   representations of as many species as possible.
   Be sure to include creatures of the rivers and
   coastal areas.

3. Research Brazilian plants. Learn about their uses in
   medicine, the food industry, or chemical production.

   ▶ Interview someone who depends in some way
   on one of these products. Prepare at least six
   questions before the interview. Ask about how
   it was before the product was developed, how
   it is now, and what may happen in the future if
   the plant becomes extinct.

   ▶ Prepare a three- to five-minute news feature
   to present what you learned to the class.

4. Research the pink river dolphin. How large do
   they grow? Where are they found in the river?
   What do they eat? How long is their life span?
   What eats them?

   ▶ Write a story about the dolphin using the information from your research.

5. Find out about the animals of Brazil. Think about
   which different biological categories each would
   fall under.

▶ Using the categories you determine from your research, make a map or web of animals found in Brazil. Use a large piece of poster board or other sturdy paper. Collect photos, drawings, and other representations and use them to illustrate your map.

6. Find out what trees in your area are best for contributing to Earth's atmosphere. Then plant a tree and have a ceremonial dedication to the regeneration of Earth's atmosphere. Write a statement about its contribution to the atmosphere.

▶ Read your statement. With some friends, put on a play, sing a song, or create a mural to honor the tree, the atmosphere, or the Amazon rain forest.

## *Food, Festivals, and Celebrations*

Brazil's people celebrate frequently and in many ways, but no festival can compare to Carnaval. The celebration began in the city of Bahia, once Brazil's capital, to honor Lent. Today, all Brazil's major cities celebrate Carnaval, and both rich and poor leave their concerns behind and enter a fantasy world of costumes, dancing, and partying. City streets are filled with people and lavish parades. The samba plays a large role in the celebrations. Samba schools, which may have as many as 3,000 performers, are formed each year to create new samba music and dances that will be judged during the parades. The performers practice enthusiastically for many weeks, then compete for the championship title.

New Year's Eve is celebrated along Brazil's beaches in ceremonial homage to Iemanjá. This goddess of rivers and other waters in an imported West African religion has similarities to the Virgin Mary. Dressed in white, thousands of people come to the beaches with flowers, candles, and gifts for Iemanjá. Drums and dancing, fireworks and bells accompany the celebration. As the new year begins, the givers

*Coconut Blancmange*

*(4 servings)*
*1 cup unsweetened grated coconut*
*1 cup boiling water*
*3 cups milk*
*6 tablespoons cornstarch*
*1/4 teaspoon salt*
*1/2 teaspoon coconut flavoring*

*Combine the grated coconut and boiling water in a bowl and let stand for 15 minutes. Heat the sugar and milk together in a saucepan, stirring until the sugar has dissolved. Slowly bring to a boil. Strain the liquid from the coconut and mix in cornstarch, stirring until smooth. Add 1/2 cup of the boiling milk and stir. Return this mixture to the pan with the remaining milk and add salt. Cook until it thickens, stirring contantly. When thick, cook over low heat an additional 10 minutes. Then add the coconut flavoring and pour into a 4-cup mold or into muffin pans for small, individual servings. Refrigerate 3 to 4 hours until set. The unmolded dessert is often served with a chocolate or vanilla sauce.*

*Homes in the northeast of Brazil are made of dried mud, built up on a frame of woven sticks. Near the Amazon River, houses are built of timber and elevated on stilts, because the river floods regularly.*

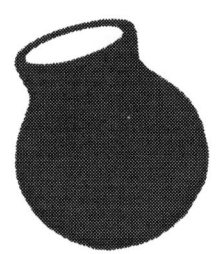

watch to be sure their gifts are carried out to sea—a sign that the goddess has accepted them and that the givers will be granted their wishes. It is a bad omen if the gifts return to the beach.

Brazil also celebrates national political holidays, such as that which honors Joaquim José da Silva Xavier. The holiday is known as Tiradentes because the hero is a dentist. He is honored as the father of Brazilian independence because he led the first revolt against Portuguese colonists in 1789.

Brazil's food, like its people, is a dynamic mix of Portuguese, Indian, and African cuisine. It includes *salgados,* salty foods sold at street-corner "launcheonettes," and *doces,* sweet foods, many of which are like the egg-based custards of Portugal and France. The national dish, *feijoada,* is traditionally served for lunch on Saturdays. It is made from black beans, sausage, beef, and pork and is served with rice, shredded kale, orange slices, and a manioc flour that has been fried with onion and egg. Brazil's answer to Coca-Cola is called *guaraná.* A favorite and common juice is chilled sap from a young, green coconut.

## Activities

1. Learn about Carnaval—when, where, why, and how was it first celebrated? How has the celebration changed over the years? What foods are associated with Carnaval? To share what you learned, choose one of the following:

   ▶ Create paper dolls dressed for Carnaval.

   ▶ Present a puppet show about Carnaval.

   ▶ With friends, present a skit about Carnaval.

2. Learn about Joaquin José da Silva Xavier and Tiradentes Day. What type of person was Joaquin? What made him a successful leader? What significant events led up to and followed the revolt in 1789?

▶ Pretend you are Joaquin writing letters to a friend before, during, and after the revolt. Include his feelings, hopes, and ideas in the letters.

3. Find out about the masks made in Brazil.

▶ Using materials similar to those the Brazilians use to make masks, create your own masks.

## Dances, Games, and Sports

The national sport of Brazil is *futebal,* or soccer, and the people support it with a passion. The world's largest soccer stadium, the Maracana, is in Rio de Janeiro and seats 200,000 people. Brazilian soccer fans can be so enthusiastic that a deep, nine-foot moat was built around the playing field in the Maracana to protect players and referees from over-zealous spectators. People around the world know the name of Pele, a native Brazilian and famous soccer player who began playing at age 15. Other famous Brazilian athletes are tennis star Maria Bueno and car racing champions Emerson Fittipaldi and Nelson Piquet.

Another Brazilian sport was originally a fight, disguised by African slaves as a dance. Forbidden to fight, the slaves added music and song to their fighting and called the dance the *capoeira*. Today this unusual sport and dance involves swinging and kicking in rhythm to music, with opponents never actually touching one another. Sometimes dancers hold knives and do elaborate back bends and agile foot movements.

Among the Xingu people, a traditional dance conveys the myth of the Jamarikumá Amazons. These legendary Xingu women fled their selfish husbands and were said to live in the jungle without men. Their story is conveyed in song and dance by women wearing bright paint and feathers.

A common Waúja dance occurs after the men's daily practice for war games, called *javari*. These

*Singer and songwriter Sergio Mendes was born in Brazil in 1941.*

competitions, held between neighboring tribes, involve a mock battle in which live opponents dodge blunted spears.

## Activities

1.  Research Brazilian soccer, its past and present. How does it differ from soccer as you or your friends play it?

    ▶ Construct a scale model of the Maracana. When you present the model to the class, tell what you learned about Brazilian soccer.

2.  Learn the myth of the Jamarikuma.

    ▶ With a friend, create a mural that illustrates the myth and the dance.

# Music, Art, and Architecture

The voices of Brazil's various cultures, especially the Portuguese, Indian, and African, have blended together to create a uniquely beautiful and rich musical heritage. Among the famous Brazilian styles are the bossa nova and the samba, rhythms that have become standard in jazz. Nowhere in Brazil is there lack of music, for the African drums beat their complex rhythms constantly, the Amazon peoples sing their stories, and every corner of the immense land has developed its own styles.

Among Brazilian classical composers, Heitor Villa-Lobos is perhaps the most prominent. His well-known works use Brazilian folk rhythms and melodies.

Brazilian arts and crafts include basket and fabric weavings, clay pottery, statuettes, leather designs and products, straw goods, hammocks, painted gourds, lace works, and art pieces of gold and silver.

O Aleijadinho, "the Little Cripple," was the most famous religious sculptor of the 1700s.

Many Amazon tribes paint beautiful geometric designs, symbolizing jungle creatures, on pots and their bodies. This is a very social art and an activity of great importance. Amazon people also use the brilliant feathers of tropical birds for headdresses, necklaces, and other decorations.

Jorge Amado is one of Brazil's most popular writers. Many of his novels are based on his early experiences in northeast Brazil. *Dona Flor and Her Two Husbands* has been translated into English.

A diversity of human talents can be seen throughout the land. In Rio de Janeiro, a 120-foot, 700-ton statue of Christ the Redeemer overlooks the city from Corcovado Peak. The coastal village of Parati contains so much superb eighteenth-century architecture that the entire town is preserved as a Brazilian national monument. In the town of Ouro Prêto (Black Gold), a visitor can see spectacular churches and homes built by those who made fortunes from the area's gold and diamonds. These and many other human creations are evidence of the creative and determined spirit of the people.

*The name Amazon comes from the Amazon warrior women of Greek legends. The Amazon River was supposedly named after these women by Francisco Orellana, who was attacked by female warriors on the river in 1541.*

## Activities

1. Research either the bossa nova or the samba. Where and when did it originate? How has it changed over the years? What is distinctive about it? What other music has been incorporated into it? What dance steps go with it?

   ▶ Make a presentation to the class that includes information, samples of music, and a demonstration of dance steps.

   ▶ Using samba rhythm write a song about the beauty of Brazil. Write it in Spanish, if possible. Perform it for your class.

2. Learn as much as you can about the geometric designs painted by some of the Amazon tribes. What materials are used? What do the designs symbolize? How are the designs made?

▶ Make a clay pot and paint geometric patterns on it. You can roll and coil polyform clay, which is available at art stores.

3. Collect examples of architecture you might find in Brazil today, including nineteenth-century colonial, Jesuit-style Baroque, and tin.

▶ Make a collage of the examples.

4. Choose three or four Brazilian poets. Find out a little about their lives and read several of their poems. Choose one poem.

▶ Read the poem aloud to the class and tell what you think the poem means. Ask your classmates what they think the poem means. Discuss your opinions.

# *Tchikao's Day*

Tchikao shivers slightly as he emerges from his morning river bath and shakes the water from his bare, coppery skin. He will return to the river after breakfast to fish with the men. Breakfast for Tchikao and his family consists of cakes his mother and sisters made the day before from cassava. The hut bustles with preparations for the last summer celebration before the rains come in September.

As Tchikao fishes with his father and other tribesmen, he thinks about his upcoming initiation as a man. In past years, this would have meant piercing his ears with an arrow shaft and gradually increasing the size of the opening until a large wooden disk could be inserted. This initiation rite is no longer done, but Tchikao's life will still change after he enters manhood. As an unmarried man, he will leave his family's home and sleep on the ground near a small fire in the center of the village. Tchikao will also be old enough to participate in log relays, a popular sport of the Kraho people and other Brazilian tribes.

As Tchikao and the men return to the village, their basketlike traps filled with fish, they sing a song

*During the winter months of July and August, little rain falls in the rain forest. Rain rarely falls in northeast Brazil, which has suffered a drought since 1977.*

about the great anaconda snake that lives in the river. At home Tchikao and his family admire their new baby. Painted with red dye and wearing bracelets and anklets of vine to ward off evil spirits, the baby is a welcome addition to the family.

Last winter one of Tchikao's brothers died of anemia, caused by a poor diet. White hunters have killed most of the region's deer, wild pigs, anteaters, and monkeys, so the Kraho cannot always find enough animals to feed the village. Many Kraho have died of smallpox, measles, and other European diseases.

Anemia will not be as common in the future, for Tchikao's tribe now owns 25 head of cattle. A communal people, the entire Kraho tribe owns and cares for the animals.

Kraho share everything in their village, even the job of governing. Each villager belongs to one of two political groups that take six-month turns governing the village. When summer is over, it will be Tchikao's family's turn to govern.

After dinner Tchikao and his family join the rest of the village in the central plaza. Tonight, as on most nights, the village people sit cross-legged on the soft sand and sing songs about the day, nature, and especially the sun. Later, the men will meet and plan the events of the next day. When the singing is over, the villagers make their way back to their homes. Climbing into his hammock, Tchikao soon falls asleep.

*Much of the Amazon Basin is unexplored. As recently as 1975, a 400-mile-long river was discovered by Brazilian mapmakers.*

## Activity

Think about some of the rituals your culture has for children to transition into adulthood. How are they similar to those of Tchikao? How are they different? How important do you think such rituals are?

▶ Choreograph a dance that represents at least two such rituals, one from Tchikao's culture and one for a similar transition from your own. Perform the dance for your class.

# How Averiri Made the Seasons and the Night

## *A Folktale of the Kampas Indians*

*The Kampas Indians wear a traditional dress called a kushma. They are especially skilled at spinning and weaving. They grow cotton and make their own cloth, which they dye in somber colors with vegetable dyes.*

In the time before this time, there was the earth and the sky and the river. There were villages and families. But there were no seasons and no night. The sky did not grow dark and there was no season when the rain fell or the river flooded. There was no time when the air warmed and the river slid back into its banks.

At this time, Averiri traveled the earth. He came to his sister's house and the women put out food. The neighbors came and they feasted on the plants of the land, the fish of the river, and the meat of the animals.

When the feasting was done, Averiri brought out his pipes, made of long hollow reeds bound together. Averiri blew into them and made music.

He made the sounds of monkeys swinging through the trees and the drumming rhythms of tree frogs. He played the screams of the macaws and the sounds of bat wings flapping. He made the whistles of forest insects and the hum of mosquitoes and put them to words and sang them. Playing and singing, Averiri made the night.

Then he made the sounds of thunder crashing and sang of the rain pounding and the river crashing over its banks. He made the sounds of feet as they sank into the sand and the melodic flowing of rivulets down the paths. With his music, Averiri made the wet season.

Taking the sounds of ripe fruit falling from high above the ground, he sang the rustle of grass with it, and put words to the sounds. He made the sounds of the hot winds blowing through the palms and sang of the fish as they swam through the quiet river. Averiri sang the song of the dry season.

And with his music, Averiri made the night and the seasons and the earth sing his songs.

## Activities

1. Many cultures have creation myths. Learn at least one of these. Compare and contrast "How Averiri Made the Seasons and the Night" with the myth you learned. How are the images in each similar? Different? How do the rhythms of language compare? The characters? The natural elements mentioned?

   ▶ Recite both myths for the class. Create art for visual aids if you wish. After you tell the myth, ask questions that will lead the class to compare and contrast the myths. If they miss important similarities or differences, point these out.

2. With a group of friends, brainstorm a list of the sounds you hear in various seasons.

   ▶ With rhythm instruments and simple flutes, create earth music for the seasons in your part of the world. Tape record your music or play it live for your class.

*Water hyacinths are gathered and burned by Indians and the ash is refined and used for salt.*

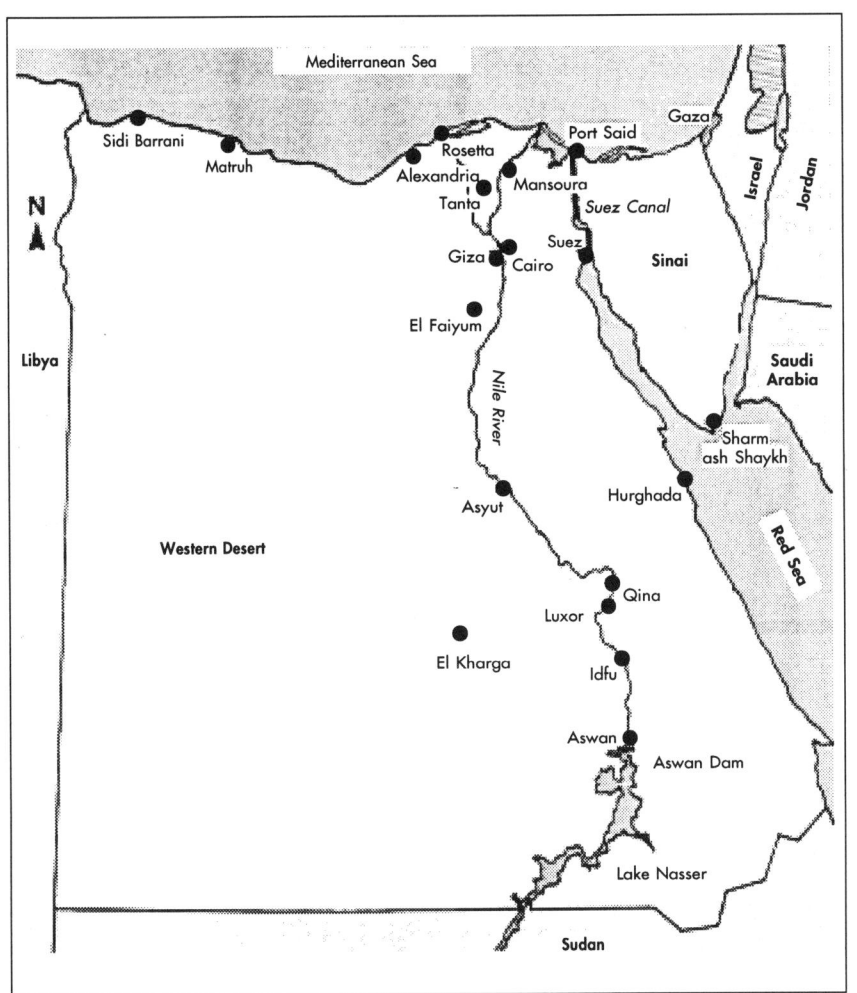

## Overview

**E**gypt is located in eastern North Africa. It is bordered on the north by the Mediterrean Sea and on the east by the Red Sea. The Nile River divides the country into the Libyan, or Western, Desert, and the Arabian, or Eastern, Desert. Oases are scattered throughout the Libyan Desert, and wadies, or dry river beds, are found in the east. Along the

By
Sue
Malletta

*The Egyptian people were among the very first cultures to develop a record-keeping system. The original hieroglyphics system had over 700 different pictures and symbols that have been found on state monuments, tombs, religious temples, and on papyrus.*

Red Sea, mountains rise to 7,000 feet above sea level.

To explore Egypt is to become fascinated by the rich human civilization that thrived in that country thousands of years ago. Despite harsh terrain and difficult weather conditions, the ancient Egyptians built magnificent structures, recorded their history, and lived in harmony with neighboring peoples.

## Historical Background

The site of one of the world's earliest civilizations, Egypt has a long and dynamic history. Human artifacts dating from 12,000 B.C.E. have been found there. Written records beginning in 3200 B.C.E. give insight into the ancient Egyptians, who settled along the Nile River and formed farming communities, created works of art, built sailing ships, and traded with their neighbors. Between 3200 B.C.E. and 333 B.C.E. Egypt was led by a series of ruling families called dynasties, which were usually headed by a pharaoh, or king.

Egypt was conquered by the Persians in 525 B.C.E., and the Persians were followed over the next 2000 years by other conquerors, among them Alexander the Great of Macedonia, the Romans, the Arab Moslems, and the Ottoman Turks. Egyptian culture, especially religion, has been influenced by each of these peoples.

The ancient religion faded when Christianity was introduced to Egypt. The Coptic Christians remain a religious minority. In about 640 C.E. conquering people brought the Islamic, or Moslem, religion to Egypt. Judaism also had its foundation near Egypt, and the Jewish people have a strong attachment to the region. Conflicts among people of these various

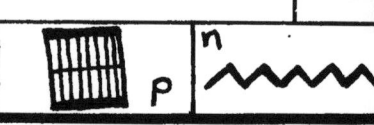

beliefs have haunted Egypt for years.

Hoping to use the area as a stronghold against the British, France invaded Egypt in 1798. Beginning in 1859 the French engineered and constructed the 103-mile-long Suez Canal, which linked the Mediterranean and Red Seas and magnified Egypt's strategic importance. In 1882 Great Britain took control of the canal and for 40 years occupied Egypt, then maintained a military presence along the Suez through World War II. In 1956 British troops withdrew and Egypt took control of the canal.

In 1948 the Jewish state of Israel was established in territory that Arab people claimed for themselves. Egypt and several other Arab countries immediately invaded, and border clashes continue to this day.

In 1953 the Egyptian army seized power and declared Egypt an independent republic. Since then changes in leadership and government have caused disunity and chaos in Egypt. Anwar al-Sadat and Menachim Begin were able to negotiate a peace accord in 1979, but Sadat was assassinated in 1981. Hosni Mubarak succeeded him as president.

Egypt's economy has suffered in recent years from high inflation rates and a large national debt. The discovery of oil fields in the Gulf of Suez, Sinai, and the Libyan Desert has significantly improved Egypt's finances, but because of ownership disputes over the Sinai Peninsula, revenue from oil production has not been consistent. The Suez Canal has also brought large amounts of money into Egypt, but political unrest has made the canal an unstable source of income as well.

## Activities

1. Egypt was the site of one of the world's earliest civilizations. What geographic and climatic conditions made this civilization possible? What other factors promoted the development of a civilization?

   ▶ After you learn why and how early Egyptian civilization developed, make a relief map of

*There were actually several Cleopatras in Egypt. The most famous one ruled Egypt as queen beginning in 51 B.C.E.*

✗ ✗ ✗ ✗ ✗

*King Tutankhamen became the ruler of Egypt at age nine.*

*The oldest blade tool site in Africa was at Kom Ombo in upper Egypt. The tools are estimated to have been made in 12,200 B.C.E. To date, no skeletons of the people who made them have been found.*

45

*Along the Red Sea, mountains rise to 7000 feet above sea level. The Sinai Peninsula, on the east, has belonged to Egypt throughout much of its history. The central location of this peninsula for trade and travel between continents has had great influence on Egypt's cultural development but has also been the source of unrest as people around the world fight for control of this strategic area.*

Egypt and the surrounding areas. Use a mixture of flour, salt, and water to show the landforms. Paint the map with water colors or thinned tempera. In the key to your map, include ways to identify the conditions and factors that promoted the development of civilization.

2. Since it is a very old and strategically located country, Egypt has been conquered and ruled by a variety of other countries. Learn about Egypt's colorful history, then select a period of 300 to 500 years you find particularly interesting.

   ▶ Make an illustrated time line of this period, noting significant events and people.

3. The construction of the Suez Canal has an interesting history. Research the canal. Who had the idea? Who constructed it? Who paid for it? What problems were encountered during construction? Afterward?

   ▶ After you learn about the Suez Canal, make a large chart or overhead transparency diagramming the construction and showing how it operates. Present and explain your diagram to the class.

4. Read current magazines or newspaper articles to find out about the most recent archaeological discoveries in Egypt. Where have these been found? What items were found? What did the findings reveal about Egyptian culture?

   ▶ Write about these in your own newspaper article or do a simulated television newscast for your class to break the news about these latest finds.

5. Several religions have close ties to Egypt. Find out as much as you can about one or more of these religions. Where did it originate? Who was its first leader? What special connections does it have with Egypt? How valid do you believe its claim to part of Egypt is? Why?

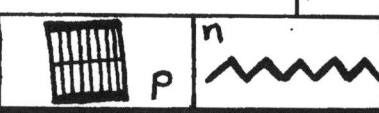

▶ Prepare an illuminated manuscript that tells the story of the religion you chose. Be prepared to present your opinion on the validity of its claim and defend your position if necessary.

6. Between 3200 and 333 B.C.E. Egypt was led by a series of ruling families called dynasties, which were headed by pharaohs. As dynasties grew weaker, the country was ruled by priests. In what other ways has the country been ruled? How is Egypt ruled today? What are the similarities and differences among the different ways of ruling? Which one would you choose to live under? Why?

▶ Choose one method of ruling and create a play in which you show the strengths and weaknesses of that method. With some friends, present your play to the class.

7. Think about what would happen if there were a ruler of Egypt, male or female, of whom no one knew. What would that person's name be? What might her or his family been like? Where did the ruler live? Imagine that your ruler has just been discovered by archaeologists.

▶ Write a story about your pharaoh or queen. Include the ruler's name, information about family members, where the ruler lived, what he or she enjoyed doing, why this ruler was highly respected, and what he or she accomplished.

8. Find out about Egyptian political history since World War II. What are some of the conflicts Egypt has faced? Why was Egypt declared a republic?

▶ Write an illustrated biography of one of the following: Anwar al-Sadat, Gamal Abdel Nasser, or King Farouk.

9. Find out about the invasions of Egypt over the centuries. What changes, such as religious shifts, occurred? Under whose rule did such changes occur?

*The Egyptian flag has three bold stripes—red, white, and black—with a center falcon emblem. The red stands for the blood shed during the revolution, the white stands for the country's bright future, the black signifies the years before Egypt became a republic, and the falcon is associated with Mohammed, the founder of Islam.*

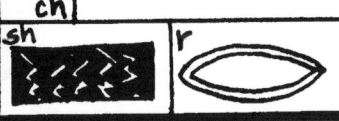

*Most of Egypt's 54 million people live along the Nile River and the 103-mile-long Suez canal. Egypt has a high population growth rate and experts estimate that the population could reach 100 million by the year 2020, with more people living in the city of Cairo than in all of Canada.*

▶ Make a chart of the invasions and subsequent rule by foreign powers. Compare the government structure under the kings with today's government in Egypt.

10. Find out about Egyptian history. What do you think were the most significant events? What events changed the course of Egyptian history?

▶ Make a time line that shows the events and their effects. Illustrate your time line. Present it to your class.

## The People

In some ways Egypt hasn't changed much since ancient times. Many Egyptian people resemble their ancestors in the ways they dress, eat, travel, and raise crops. But Egyptian lifestyle, religion, and attitudes have undergone many changes since ancient days.

Ancient Egyptian society consisted of a working class, the Fellahins, and a ruling class, made up of kings (pharaohs) and queens. In ancient times, Egypt fluctuated between prosperity and poverty, depending on the strengths and weaknesses of its rulers. Believing in life after death, the ancient Egyptians built monumental pyramids and tombs, structures that were intended to safely house Egyptian rulers after death.

The ancient Egyptians were among the first to develop a calendar. The Egyptian year began with the reappearance of Sirius, the brightest star in the sky, around June 20. This date coincided with the annual flooding of the Nile.

The Egyptians relied on the Nile River for their survival. It supplied them with water and helped keep the land fertile for farming. It also provided mud for building houses and was home to plants and animals that people needed for food and other uses.

Today a large number of Egyptians live in urban areas and work as unskilled laborers, but some still live in small mud homes along the Nile as their ancestors did. The Bedouins, a nomadic people, also live

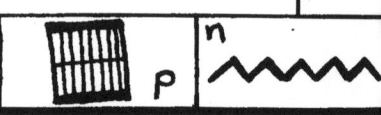

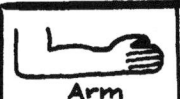 

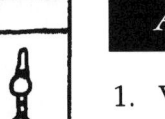

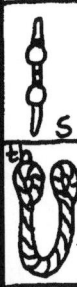

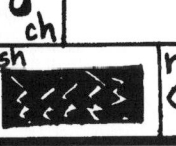

much as their ancestors did, roaming the desert, herding sheep and goats, and living in tents.

The majority of Egyptians are Sunni Muslims, and Cairo is a great center of religious study. Islamic doctrines once controlled both spiritual and governmental affairs in Egypt, but today the religion has mostly a spiritual influence.

## Activities

1.  When most people think of Egypt, they think of pyramids. Learn about pyramids and select one on which to become an expert.

    ▶ Build a cutaway model of the pyramid you select, putting authentic decorations and objects inside. Be sure to include the inner chambers and secret passageways. Be prepared to share your expertise by giving an oral "tour" of your model.

2.  Research a pyramid, mastaba, or new tomb. Imagine you are designing this for yourself. What items would you include so archaeologists in the future would know something about who you are?

    ▶ Sketch a plan for your pyramid, mastaba, or new tomb.

3.  Research the mummification process. What materials were used? How have mummies contributed to our knowledge of the Egyptian culture?

    ▶ Make a drawing of a mummy case and use Egyptian symbols to tell about the interests or accomplishments of the person who was mummified.

4.  Learn about the Nile River and its relationship to the lives of the Egyptian people in ancient and modern times. How did it sustain life? How does it sustain life now? To what uses have ancient and modern people put the Nile? What are the effects of modern dams?

    ▶ Develop a board game based on the history of the Nile. Be sure that people playing the game will learn some of this history.

*Common Egyptian words and phrases*

*Marhaba!*
*(mar-HA-ba)*
*Hello! Welcome!*

*Maa salahma*
*(MA-a sa-LAH-ma)*
*Goodbye*

*Alf Shukre*
*(alf-SHUK-re)*
*Thanks a lot*

*Minfahdluk*
*(min-fud-LUK)*
*Please*

*Aiwa. La.*
*(I-wah. La.)*
*Yes. No.*

*Isstyak?*
*(iz-ZI-yak)*
*How are you?*

*There are 28 consonant letters in the Arabic alphabet, which is read from right to left. Vowel sounds are made by adding small extra dots and lines.*

*Today the basic unit of money is the Egyptian pound, which is divided into 100 piastres. Egyptians use 1-, 5-, 10-, 20-, and 100-Egyptian-pound bank notes and two silver coins valued at 5 and 10 piastres.*

5. Learn about an Egyptian pharaoh or queen, such as one of the Cleopatras, Tutankhamun, Cheops, Hatshepsut, Nefertiti, or one of the Ramses. Find out about the person's life and the lifestyles of people in Egypt during his or her rule.

   ▶ Develop a skit based on this information. Be sure that the skit gives the audience a lot of information about Egypt at the time of the ruler you choose.

6. Find out the meanings of several words related to Egypt, such as pyramid, mastaba, mummification, gold, chariot, jewels, throne, natron, canopic jars, Sphinx, papyrus, lotus, desert, Nile, and other words you learn while studying Egyptian culture.

   ▶ Create a word find (on the computer if possible) using the words.

7. The Egyptians built pyramids, developed hieroglyphics, made papyrus scrolls on which to write, developed a calendar, and developed algebra and trigonometry. Why do you suppose this group of people made so many contributions to the world? Research Egyptian history, spend some time thinking, and then decide what factors made possible Egyptian discoveries and inventions.

   ▶ Write an essay at least five paragraphs long that states and explains your belief and gives reasons and examples to support it.

8. Men and women have distinct roles and rights in Egypt. Find out about the lifestyles of modern Egyptian men and women. How are they different from each other? How are they different from the lifestyles of men and women in the United States?

   ▶ With other classmates, set up a panel to discuss the differences. Be sure that there is at least one person representing each role (Egyptian man, Egyptian woman, U.S. man, and U.S. woman). Some students may have to advocate positions with which they don't agree.

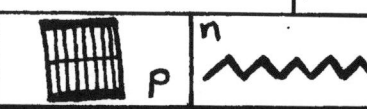

9. Find out about hieroglyphics. What do some of the pictures represent? How did they eventually become an alphabet?

   ▶ Design a picture for each letter of the alphabet and write a letter in your secret code to a friend.

10. Research the Rosetta Stone. Why was it significant? What knowledge has it given us?

    ▶ In a chart, poster, or some other medium, report your findings to your class.

## Wildlife and the Environment

Egypt has a variety of animal life. The cobra is native to Egypt, and the desert is home to lizards, gazelles, camels, goats, and sheep. Hyenas, jackals, boars, mongooses, wild asses, and jerboas live in the Nile Delta and the mountains along the Red Sea. Hippopotamuses and crocodiles are found in upper Egypt.

The Aswan High Dam has had both positive and negative environmental effects. The dam has created more arable land, extended the growing season, and increased farm production, and it provides hydroelectic power to the nation. The dam, however, has also stopped the natural flow of silt, causing farmers to use artificial fertilizers and allowing mineral salts to accumulate in the soil near the river. The fish population has decreased drastically, and the marine life in the Mediterranean Sea is changing as a result of the changes in the river's flow. Also, schistosomiasis, an infectious disease, has dramatically increased since completion of the dam.

In 1979 Egypt established a Wildlife Service to protect and preserve the nation's wilderness. Many protected sites are owned by private research institutions. Despite some progress, however, overpopulation, hunger, and pollution remain major problems for the Egyptian people. Cairo, the largest city in Africa, is one of the world's most polluted cities, and many of its inhabitants are homeless.

*The seemingly inhospitable desert environment contains very special plants and animals that have evolved through thousands of years to survive the harsh desert conditions. Within Egypt, the Nile River divides the Sahara Desert into two areas called the Arabian Desert and the Libyan Desert. Wadies, trenchlike formations, are found on the eastern Arabian Desert, and the Libyan Desert has three oases created by seepage from the Nile.*

✱ ✱ ✱ ✱ ✱

*The Nile River is the longest river in the world.*

✱ ✱ ✱ ✱ ✱

*There is enough stone in the Aswan Dam to build 17 Great Pyramids.*

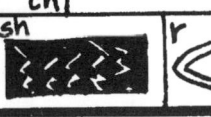

51

*The vast Sahara Desert spans North Africa from east to west, covering all of Egypt. The Sahara Desert has spread to the point that today it covers most of northern Africa. It is advancing southward.*

* * * * *

*The Sahara Desert covers about three million square miles, which is about one-third of the African continent.*

* * * * *

*Parts of the western desert are hyperarid, which means that entire generations pass without seeing rain.*

## Activities

1. Learn about the different animals that were re-vered and honored in ancient Egyptian times.

   ▶ Create animal puppets and tell a traditional Egyptian folktale or make up your own story based on the Egyptian folklore.

2. Schistosomiasis is a serious infectious disease that has increased since the Aswan High Dam was completed. Research the disease and the condi-tions that favor its spread. Learn about the effects of the dam on the environment. How, if at all, are the disease and the dam related?

   ▶ Make a large chart that shows the schistosomiasis cycle and indicates what relationship exists be-tween the dam and the disease.

3. Find out what Egypt looked like before the Aswan High Dam was built. Compare it to how Egypt looks today. What has the lake created by the dam covered?

   ▶ Draw a map showing the land in Egypt before the Aswan Dam was built. Color the area once flooded each year by the Nile. Then draw a map showing Egypt since the dam's construc-tion. Make a list of the positive and negative impacts of the dam.

4. Become an expert on one of Egypt's native ani-mals. Where does it live? How are its needs spe-cifically related to its environment? What does it eat? How does it live, in a group or by itself? How is modern civilization affecting it?

   ▶ Build a diorama based on what you learned about the creature, its life, habits, and environment.

5. Imagine that you are part of a hunting expedition along the Nile. What weapons do you bring? What

animals are you hunting? Do you find your prey or does your prey find you? What would happen if your papyrus boat was overturned by a crodile or a hippopotamus?

▶ In small groups, perform a short mime that depicts a hunting expedition scenario.

## *Food, Festivals, and Celebrations*

The paintings, inscriptions, and dried food found in pyramids and ancient tombs tell us a lot about the foods of ancient Egypt. Today, Egyptians eat many of the same foods, such as beans and onions, cereals and bread, fish and fowl from the Nile, chicken, lamb, and goat, and native fruits such as figs, dates, olives, and pomegranates. Foods are cooked with a mixture of spices such as coriander, cumin, rosemary, and sage.

Beer and bread are basic items in the Egyptian diet. The flour for making bread is hand ground between stones and then mixed with water to make dough. Beer is made by crumbling pieces of lightly baked bread into water and letting it ferment. Egyptians also enjoy goat and buffalo milk, wine, strong dark coffee and tea, and fruit juices made from pomegranates and quinces.

During ancient times, Egyptians held festivals to honor their various gods. Plays told stories about the gods, and each celebration involved dancing, music, and special food. Egyptians' celebrations are still focused on religious beliefs. During Ramadan, an Islamic holiday, people fast from sunrise to sunset and read the Koran. They continue this ritual for an entire month. A new moon brings an end to the fasting and the beginning of a three-day festival called Id al-Fitz. This time is joyous; people eat special foods, visit friends, exchange gifts, and wear new clothes.

*Pomegranate*
*Seed Salad*

*1 pomegranate*
*3 tangerines, sectioned*
*2 grapefruits, sectioned*
*1 kiwi, sliced*
*Dressing*
*2 tablespoons honey*
*juice of one lemon*

*Place pomegranate seeds aside and mix other fruit gently. Sprinkle seeds into fruit mixture and cover with honey/lemon dressing. Note: Grenadine syrup is made from the juice of the pomegranate.*

> **Popular festival foods:**
>
> **Wara Keinab** – stuffed grape leaves
>
> **Toshi** – mixed vegetables soaked in a brine until pickled
>
> **Laban Kabadi** – yogurt which is served plain as a snack, with sugar as a dessert, or dried as a creamy cheese
>
> **Baklava** – thin filo dough that is layered with honey and nuts. A similar dessert called **Konafa** is made with shredded wheat instead of filo dough and is served at Ramadan.

## Activities

1. Research one of the ancient Egyptian gods. Of what part of life was this god in charge? How did the people try to gain the favor of this god? What holiday(s), festival(s), foods, or celebrations honored him or her?

   ▶ With friends, create and present a play or a puppet show that tells a story about the god. Make the costumes and information as authentic as you can.

2. Ramadan is an important time for many Egyptians. Learn as much as you can about Ramadan. Why is it observed? When? For how long? What customs are traditionally followed during Ramadan? What is the significance of the various customs?

   ▶ Write diary entries that an Egyptian person might make of his or her thoughts during Ramadan and Id al-Fitz.

## Dances, Games, and Sports

Egyptian children and adults have enjoyed playing games since ancient times. Tomb paintings show us that children played *khuzza lawizza,* or leap frog, ball games, and tug-of-war. Children had animal pull toys with moveable jaws, spinning tops, and wooden dolls with hair made of twine.

Adults played a game called *senet,* a board game that symbolizes the struggles against the forces of evil. Another board game found in the tombs of the pharaohs was called the Snake. This board was round and coiled like a snake, and players competed to be the first to move their stone marbles or counters into the center of the board.

Ancient nobles and pharoahs took great pride in their hunting skills. Hunting and fishing remain recreational sports, but many families also rely on these activities to provide themselves with food. Modern

*Soccer is the most popular Egyptian sport.*

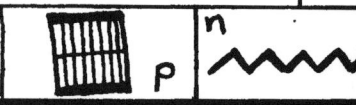

Egyptians also enjoy a variety of sports and games. Soccer is the most popular spectator and group sport in Egypt.

## Activities

1. Find pictures of and information about ancient Egyptian toys depicted in tomb paintings.

   ▶ Design and construct a toy or doll similar to those ancient ones.

2. Select a topic related to your study of Egypt. Become an expert on this topic, and learn about the game "the Snake."

   ▶ Create a board game based on your expertise. Make the board round and coiled like a snake, and design the game so that players learn about Egypt while playing.

## Music, Art, and Architecture

The harp, one of the earliest known stringed instruments in the world, dates back to ancient Egypt. Tomb paintings depict the primitive harp being played for the pharaohs. Early harps had a varying number of loose-fitting strings that produced only low-pitched sounds.

The lyre, another early stringed instrument, appeared in Egypt around 1500 B.C.E. The Egyptian lyre was U-shaped and had between five and eleven strings. It was used to accompany singing, much like a modern guitar or piano.

Egypt's famous pyramids were built between 2686 and 1786 B.C.E. These ancient monuments rank among the largest structures in the world. The pyramid of Khufu, the Great Pyramid, is taller than a 40-story building and covers an area larger than ten football fields.

Many questions about the pyramids remain unanswered. Most people accept the theory that they were

*The understanding and reading of hieroglyphics was lost until a Frenchman named Jean-Francois Champollion discovered the Rosetta stone in 1799.*

❅ ❅ ❅ ❅ ❅

*Scribes were respected and honored. They did not participate in national labor projects or pay taxes and could even reach the status of a nobleman or king.*

*Because of the Nile, Egypt is one of only two Middle Eastern countries that has an adequate water supply within its boundaries. This is partly why Egypt is the most populated Middle Eastern country and the second most populous country in Africa.*

♯ ♯ ♯ ♯ ♯

*In Egypt's summer, temperatures may exceed 110° F in the daytime but drop drastically in the evenings. High winds from the desert, called khamsins, often bring extreme temperatures to the area.*

built as tombs for pharoahs and other important people, though some have suggested that the pyramids had other purposes. Over the years, many pyramids have been robbed of their treasures, so much of what we know comes from studying the artwork and murals on the chamber walls.

The pyramids show that early Egyptians understood some important scientific and mathematical principles. The base of the pyramid of Khufu is almost perfectly square. Its sides are aligned on exact north-south and east-west lines. Many years after the pyramids were built, Greek mathematicians proved mathematical theories that the Egyptians used regularly.

## Activities

1. The harp and lyre, both stringed instruments, were used in ancient Egypt. Learn as much as you can about these early musical instruments. How did early harps differ from modern harps? How did their shape affect their sound? How do harps and lyres differ from each other?

   ▶ Based on what you learn, construct a harp, a lyre, or one of each. Prepare a demonstration of how the instruments are played. Also tell your audience how the early instruments have evolved and where most modern ones are used.

2. Become an expert on the various theories about how and why the pyramids were built. Develop criteria by which to evaluate these theories. Using these criteria, select the theory you believe to be most valid.

   ▶ Write an essay that presents and supports your choice. The essay will have at least five paragraphs. Be sure to include the criteria, to examine each theory in light of the criteria, and to include your conclusion and examples or reasons as support.

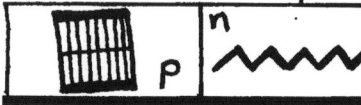

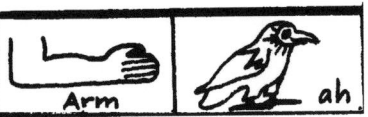

3. Find out about modern Egyptian music, art, and architecture. How is it influenced by the cultures of peoples that occupied Egypt in the past? How is it influenced by Western traditions?

   ▶ Create a mural that includes examples of ancient Egyptian buildings and of modern Egyptian buildings. Include on the mural the dates the buildings were probably built.

4. Study Egyptian symbolism. What do some of the symbols mean? Which do you find the most appealing?

   ▶ Make clay or wire jewelry using the symbols you discover.

## Ezzat's Day

Ezzat is a nine-year-old boy who lives in Om Khenan, a small village 17 kilometers south of Cairo. He lives in a three-room brick house with his mother, father, grandmother, and two sisters. They raise chickens, goats, and corn on their small farm next to the Nile River. Every morning, Ezzat gets up at 6:00 to feed the goats and to gather buckets of water from the river for cooking, drinking, and bathing. He and his oldest sister carry the buckets on their heads.

Ezzat is fortunate to live within walking distance of his school, and he is glad his parents think it's important that he learn to read, write, and do arithmetic. Some of his friends do not go to school. Instead they work in the fields and help their families with daily tasks. Most Egyptian girls do not go to school either. They cook, sew, and care for younger children, or work in the fields.

In the morning, Ezzat goes to the only school in the village. Other children use the same classroom in the afternoon. After school Ezzat returns home to a meal of bread, boiled beans, mutton, and goat's milk. Later he enjoys playing cards with his friend Mohammed or playing soccer with other children.

*Only 5 percent of Egypt's 400 thousand square miles is arable; the arable land is along the banks of the Nile River.*

❆ ❆ ❆ ❆ ❆

*Because of the small amount of arable land and the large population in Egypt, as much as two-thirds of the country's food has to be imported.*

*One of Egypt's most successful crops has been cotton. Egyptians also harvest figs, grapes, pomegranates, and a variety of vegetables and grains from their land. A single date palm yields 600 pounds of dates a year.*

On Friday Ezzat goes with his father to a mosque to pray. All Sunni Muslim people kneel five times a day and face east, the direction of Mecca. Many people in Ezzat's village have traveled to Mecca and have painted pictures of their journey on the outside walls of their clay homes.

## Activity

What does Ezzat's day tell you about Egyptian values, culture, and economy? How is his day different from yours? How is it similar?

▶ Write a letter to Ezzat. Tell him about a typical day in your life. Tell him what you find most interesting about his life. Then write about what part of your life you would like to trade for a part of his life.

# The Crocodile and the Baboon

## An Egyptian Folktale

Once upon a time a crocodile family lived among the papyrus reeds of the Nile River. They lived on the fish and fowl that inhabited the river.

One day, as the crocodiles lay sunning themselves and watching playful baboons swing from palm tree to palm tree, the mother crocodile said to her son, "I want a heart of a baboon for dinner. Go get me one and you shall be the best son I've ever had."

"How am I to catch a baboon in a tree when I can't climb and the baboons never come to the river's edge?"

"Put your wits to work," replied his mother. "You'll find a way to outsmart the baboon if you really put your mind to it."

At last, the son had an idea. "I know what I'll do. I'll convince a baboon to cross the river on my back and feast on the wonderful fruit of the island." Slowly,

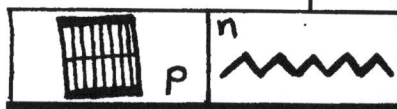

he swam to the river's edge and called out to the baboons. "Would you like to cross the river and taste the delicious fruit that grows on the island?"

One of the baboons thought the idea sounded marvelous, and she asked, "How am I to cross the river when I don't know how to swim?" The friendly crocodile replied, "Just jump on my nice firm back and I shall take you to the island so you can feast on the scrumptious fruit!" Unaware of the crocodile's plan, the baboon quickly crawled down the tree and hopped onto the crocodile's back.

Not far from shore, the delighted crocodile dove deep into the water, which frightened the little baboon half to death. When he returned to the surface, the sputtering, choking baboon asked why he dove into the water and nearly drowned her.

The crocodile chuckled and said, "My mother wants a nice warm baboon heart for dinner tonight and I have tricked you to come with me to the island."

Quickly the baboon said, "I wish you would have told me you only wanted my heart, because I would have brought it with me today. Unfortunately, I left it up in the tree. Please, just take me to the island, then I'll get my heart for you."

"No!" answered the impatient crocodile. "I'll take you back to the tree immediately and then we'll see about the island fruit."

As the baboon scrambled up the tree, she called back, "My heart is way up here! If you want it you will have to come up here to get it."

### Activity

The crocodile, the baboon, and the Nile River make this story fit Egypt. What do you think the moral to this story is?

▶ Create and write a fable or folktale that fits where you live. Be sure that your tale also has a moral, a lesson to be learned.

*Many homes are made of mud bricks and have grass or thatched roofs.*

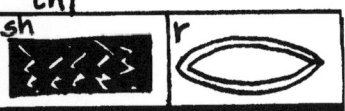

59

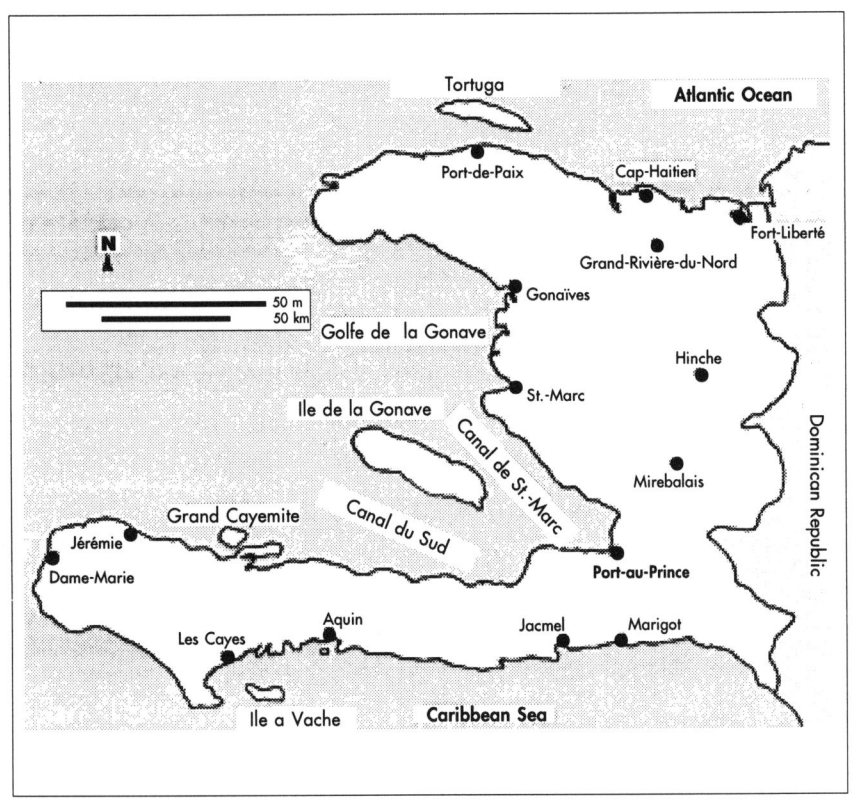

## Overview

Haiti's story is full of contrasts—physically, politically, and historically. The country is quite small—only 10,714 square miles—but contains many different climates and land features. The Arawak Indian word *Haiti*, which means "land of the mountains," suits this country where two-thirds of the land is mountainous and the remaining

third is semiarid and not well suited to farming. Sharp peaks and deep valleys filled with rushing rivers and waterfalls make overland transportation slow.

Shaped like a lobster's claw, Haiti occupies the western third of the island of Hispaniola, sharing a border with the Dominican Republic to the east. The island is southeast of Cuba and east of Jamaica. The Atlantic Ocean is to the north and the Caribbean Sea to the south. Hispaniola is part of an island group called the Greater Antilles, or West Indies.

*Hispaniola was Christopher Columbus's first landfall in 1492.*

## Historical Background

Before Columbus visited Haiti in 1492, the population was mainly Taino. Later a French colony, Haiti was the site of the only successful slave revolt in the Western Hemisphere. The revolt isolated Haiti from other European colonies and the United States, which were dependent upon a slave economy. Haiti was left to develop in isolation, with virtually no trade or contact with the international community.

After the revolt, the French planters left the country. The offspring of the planters and their enslaved Africans, the mulattoes (people of mixed race), created their own version of French culture. The urban mulattoes, with their French-based culture, became the elite in Haiti, with black people forming the working and servant class.

The former enslaved Africans on Haiti, most of them African born, continued to speak French, mixing it with English, Spanish, and African words to create a new language called Creole. Although Creole-speaking

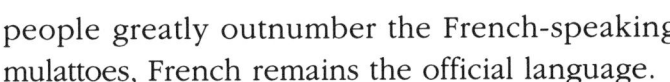

people greatly outnumber the French-speaking mulattoes, French remains the official language.

The people also continued to practice Roman Catholicism, but they blended in elements of the tribal religions they had brought from Africa. This combination has become known as voodoo.

Haiti's present population is 95 percent black. Although the dictators Francois and Jean-Claude Duvalier redistributed some of the nation's wealth, there is still a huge gap between the few millionaires who control Haiti's government and the masses of poor who have no material wealth at all. The 23 percent literacy rate in Haiti reflects the fact that most blacks have had no formal education and are unable even to speak French, much less to read or write it.

By the 1980s, many Haitians felt they could no longer live in their native land because of political and economic oppression. They began a desperate migration to the Bahamas and the United States in small fishing boats. The U.S. Coast Guard intercepted some 35,000 of these "boat people" in 1991 and 1992 and, despite protests by human rights groups, returned them to Haiti. Many other Haitians completed the ocean journey, however, and are pressing the governments of both the Bahamas and the United States to relax immigration regulations and allow more Haitians to enter these countries.

Despite the fact that the majority of them live with no prospects of comfort or ease, the Haitian people have a rich culture and spirituality. The dancing, singing, and artistic visions of the Haitian people speak of their deep-seated joy of life. The Haitians have made creative decisions to deal with their problems, and despite the complexity and contradictions within Haiti's society, its people celebrate their diversity.

## Activities

1. French is the official language of Haiti, even though more Haitians speak Creole than speak

*The Citadelle Laferriere was built by the reputedly mad King Christopher during his reign in the early 1800s. The fort was built to protect the new republic from recolonization by European countries or enslavement by mulatto leaders. Twenty thousand men are said to have died from overwork building it.*

French. Seek information about why this situation exists and how it has come about.

> ▶ Develop a skit based on the information you gather.

2. Find out about French white planters, free mulattos, and black slaves. Where did they meet? How did they address each other? What were each group's concerns? What do you talk about?

> ▶ Create a play in which each of you takes on one of the roles. Put the play on for your class.

3. Haiti was the site of the only successful slave revolt in the Western Hemisphere. Research this revolt, looking for answers to the following and your own questions: Who led the slaves to revolt? What did the slaves feel were the most important issues or problems? How did slaves communicate their plans to revolt? How was the revolt accomplished? What changes did the revolt bring about? Based on your research, identify the three most important elements of this revolt.

> ▶ Prepare an oral presentation of these elements, explaining why each was important and how it contributed to the success of the revolt. To add visual interest to your presentation, use overhead transparencies, posters, or other visual aids to help your audience understand your points.

4. Find out about the division of wealth in Haiti. What percentage of the population is wealthy? What makes them wealthy? Why are the poor poor? Find out about the division of wealth in the United States, as well.

> ▶ Make a graph showing your findings.

5. Research life in Haiti in the 1980s and 1990s, focusing on political and economic oppression. Take a stand on whether or not the United States and other countries should allow immigration of Haitians fleeing this oppression.

**Proverb**

*The little fellow does what he can; the big fellow does what he wants.*

▶ Write a letter to the editor of your local newspaper, stating your position and giving evidence or reasons to support your position. With several interested friends, organize a panel discussion about Haitians trying to enter the United States.

6. Find out about Haitian history. What do you think were the most significant events? What events changed the course of Haitian history?

▶ Make a time line that shows the events and their effects. Illustrate your time line. Present it to your class.

7. Find out how breadfruit came to Haiti. Pretend you are a sailor under the command of Captain Bly.

▶ Write a paragraph about how he treats the crew.

8. Find out what foods are native to Hispaniola. Then find out what foods were introduced and from where they came.

▶ Make a list for each category. Explain the uses and why the foods are important.

9. Research current agricultural and industrial practices in Haiti. What are the main exports? Imports? Where do most Haitians work? What kinds of wages do they earn? What tools do they use?

▶ Write a proposal that suggests possible alternative agricultural or industrial methods. The suggestions must be environmentally sound and economically beneficial.

*The Arawak invented hammocks.*

## The People

The first residents of Hispaniola called themselves Taino, meaning "good people." More than a thousand years ago, they migrated from South America to the islands of the West Indies by canoe. The Tainos, part of the Arawak tribe, had a peaceful culture. They

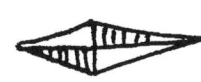

*Enslaved Africans were stolen from their families and resold as their masters wished. In fact, the treatment of enslaved Africans was so harsh that most died before having children. Children who survived to adulthood could be separated from their parents and sold to a different plantation.*

supported themselves by fishing and agriculture. Beginning in the early 1400s, the warlike Carib people, who the Arawaks called cannibals, came north to raid the Arawak settlements. Looking for allies, the Arawaks eventually befriended the Spanish sailors left behind by Columbus in 1492. Instead of receiving protection, however, the Arawaks were wiped out by European diseases and harsh treatment by Spanish and French colonists who followed the explorers. The Caribs refused to be enslaved by the colonists and fled to other islands after numerous battles.

The French and Spanish colonists needed workers to run their huge plantations, which grew crops such as sugarcane and coffee beans. To fill this need, the growers began to import enslaved Africans from what are today Ghana, Togo, Benin, Nigeria, and Cameroon. The Africans were mostly members of the Yoruba tribe, which had strong cultural traditions based on respect for and worship of the land. The enslaved Africans brought with them the rituals and beliefs that would later be blended with Roman Catholicism to become what we know as voodoo.

Europeans continued to rule Hispaniola, but a separate society, consisting of the mulattoes and the pure African slaves, also developed. By the late eighteenth century, Haiti had 500,000 blacks, 30,000 whites, and 27,000 mulattoes.

Today, the conflicts between races in Haiti continue. The nation has a complicated social structure based on skin color and economic standing. Mulattoes remain the elite in Haiti, while the blacks live in poverty and continue to grow poorer. Haiti is the poorest country in the Western Hemisphere and is highly dependent on foreign aid.

The spirit world overlaps the day-to-day world of Haitians, who believe that good and evil spirits live among them in mountains, trees, rainbows, and snakes. These spirits are always watching. The voodoo religion includes rules of conduct, with severe punishment for wrongdoing. Papa Doc Duvalier's secret police officers were called Ton Ton Macoutes,

which translates loosely into Bogey Men, and were thought to have great voodoo powers and so had control over the people.

Voodoo religion permeates daily life in Haiti. Followers worship a supreme being, who is thought to be approachable only through lesser gods called *loa*. The loa are said to have strong personalities. A *houngan* (priest) or *mambo* (priestess) presides over voodoo rituals. People pray by chanting, dancing, and singing in a holy place called a *hounfor*. During the ceremony, the loa replace believers' souls so the loa can help the people solve problems. Worship can take place on any day, although throughout the year there are special voodoo festivals loosely based on the Christian calendar.

## Activities

1. Find out about the countries from which today's Haitian people originate.

   ▶ Draw an immigration-emigration map to show the origins and destinations of the Haitian people.

2. Learn about the lives of the very poor and the very rich in Haiti. How is the ability to read and write related to the lives of the poor? The rich? What effects would an increase in the literacy rate have on the lives of the poor and the rich?

   ▶ Create a colorful mural that illustrates life for both classes of people now and in the future if the literacy rate were to increase significantly.

3. Find out about proverbs. What purpose do they serve in a culture? Why are they passed down through generations? Choose two proverbs from your own culture and two from a Caribbean culture that mean the same or nearly the same thing.

   ▶ Explain what they mean to your class. Allow your classmates to state their opinions about whether the proverbs are good or bad.

*Today Haitians are strongly attached to their home villages and have large extended families. In community groups called coumbites, people help each other harvest crops, take care of children, and build houses, often making a party out of the work.*

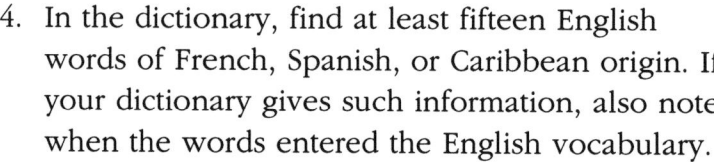

"*We are quite like the American, transplanted and stripped of traditions, but there is in the fusion of the European and African cultures which constitutes our national character, something that makes us less French than the American is English.*"

—*Hau*

4. In the dictionary, find at least fifteen English words of French, Spanish, or Caribbean origin. If your dictionary gives such information, also note when the words entered the English vocabulary.

   ▶ Write a short story about Haiti in which you use at least ten of the words you researched.

5. Learn about the development of voodoo in Haiti. What elements of Catholicism are evident? What practices stem from religions practiced in Africa? Why do you think some movies portray voodoo negatively? What are some of the positive aspects of voodoo?

   ▶ Create a script and videotape or a story in which you show the positive aspects of voodoo.

6. Find out what elements of Taino and other native cultures are evident in Haitian culture. What elements of African and European cultures are evident? Which has had the strongest influence?

   ▶ Create a museum of modern Haitian culture that displays the influences from Haiti's past. Create a brochure for museum visitors that explains those influences.

7. Pretend you have been kidnapped and taken from Africa to be a slave in Haiti.

   ▶ Write a letter to your family, who was left behind, telling what happened on your voyage and what life is like on a plantation.

8. Imagine you are the child of a plantation owner. Find out what your daily chores would be if you were a girl. What would they be if you were a boy? The son of slaves? The daughter of slaves?

   ▶ Make four lists of duties, one from each of the viewpoints listed above.

9. Research the class structure in Haitian society. What are the different groups? How did the different groups develop? What group has the most political power? How difficult is it to become

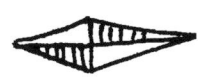

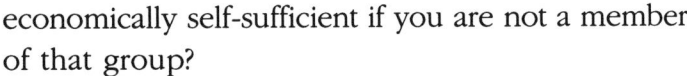

economically self-sufficient if you are not a member of that group?

▶ With a group of friends playing the different people, present a news talk show to your class in which an interviewer asks questions of members of the different classes. Prepare questions having to do with economic status, political status, educational opportunities, and other topics.

## *Wildlife and the Environment*

Unfortunately, Haiti is plagued by environmental problems that began early in the country's history. With too many people and too little land, Haiti simply does not produce enough food to feed its people. With no future in farming, many young people crowd into the cities, where they live in cardboard and tin shacks. Diseases such as tuberculosis, malaria, and AIDS are serious problems in urban areas.

Before Haiti's land was dominated by intensive agriculture and other human uses, it was home to a great variety of birds, small mammals, reptiles, and amphibians. Some rivers may still have crocodiles, but most wildlife species native to Haiti are gone.

The typical Haitian farmer has only a hoe, a machete, and a digging stick as tools. Manure from livestock provides the only fertilizer for the soil. Haitian farmers have traditionally used slash-and-burn farming practices, but after almost two hundred years of using this method, many lands are reduced to scrub, unable to support crops or native vegetation. Plants whose roots that once held soil in place are gone, too, and erosion is a major problem in Haiti.

Once richly forested, Haiti now retains only 7 percent of its original pine and hardwood forests. Birds and other wildlife that depended on the trees for habitat and food have been reduced to small numbers or completely wiped out. Pollution and soil erosion also affect the breeding grounds of marine organisms

*"I have celebrated our birds, our fertile countryside,*

*Our banana trees bent over with bunches of fruit*

*And the logwood in flower perfuming our mountains*

*And the great fans of our green palm trees."*

—Oswald Duran

*Haiti has more mountains than Switzerland.*

close to the land. With overfishing and the loss of clean water, marine life is threatened.

Recently, reforestation workers started to plant fast-growing trees, which are intended to be cut within a few years, specifically for firewood. These trees are often planted along field borders, in between other plants, and in backyards. They "fix" nitrogen, which means they help enrich the soil, making it more fertile.

Fortunately, recycling is not a fad but a way of life to Haitians. They use everything. Tin cans are turned into musical instruments, oil drums into gates, palm fronds into mats and hats. The ingenuity of the people could help reverse Haiti's environmental problems, if the people only had the financial resources to implement their ideas.

## Activities

1. On a globe, find the locations of Earth's coral reef systems. Then research a form of sea life native to Haiti.

   ▶ Write a report or create a song that shows your findings.

2. Research the natural history of Haiti: the forests, wildlife, and resources the land originally had and what has happened to them.

   ▶ Using an opaque projector or other means, draw two maps of Haiti on tagboard 12" x 18" or larger. On one map, include the original forests, creatures, and other features. On the other map, show what remains of these resources. Write several paragraphs to explain the maps. Include the following in the paragraphs: the effects of overpopulation, the effects of slash-and-burn farming, the effects of little education and money, and the effects of few natural resources.

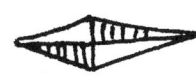

3. Even though most native Haitian wildlife species have disappeared, sea life around the island is varied and plentiful. Research to find out why the sea life has not been as greatly affected as the wildlife on land and in the rivers. How might the sea offer some help in feeding Haiti's people?

   ▶ Develop a plan by which sea life could be used for food but not depleted. Prepare a film-strip or video that presents the plan. Be sure to include the following:

   *steps for increasing the harvest of sea life*
   *precautions to avoid damaging the environment and reducing the number of sea creatures*

   *benefits and possible problems of the plan*

4. Find out about one of the typical landscapes in Haiti. What kinds of geographical features does it have? What plant life? What wildlife?

   ▶ Create a landscape with soil, rooted plants, and rocks. Make sure it has elevation. Using a watering can, show erosion by water. Remove rooted plants and repeat the experiment

5. Find out about different types of houses built in Haiti. What materials are used for each? Which materials are readily available?

   ▶ Make a replica of a house from stiff paper, one from glued ice cream sticks, one from dried mud, and one from stacked bricks. Use a large floor fan and watering can to simulate a hurricane. Write a brief report describing what happens to the various houses. Discuss what construction materials you recommend for hurricane country.

6. Learn about slash-and-burn farming. What are its advantages? Its disadvantages? Why is it practiced in Haiti? What are long-term effects of the slash-and-burn technique?

   ▶ Create a large poster that illustrates answers to these questions.

*Haiti and the Dominican Republic share the only land border between countries in the Caribbean Sea.*

7. Although small, Haiti has a variety of biomes. Learn about three of these biomes.

   ▶ Construct a diorama of each of them. Write at least one paragraph about each diorama. Include the following in the paragraphs:

      *major weather elements*
      *plants and animals*

8. Find out about several different ocean habitats surrounding Haiti: open ocean, reef, tidal communities, and shore communities.

   ▶ Create a large mural that shows the various communities. Ask each student to cut a sea creature from paper; attach the creations in the appropriate place on the mural.

## *Food, Festivals, and Celebrations*

Like many other Caribbean cultures, Haiti celebrates Mardi Gras, a weeklong series of parties and parades that ends on Ash Wednesday, the first day of Lent in the Catholic religion. Lent is a 40-day period of sacrifice and fasting. During Mardi Gras people drop their daily routines and indulge in food, drink, and dancing.

Each neighborhood or village organizes a band that includes drummers, flute players, and whistlers. The musicians write songs, usually about how to forget daily problems and have fun. The people design elaborate costumes and masks that depict government officials, voodoo spirits, and animals. The bands play music and the people dance in the streets day and night, falling down in exhaustion and getting back up to dance some more when they have rested. The urban elite watch the parades from grandstands or from the balconies of their mansions. They spend money on costumes and fancy parties and compete with each other to see who has the most elaborate entertainment.

Haiti also has many celebrations (practically one every week) to commemorate its history. Major holidays include Pan American Week, which recognizes Haiti's

*English words derived from Arawak: potato, maize, tobacco, canoe, hurricane, barbecue, cannibal, cassava*

connection to other countries in the Western Hemisphere, All Saint's Day, which is like our Halloween, all the traditional Christian holidays, and many voodoo ones. Most holidays include music and special get-togethers with family and neighbors.

The main staples of the Haitian diet are rice and beans, supplemented by foods such as maize, tomatoes, okra, breadfruit, cassava, sweet potatoes, and taro root. People who live near the coast eat fish. Tropical fruits, such as mangoes, coconuts, citrus, papaya, and several kinds of bananas, provide some variety. Animals—chicken, goats, and cattle—are saved for voodoo ceremonies and other special occasions, at which meat is shared throughout the community.

This dish is the daily favorite: ▶

## Activities

1. Learn about Mardi Gras as it is celebrated in Haiti. Be sure to find out about the food, costumes, music, and dances that are a part of Mardi Gras.

   ▶ With some friends, present a "slice of Mardi Gras" to the class. Involve the class in as many Mardi Gras activities as appropriate. Remember the food, costumes, and music.

2. Pretend you are a member of the urban Haitian elite.

   ▶ Keep a detailed diary of your life during the week of Mardi Gras.

3. Find out about some of the costumes and masks used in Mardi Gras.

   ▶ In a small group, design and create costumes and masks for a Mardi Gras fashion show. Use Caribbean music to put on your show.

4. Find as much information as you can about Haitian holidays. Choose one of the holidays to research in depth.

### Rice and Peas

*Boil rice. Cook onions and chili peppers in salt pork. Add cooked kidney beans and rice to pork mixture and heat. Delicious and good for you, too.*

▶ Using your research, create a large poster that will share what you learned about the holiday. Write a three- to five-paragraph composition that compares and contrasts the holiday to a holiday commonly celebrated in the United States or to one you and your family celebrate. Be sure to include the following: why each holiday is celebrated; how each holiday is celebrated; the clothing or costumes worn; and the food, music, or dance that is used.

# Dances, Games, and Sports

The national dance, the *merengue,* combines the formal French minuet with freewheeling African tribal dances. Mulattoes learned the minuet from the white elite in colonial times. After the revolution, they combined it with ritual African dances. The merengue is sometimes called "the wooden leg dance" because one leg stays stiff while the body and the other leg move freely. This rhythmic strut is a part of celebrations at all levels of Haitian society.

Dance is also an integral part of voodoo worship because Haitians believe that loa can enter the body during dance. Drummers control the tempo of the rituals using three drums, each representing a different aspect of the spirit world. *Bamboche* is the Creole word for party, where music and dance are always present.

Hello *in French, Haiti's national language, is* bonjour.

### Activity

Find out about the merengue. How does one dance it? What are some of the variations?

▶ Teach some of your classmates how to do the merengue.

# Music, Art, and Architecture

Besides drums, Haitian musical instruments include bamboo flutes, Marine Corps whistles, *lambis,* or conch shells, and accordions. People make their own percussion instruments from whatever is at hand. Rocks inside of tin cans are common rhythm instruments. People make ingenious homemade horns and basses, too.

The people also sing and drum at work. Many songs are composed in the fields or on assembly lines to make the work go faster. There are special songs for building houses, harvesting sugarcane, and putting children to sleep. Three favorite songs in Haiti are "Haiti Cherie," "Panama'm Tombe," and "Choucoune."

Like the rest of Haitian life, the arts blend European and African ideas to form a vital new self-expression. Until the 1920s, French culture dominated the arts in Haiti, and Haitian artists followed the classical European art trends. A distinctive Haitian art form did not develop until during the U.S. Marine occupation, when an American opened the Centre d'Art in Port-au-Prince. This painter, DeWitt Peters, recognized genius in the art of the common people and wanted to encourage its production.

The Centre d'Art became a learning institution and retail center. Artists and craftspeople streamed there from all over the island to get supplies and to learn how to paint their visions of African myth, voodoo gods, Bible stories, and village life. These Haitian folk paintings are characterized by bright colors and complex composition.

Some artists turn oil drums into metal sculpture or carve wood to resemble the ideal natural world. Others use painted papier mâché to depict fishermen, loaded buses, and the animals of Africa. Such voodoo ceremonial objects as flags, altar covers, and ritual containers are embellished with sequins and beads. Wooden storage boxes are painted and varnished.

During the same period that folk art was revived, writers began to use the Creole language, moving

*Haiti's national palace is named the White House.*

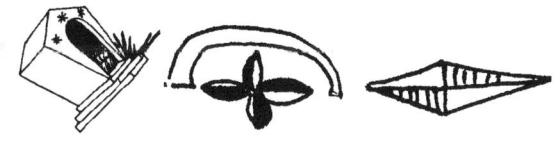

*An average tourist in Haiti spends in two days what the average Haitian earns in one year.*

away from the French literary tradition. Poets and novelists wrote about daily life and the importance of their African heritage.

In rural Haiti storytelling is the main source of entertainment. The same stories, with variations, have been told for generations and are like our fables, frequently including a lesson. Storytellers compete for the right to speak by shouting out "cric" as soon as one story ends. If the audience responds with "crac," the person shouting "cric" is allowed to tell a story. If no one yells "crac," another person shouts "cric" and awaits the "crac" to proceed. Audiences are an important part of the story, supplying sound effects, dance, and song. In "Owl" the storyteller dances when the refrain is repeated, and a member of the audience sings.

## Activities

1. Research some aspect of Haitian culture: art, music, dance, food, folklore, or other traditions.

   ▶ Create an advertisement in which you present the information about cultural elements you research. The advertisement should convince people to visit Haiti. Be sure to include the following: the way in which the tradition reflects Haitian life and personality, its uniqueness, and similar elements from other cultures.

2. With one or more friends, learn about Haitian musical instruments and songs.

   ▶ Construct one or more instruments from everyday materials. Then perform a Haitian song for the class using the instruments. When you perform the song for the class, be sure to tell them about the history and background information. Explain how you made the instruments, how you make the sound and vary it, and to what Haitian instruments each is similar.

3. Find out about the ways in which Haitians recycle materials into musical instruments.

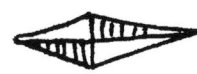

- ▶ Make a drum from tin cans or canisters or other found materials. With some friends, use your homemade rhythm instruments to make a variety of rhythms for your class.

4. Listen to Harry Belafonte recordings. What songs are about people, work, or the environment?

   - ▶ Make a chart in which you categorize the songs accordingly.

5. Listen to some recordings of Miriam Makeba. Does she make sounds that are not in your language? Find out what the sounds mean.

   - ▶ Prepare a list of the sounds and their meanings to share with your class.

6. Haitian songs are often about work.

   - ▶ Make up a work song about doing math or cleaning up the classroom.

7. Haitian art is very distinctive and colorful. Use resource books to educate yourself about this lively art form. When you feel you "know" Haitian art, ask yourself these questions: What element contributes most to making this art unique? What element contributes most to making this art similar to other Haitian art forms and art forms in other cultures? What does the art "say" to you? Choose a medium that you think would be fun to dabble in. Plan how to best express something you want to say.

   - ▶ Create a piece of art in the Haitian style that depicts Haitian life. Display and enjoy your work.

8. During the 1900s, Haitian writers began to develop their own literary style. Read one or more stories written after 1940 by Haitians. What characters or events do you think are unique to Haitian literature?

   - ▶ Alone or with friends, prepare a puppet show based on a Haitian story.

*More than a million Haitians have fled their government's oppressive regime. As many as 600,000 have gone to the United States; 400,000 to Canada; 25,000 to the Dominican Republic; 20,000 to Martinique and Guadeloupe; and 20,000 to Guyana. Another 15,000 have migrated to Venezuela, Surinam, Africa, and France.*

## Aurora's Day

Aurora Hector wakes up as usual, just as the mountaintops surrounding her village begin to color with sunlight. She lives in northern Haiti, just inland from the port of Cap-Haitien, about 3,000 feet above sea level in what was once dense jungle. Fruit trees and scrub bushes surround Aurora's house and drip moisture during the rainy season downpours.

Although Aurora is only nine years old, she is a responsible and respected worker in her family. Because she is the oldest daughter, she is up first, fanning the coals of last night's charcoal fire to heat leftover beans and rice for breakfast. The morning is cool, but she wears only a loose dress that hangs above her knees. Today she will take her sandals down from the shelf and wear them to town. The prospect of a journey to Cap-Haitien sends her running back into the house to wake her seven-year-old sister, Hortense, and her two younger brothers. Hortense will stay behind with the boys, playing games with other village children, many of them relatives. Old aunts, uncles, and grandparents will watch the children as they play naked in the stream, racing stick boats.

The children take care of the family's animals, finding choice bugs for the chickens and taking the goats to fresh grass. The cow that Aurora had known her whole life was sacrificed to Baron Samedi this year in a voodoo ceremony sponsored by her father. Aurora was proud and the meat was delicious.

Her father, Darien, has spent all week at the artist's market in Cap-Haiten, selling his mahogany wood carvings of birds that he imagines live in Africa. Though he has never seen these birds, he makes the deep red wood come alive. If his artwork sells well to the tourists who come on cruise ships to the port, he will buy a new goat.

As Aurora sweeps the packed dirt entrance to her family's straw-roofed hut, her mother, Renee, returns

from the stream with two plastic buckets full of water. The family will drink the water and use it to wash with for the day. Renee has already picked two baskets of mangoes, which she and Aurora will carry on their heads 3 1/2 miles to the bus stop.

Kissing the younger children goodbye, Aurora and her mother begin to sing as they hurry down the steep path to the road below, where they can see the beautifully painted bus arriving with neighbors already aboard. The journey to town will be long and slow, but the excitement of selling mangoes, seeing her father, and coming home in time for a Coumbite house-raising for her aunt makes Aurora dance despite the weight on her head.

## Activities

1. Interview one or more nine-year-old friends, neighbors, or relatives. Include the following in the interview: What responsibilities do you have? How do you spend a typical day? How are you learning what will be required of you when you are an adult? What do you do for fun?

   ▶ Write an essay that compares and contrasts Aurora's life with that of the nine-year-old(s) you interviewed. Describe what effects you think the current lifestyle of the children will have on them when they are 18 years old.

2. Find out about the typical day of a Haitian child. Compare your typical day to the child's.

   ▶ Make a pie chart of how much of your day is spent in school, chores, and play. Make another pie chart of a day in the life of a Haitian child. Compare the two.

# *The Owl*

### *A Haitian Folktale*

Owl thought of himself as ugly, but one night he spoke to a girl who seemed to like him. He returned the next night, and the next, and the next. One evening, after he had left, the girl's mother asked her daughter why Owl never came to visit in the daytime. Owl had told the girl that he worked all day and could not come to visit before sunset.

The mother felt the family had to see Owl's face before they could consider letting him wed their daughter. So she invited him to a Sunday afternoon dance in his honor. Though Owl was pleased about the party, he was frightened that the girl would see his face and no longer love him.

He convinced his friend Rooster to come to the dance and give him courage. But when Owl saw Rooster that afternoon, so handsome and fashionably dressed, he was filled with shame. He insisted that Rooster ride ahead and tell the party guests that Owl had an accident and would come later. After sunset Owl rode to the party, snuck in, and said to Rooster, "Tell me when the sun begins to rise, so I can hide before it is light."

The girl was very happy Owl had come and proudly introduced him to all her relatives. "Come and dance," she said as she pulled him to the center of the party.

> *Dong ga da, Dong ga da, Dong ga da,*
> *Dong ga da, Dong ga da, Dong ga da. Eh–ee–oh.*
> *Owl danced and he danced very well.*
> *Dong ga da, Dong ga da, Dong ga da,*
> *Dong ga da, Dong ga da, Dong ga da. Eh–ee–oh*

When he looked up from his dancing, he noticed Rooster was dancing so hard that he was not watching for the sun. Owl excused himself from his partner and ran to a clearing to look for the dawn. He returned to dance.

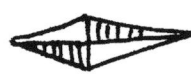

*Dong ga da, Dong ga da, Dong ga da,*
*Dong ga da, Dong ga da, Dong ga da. Eh–ee–oh*

He tried to excuse himself again but the girl said, "Stay with me," so they danced and danced and danced.

*Dong ga da, Dong ga da, Dong ga da,*
*Dong ga da, Dong ga da, Dong ga da. Eh–ee–oh*

They danced until the sun moved high into the sky, and the mother cried, "Now we can see your face!" and Rooster crowed "Kokioko." Owl tried to cover his face with his hands, and he ran to his horse. The girl cried, "Wait, Owl, wait!" When he lowered his hands to untie his horse she saw what she thought was the most fiercely handsome face in Haiti. "Owl!" she cried again, but Owl had already galloped away and never returned. The lonely girl married Rooster. But in the mornings when he crowed "Kokioko–o–o," she thought about Owl.

## Activity

Folktales may teach a lesson, or moral. What do you think the moral of "The Owl" is? Read or review six to eight Haitian fables or folktales.

► Record the name of each and write its moral in a complete sentence. Find an interesting way to share these morals. Possible ways to share include illuminated manuscript, "papyrus" scrolls, murals, or posters.

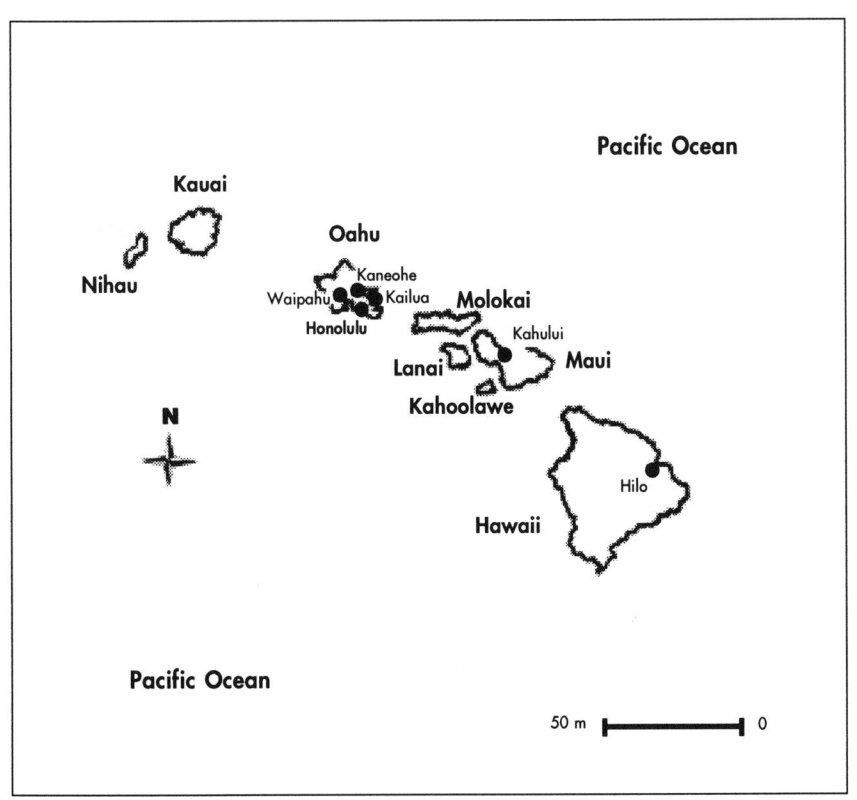

## Overview

**M**ention Hawai'i and the mind fills with images of tropical rain forests, balmy trade winds, and hula dancing. This beautiful island chain in the middle of the Pacific Ocean holds a certain magic for all who visit. Surrounded by the open sea, Hawai'i seems the most remote of all land forms, and this factor has been significant in both its natural and human

history. Honolulu is 2,397 miles from San Francisco, and the nearest inhabited land to the west is Guam, almost 3,000 miles away.

Of the approximately 132 islands, which were formed by volcanoes, only seven are inhabited. Hawai'i's isolation means it must import everything it needs, and it is particularly vulnerable to fluctuations in the cost of shipping and air travel. It is one of the most expensive places on Earth to live.

## *Historical Background*

Hawai'i's human history begins with the early expert navigators who first discovered the island chain. Polynesians from the Marquesas Islands, and later from Tahiti, crossed the uncharted Pacific Ocean in large double-hulled canoes. For more than 1,000 years, Polynesians inhabited the islands, which were unknown to the Western world. Then, in 1778, an English sea captain, James Cook, stumbled upon the islands while sailing from the Society Islands to the northwest coast of America.

As European traders began coming to the islands in greater numbers, a native chief, King Kamehameha, established his domain over all the islands. He began trading with the foreigners, exchanging sandalwood for gold and arms. The influx of Europeans brought changes to Hawai'i. Many Hawai'ians died of diseases to which they had no resistance. The population, an estimated 250,000 to 300,000 when Cook landed, fell to 56,897 by 1872, a figure that included a large percentage of nonnative newcomers.

In 1820 Protestant missionaries braved the hard journey from New England to Hawai'i. These stern New Englanders wanted to convert the natives to Christianity. In addition to bringing Western religion,

*The federal government employs more people in Hawai'i than does any other organization.*

they also introduced plantation agriculture, wrote down the Hawai'ian language, made the women wear muumuus (long, loose dresses), and forbade the hula dance, ignoring its sacred nature and significance as a method of relating history. New England businessmen brought Chinese, then Portuguese and Japanese, and later Filipino workers to Hawai'i to work the sugarcane and pineapple plantations.

*Hawai'i is in the Pacific Ocean, about 2,400 miles southwest of California.*

Although the Hawai'ian monarchy continued to reign, American businesses were gaining influence and power in Hawai'i. In 1893 a group of sugar growers and landowners made Queen Lili'uokalani a prisoner in the Iolani Palace and forced her to abdicate the throne. This takeover, led by Sanford Ballard Dole, the son of an American missionary, ended the monarchy forever.

On July 4, 1894, Dole and his followers formed the Republic of Hawai'i, with Dole as president. The islands were then annexed by the United States in 1898 and made a U.S. territory in 1900. Dole was appointed governor and Prince Kuhio, a nephew of Queen Lili'uokalani, became one of Hawai'i's first delegates to Congress.

The United States recognized the strategic importance of Hawai'i as a military outpost, and in 1908, Congress approved construction of a gigantic naval base at Pearl Harbor on O'ahu. This military base was the scene of the Japanese bombing on December 7, 1941, that drew the United States into World War II.

Hawai'i became the fiftieth state on March 12, 1959. The resident population is now more than one million. Native Hawai'ians constitute less than 20 percent of this number, and only ten thousand of those are direct descendants of the early Polynesian settlers. Finally recognizing the unjust takeover of the Hawai'ian government in 1893, the United States government in 1993 officially apologized to the Hawai'ian people for overthrowing Queen Lili'uokalani. In recent years native Hawai'ians have organized a strong movement for independence.

*O'ahu, third in size
among the islands, is
home to more than
three-fourths of
Hawai'i's people and
the only skyscrapers
in Hawai'i.*

❦ ❦ ❦ ❦ ❦

*Kaua'i, the oldest
island, is called
"the Garden Island."
Mt. Waialeale, its
highest peak, has been
called the wettest
place on Earth.*

## Activities

1. The earliest people to settle in Hawai'i were expert Polynesian navigators who crossed the uncharted ocean in double-hulled canoes. Research early navigational methods. How did sailors know where they were and how to get where they wanted to go?

   ▶ Make a large map that includes the Marquesas Islands and Tahiti as well as Hawai'i. Show possible routes from the former to Hawai'i. To accompany the map, draw or construct models of early navigational instruments and sailing vessels. Provide a written explanation of how these worked. Or create a chart showing the constellations they would have used to find their way.

2. Learn as much as you can about King Kamehameha. How did he gain power over all the islands? How did he rule and communicate with the various islands? How did the people feel about him? Pretend you are an English merchant who wants to trade gold and weapons for sandalwood.

   ▶ With one or more friends, prepare a skit that demonstrates what you have learned about the king and his kingdom. Your approach and sales pitch to the king and his responses should give information and clues about his reign.

3. The Protestant missionaries who arrived in Hawai'i in 1820 significantly changed life on the islands. Learn about the missionary period. What was accomplished? What aspects of Hawai'ian culture were lost, or at least forbidden?

   ▶ Develop two diaries, one that reflects a missionary's view of these events and one that reflects the beliefs and feelings of a Hawai'ian whose life is being changed. In the diary entries, be sure to include the positive and negative effects of the changes.

4. In 1778, Captain James Cook "discovered" the Hawai'ian Islands. Research Captain Cook. Find out about his journeys and his character.

   ▶ Make an illustrated time line of Hawai'ian history from 1775 to 1900. Mark in some way those events that were related directly to Cook's discovery. Be able to give an oral explanation of what you think is the most important event of this time period, including why it is the most important.

5. Imagine you were on The Discovery with Captain Cook. In your library, find the actual journals of Cook and his crew.

   ▶ Write a journal as you experience meeting Hawai'ians for the first time.

6. Learn about the plantation agriculture that the New England Protestant missionaries brought to Hawai'i. How did it work with crops that grow well in Hawai'i, such as sugarcane and pineapple? Why was it necessary for the New Englanders to bring in workers for the plantations?

   ▶ With two or three friends, develop a mock plantation owners' meeting to discuss problems, needs, and profitability of your plantations. Be prepared to answer questions the class may have following the presentation.

7. Learn about Sanford Ballard Dole. Where was his family originally from? Where and when was he born? How did his upbringing and education prepare him to be a leader of the American takeover of Hawai'i? What were the main reasons he wanted the Hawai'ian monarchy destroyed?

   ▶ Make an outline of a speech Mr. Dole might have prepared to convince other Americans to support him in his move for power. Organize the speech to support your requests for help; make the speech persuasive.

*Mau'i, the second largest island, was once two separate land masses. Erosion from mountain slopes formed the isthmus that joins them.*

§ § § § §

*Moloka'i, shaped like a shoe, is a quiet place where many traditional ways of life have been preserved.*

§ § § § §

*Hawai'i, the newest and largest of the islands, has an active volcano, coffee farms, and fields of sugarcane.*

*The newest of the fifty states and the only state that is completely surrounded by water, Hawai'i is unique for many reasons: It is the only state that was once an independent kingdom.*

8. Research the life of Queen Lili'uokani of Hawai'i. What were her family origins? How was she prepared to become queen? What were her duties? How was the monarchy organized?

   ▶ Write diary excerpts from different periods of the queen's life: as a young girl, a young woman, queen, and as a woman who was forced to abdicate her throne. Be sure you include her feelings as well as the events that were taking place. Plan and present a play or series of skits leading up to and following the forced abdication of Queen Lili'uokani. Include scenes based on the following events: Sanford Ballard Dole's rise to power, Queen Lili'uokani's imprisonment in Iolani Palace, the abdication, and the naming of Dole as president of the Republic of Hawai'i.

9. In 1993 the U.S. Government officially apologized to the Hawai'ian people for overthrowing Queen Lili'uokalani in 1893. Learn about what led up to the apology. Who led the movement? How did the people bring the apology about? What, if anything, did the apology accomplish? Take a stand on the fairness of and need for the apology.

   ▶ Prepare and deliver a speech that presents and supports your beliefs regarding the apology.

10. Find out about Hawai'ian history. What do you think were the most significant events? What events changed the course of Hawai'ian history?

   ▶ Make a time line that shows the events and their effects. Illustrate your time line. Present it to your class.

## *The People*

Early Hawai'ian society relied upon a strict caste system to determine each person's role. Station in life was determined by ancestry and birth. The law of the land, or *kapu* system, had many rules and was strictly

enforced. For example, a commoner who carelessly let his or her shadow fall upon the body or even the path of a chief could be put to death. If a person who broke kapu could reach the *heiau* (temple) in one of the refuge cities before being caught and put to death by pursuers, however, he or she could be purified by a priest. Once purified, the person would be absolved of the infraction and allowed to live.

From all accounts, the Hawai'ian *ali'i* were treated as a breed apart from the common people. Larger than the average people, they were also stronger. The king had to prove he was the strongest person and therefore able to defend himself and his people against all enemies. But there was more to this royal line than superior size and strength. The ali'i learned the languages, culture, religion, and science of the European visitors to Hawai'i. They learned to negotiate and trade with the foreigners and smoothly made the transition, in less than four decades, from ruling an isolated, simple culture to consorting with European leaders.

Common men and women were given tasks according to their gender. Men cooked, fought, fished, built houses and canoes, and made implements and utensils. They also made feather robes, farmed, and were priests. Women made cloth, wove mats and baskets, and raised children. There was no routine work schedule and no money.

The common people were like tenants in a feudal system. They were required to work for the chiefs, contributing goods and labor and paying taxes in the form of foods, cloth, mats, and feathers. The common people also fought, built roads, and cleaned irrigation ditches—whatever needed to be done in the community.

Before the missionaries came, people did not work according to a specific schedule. But the missionaries established a seven-day work week, and people were required to work one day a week for the king and one day a week for a local overseer. Although physically strong and trained to be warriors, the Hawai'ian people were docile and obedient to the

*Hawai'i's population is a multicultural mix of Caucasian, Asian, and Polynesian peoples. No group is a majority. Though Hawai'i is part of the United States, the English spoken there includes words and phrases from seven or eight languages.*

*Of the fifty states,
Hawai'i has the
highest percentage of
people who have more
than one job and the
highest percentage of
two-income families.*

king and his commands. This habit of obedience made the Hawai'ians very susceptible to the demands of the missionaries, who told the Hawai'ians that many elements of their traditional society were shameful and needed to be changed. The sacred hula dance was forbidden and thus much of the oral history passed on during the traditional dance was lost.

In the decades following Hawai'i's initial contact with the outside world, wave upon wave of immigrant groups flowed into the region. Today, Hawai'i is a society of minorities, with no ethnic group predominating. The largest single group traces its origins to southern Japan and Okinawa. Other major groups include Europeans and European Americans, Filipinos, Chinese, and native Hawai'ians. This mix of cultures is evident in Hawai'i's present food, music, language, and celebrations.

## Activities

1. Learn about caste systems in general and the early Hawai'ian caste system in particular. How do caste systems develop? Are there caste systems in this country? Why do they continue? How were the castes in Hawai'i identified?

    ▶ Write and produce a play based on the Hawai'ian caste system. Be sure to include the following elements:

    *The ways in which members are assigned to a caste*

    *Rules, tabus, privileges, and duties assigned to each caste*

    *Situations in which members of various castes must interact*

    *A debriefing following the play:*

    How did participants feel during the play? Why did they feel in these ways?

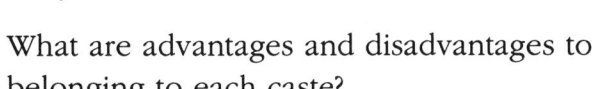

What are advantages and disadvantages to belonging to each caste?

What advantages and disadvantages does the caste system have for a society?

2. Research the Hawai'ian kapu system. Who enforced the rules? Who benefitted most from the kapu system?

   ▶ Develop a board game based on the kapu system. Design the game so that a variety of types of people (men, women, priests, commoners, chief) are included and so people who play the game will learn about kapu.

3. Find out about the traditional roles of men and women in Hawai'i before the mid-1800s. Analyze your household or that of a friend in regard to task responsibility. For example, who does the laundry, the cooking, and so on?

   ▶ Make a large chart that shows the traditional Hawai'ian roles by gender and those of the household you analyzed. List similarities and differences you observed and your conclusion as to which is the better situation and why it is better.

4. Learn about feudal systems. What frustrations do common people have in such a system? What advantages do they have? Explain how the tenants and the chiefs got what they needed to survive.

   ▶ Develop a large poster map of a feudal chief's land, including the following information:

   *where the tenant lives*
   *how the land is used*
   *where the chief lives*
   *how the chief and his holdings are protected*
   *the duties of the tenants*
   *the responsibilities of the chief*

*The 250,000-acre Parker Ranch on the island of Hawai'i is the largest privately owned cattle ranch in the world.*

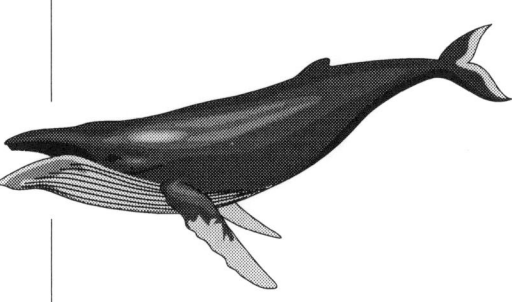

5. Learn about the sacred hula dance and what its movements mean and the stories they tell.

   ▶ Prepare a demonstration of the hula dance to share what you learned. Use Hawai'ian chants or record music.

6. One of the Hawai'ian missionary accomplishments was to codify and write the Hawai'ian language, which made written records and history possible. On the other hand, by banning the sacred hula dance, the missionaries caused much of the oral history to be lost. Learn as much as you can about these losses and gains, then decide whether more was lost or gained through these changes.

   ▶ Write an editorial stating and supporting your conclusion or, with another student, present a debate. Include the following information

   *specific gains and effects*
   *specific losses and effects*
   *your opinion*
   *support (reasons) for your opinion*

7. Research immigration to Hawai'i during the last one hundred years. Learn about the tradition, culture, and languages various groups brought to Hawai'i. Choose three to five current Hawai'ian practices.

   ▶ Make a large chart that illustrates the following:

   *the custom*
   *its country of origin*
   *how, if at all, it has changed in Hawai'i*

8. Find out about Father Damien. What did he do for Hawai'ian people? How did he die? When did his ministry occur?

   ▶ Write a short biography of Father Damien. Use it as the focal point of a presentation. Include in your presentation a map of Hawai'i on which you indicate where the colony was.

*The rainfall and vegetation in the great rain forests on the windward side of all the islands are essential to Hawai'i. The rain provides water for drinking and agriculture. Forests catch the water and prevent it from running off the rocky soil and back into the sea.*

# *Wildlife and the Environment*

Scientists believe that the hoary bat and the monk seal were the only mammals living on the Hawai'ian Islands before settlers arrived. Marine mammals such as whales and dolphins have lived in Hawai'ian waters since ancient times. Domestic animals were introduced by the Polynesians and Europeans. The mongoose was introduced in 1883 and has nearly decimated the ground bird population. Today deer, wild boars, wild goats and sheep, rats, frogs, toads, and mongooses are among the wild animals found in Hawai'i. In some areas, efforts are being made to restore native species.

The Hawai'ian Islands are inhabited by 150 species of birds. About 40 of these species were introduced from other places. Several are rare species found nowhere else in the world. About seven hundred species of fish swim in Hawai'ian waters. The coastline is bordered by coral reefs, which provide a habitat for large numbers of marine animals. Many brightly colored fish live inside the reefs, and many species abound inside tide pools.

Although hundreds of species of orchids grow in Hawai'i, only four of these are native. A few native wildflowers and wild plants persist in the mountains above 1,500 feet. Below that, virtually all native plants have been replaced by species introduced by humans.

The balance of nature in Hawai'i has been upset at every level since the arrival of Captain Cook. Indigenous plants and original rain forests were destroyed, first by the overharvesting of sandalwood and then by the introduction of livestock.

As the rain forests receded, plantation owners, who were concerned about the loss of rainfall, randomly reseeded the forests with little concern for the consequences. Seeds were gathered from trees all over the globe. Many species were poisonous or, like the Himalayan blackberry, untamable. In fewer than 150 years, humans destroyed a forest and an ecosystem that took twenty to thirty million years to evolve.

*The Hawai'ian hawk lives only in Hawai'i and is an endangered species.*

*Each of the islands contains within it a great lens-shaped body of fresh water, an artesian well, beneath the inactive volcanoes.*

In the old days, the simple hook and net fishing methods of the Hawai'ians did little to threaten the vast numbers of species there. But today, the fish populations of the reefs nearest to shore have been reduced by overfishing, bleaches and detergents spilled into the water, free-floating fishing lines and nets, and plastic litter.

Other environmental threats come from active volcanoes. Lava seeps down the mountainside, sometimes destroying beaches and whole subdivisions in its slow but steady wave. When it hits the ocean, the steaming lava sends up a cloud of sulfuric gas that seriously affects Hawai'i's air quality.

Some people have suggested harnessing the volcanoes' geothermal energy for electric power. This would help free Hawai'i from its dependence on imported oil and would provide a clean and local power supply for all the islands. Opponents point out the dangers involved with a highly unstable power source, and some believe that the spirit of Pele would not stand to be bound. These arguments have brought geothermal power development to a standstill.

## Activities

1. Find out about Hawai'i's geographical elements. Where are the tallest mountains? Where are the islands' sources of fresh water?

   ▶ Build a large, three-dimensional model of the Hawai'ian Islands. Use clay or dough to shape the volcanoes, sugar or salt for the beaches. Remember that some of the beaches are made up of black sand.

2. Since Captain Cook's arrival, many or most of those coming to Hawai'i have upset the balance of nature at some level. Select a time period or a group of people on which to focus. Learn what impacts on the environment are related to the time or the group and the long-term effects of the impacts. What lessons could be learned from your

study? Imagine that you lived during that time.

▶ Write a news article or create a filmstrip about the sandalwood tree on Hawi'i. What did it look like? Where was it found? Who wanted it? Where did it all go? Are there any left? Bring sandalwood to class if you can. Design a campaign to present to the public the information and a plan for prevention or a remedy.

3. Many plants, animals, and birds have been introduced "successfully" to Hawai'i. Choose a species to research. Why was it brought to Hawai'i? Why did it do well or thrive? What benefits does it offer? What drawbacks?

▶ Make a film strip or a video that tells about the species in Hawai'i.

4. Find pictures of Hawai'ian fish that live on the coral reef.

▶ Make a painting or a drawing of what you would see if you were snorkeling.

5. Hawai'i was formed by volcanic activity, yet active volcanoes pose environmental problems. Learn about the destructive and constructive aspects of active volcanoes in Hawai'i today.

▶ Illustrate what you learn by constructing a diorama detailing the environmental impact of active volcanoes or showing the cycle that begins with an eruption and comes full circle, when plants and animals inhabit the eroded lava.

6. If the Hawai'ian people could harness the geothermal energy of their volcanoes to produce electrical energy, many of their economic and environmental problems would be solved or alleviated. Investigate geothermal energy and the possibilities of putting it to practical use.

▶ Develop a slide or tape presentation about these possibilities. Be sure to include the following:

*It is possible to scuba dive in the ocean and snow ski in the mountains on the same day on Hawai'i.*

*positive and negative aspects and effects*

*possible problems*

*recommendations as to whether the Hawai'ians should or should not harness volcanic energy*

7. Divide into small groups. Have each group choose and research a different life form or ecosystem from the Hawai'ian Islands area. This might include an endangered species, a rain forest, a volcano, or the coral reef.

   ▶ Present a panel discussion telling of the changes and environmental concerns of your topic.

## *Food, Festivals, and Celebrations*

Hawai'ians enjoy many celebrations. These include the Chinese New Year, which begins with fireworks and involves dragon dances and many street carnivals, and Prince Kuhio Day, acknowledging Hawai'i's delegate to Congress from 1902 to 1922. The Merry Monarch Festival is a competition among the best hula schools from all the islands and is held in April in Hilo, Hawai'i. To greet spring, Lei Day is celebrated on all the islands on May 1. The day features lei exhibits and competitions.

King Kamehameha Day is a cause for parades and pageantry in June, on a day set aside as a state holiday to honor Kamehameha I, who united the kingdom of Hawai'i. Bon Odori Festival is a Buddhist festival of souls celebrated on all the islands in July and featuring colorful dances and floating lantern ceremonies.

Hawai'ians enjoy a variety of foods, such as *ahi* (tuna), chicken *luau* (a stew made from chicken, taro leaves, and coconut milk), *haupia* (coconut pudding), *laulau* (a bundle made of butterfish and pork and steamed in leaves), and tropical fruits such as papaya, mango, and guava. Also common are Japanese foods, such as *saimin* (long, thin noodles and vegetables in

*Aloha means "hello," "goodbye," and "I love you" in Hawai'ian.*

a broth), *sashimi* (raw fish sliced thin, served with soy sauce), and *sushi* (raw fish served with vinegar rice and Japanese horseradish), as well as Chinese foods such as *dim sum* (Chinese dumplings) and *kim tee* (very hot pickled cabbage), and some Portuguese foods such as *malasada* (deep-fried doughnuts, without holes, dipped in sugar) and Portuguese sausage.

## Activities

1. Learn about the Chinese New Year as it is celebrated in Hawai'i. How long does it last? What is included? What are the reasons or history of the celebrations? Interview your parents, neighbors, grandparents, and or adult friends, asking them how they celebrate the beginning of a new year. What similarities and differences do you notice between the Hawai'ian celebration and that of the people you interviewed?

   ▶ Make a large, two-circle Venn diagram that illustrates your observations. Put the Hawai'ian customs in one circle, your family members' and friends' in the other, and the customs common to both in the overlap.

2. Prince Kuhio Day honors the prince who was a delegate to Congress from 1902 to 1922. Learn about this prince, his accomplishments, and the celebration. Select another person who is honored by his or her country as a statesperson or leader. (Abraham Lincoln and Martin Luther King, Jr., are two examples.)

   ▶ Write an essay that briefly introduces Prince Kuhio and the person you chose and explains why each is honored. Explain how the celebrations are or are not appropriate to what the person stood for.

3. Learn about the Bon Odori Festival. What is its origin? What do the ceremonies stand for, and why are they meaningful to participants?

*Many of the plants and animals found in Hawai'i exist nowhere else on Earth. It is the southernmost state, the westernmost state, and the only state that is not part of the mainland.*

▶ Make a large crayon resist painting that depicts the bondances or the floating lantern ceremony.

4. The Hawai'ian Thanksgiving is Makahiki. Learn about this holiday and its history. How is Makahiki different from and similar to a traditional mainland U.S. Thanksgiving?

▶ Prepare a skit in which you and a friend present the two holidays by taking the part of a person who is celebrating one of the holidays. For example, you might begin by dressing like a Hawai'ian person, introducing yourself by your Hawai'ian name, and telling about the history of Makahiki. Then your friend might introduce him or herself and tell why the first U.S. Thanksgiving was celebrated. Continue alternating with food, traditions, and other information about the holidays.

# Dances, Games, and Sports

Both men and women learn the hula dance, originally a type of prayer, but only men performed in the temple. Dancers were trained under strict supervision of a *kumu,* or priest. Traditional Hawai'ian hula dancers wore a *pa'u,* a sarong-type skirt (not a grass skirt), tied at the waist.

Surfing, above all sports, belongs to Hawai'i. With no continental shelf to slow down the swells, fast-moving waves can come out of deep water and hit the shallow coral reefs with explosive power. The north shore of O'ahu is considered the "Mount Everest of surfing." The high winter surf is the most challenging.

Although the origins of surfing are lost in prehistory, the ancient Hawai'ians developed the sport to a degree unmatched anywhere in the world. Early surfers had to be very strong because the first surfboards were made from solid wood and could weigh 100 to 150 pounds. Surfers were among those who took the

> *"The hula is the Heartbeat of the Hawai'ians. You stop the Hula, you stop the Heartbeat."*
>
> —*Kalakaua, the "Merrie Monarch"*

nails from Captain Cook's boats when he first dropped anchor.

One man who made surfing popular throughout the world was Duke Paoa Kahanamoku (1889–1968). Born in Haleakala, Mau'i, a direct descendant of the royal ali'i, the Duke grew to be a champion swimmer. He won the 100-yard freestyle race at the 1912 and 1920 Olympic Games and held the world record for almost 20 years. He was also world famous as a surfing champion. A surfboard sculpture, dedicated to Duke in 1989, stands near Waikiki Beach.

Lighter, smaller surfboards were made beginning in the 1940s. Boards are now designed to suit every purpose, from learning on gentle swells to riding the big waves. Surfers also have their own vocabulary: "Lip" refers to the leading edge of a breaking wave, "curl" is the lip of a wave when it's falling in an arc, and a "hollow wave" is one in which the lip pitches out, creating a tube.

Whatever advances are made in equipment, today's surfer waits, just as the fifth-century surfer did, for the perfect wave. In the end, it is the wave that hurls the surfer either toward the shore or under the water in a churning fury; waiting for the perfect wave is all that matters.

*"All my life I have studied and danced the hula. I can honestly say that I have accomplished many of my goals in life because of it. Winning various titles and honors in hula has made me a positive role model among many younger generations of dancers."*
*—Kapualokeokalaniakea*
*Dalire*

## Activities

1. Surfing is a very old sport. Learn about the sport and how it has evolved through the centuries. Learn what skills were and are needed for surfing on different types of boards.

   ▶ Make models of surfboards, from early to modern. Be sure your models exhibit the changes and constants in shape, material, and size. Present the models and explanations to the class.

2. Research surfing, concentrating on what makes a perfect wave.

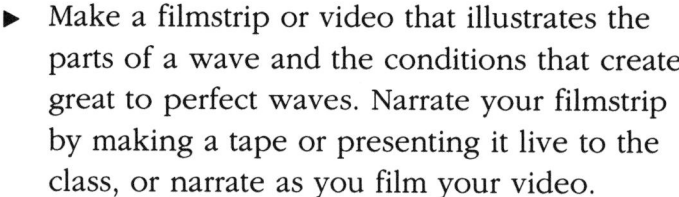

> ▶ Make a filmstrip or video that illustrates the parts of a wave and the conditions that create great to perfect waves. Narrate your filmstrip by making a tape or presenting it live to the class, or narrate as you film your video.

3. Find out about Duke Paoa Kahanamoku, the champion swimmer and surfer. Choose a period of his life you find particularly interesting

> ▶ Write diary entries he might have written during the period. Remember to include not only what he does but also what he feels and thinks.

4. Most people on mainland United States think the hula is performed by women wearing grass skirts. Research the hula. Where and when was it traditionally performed? Who performs it? Why was it traditionally performed? What did the people wear?

> ▶ Make an illustrated time line of the use of the hula from earliest times to the present.

## *Music, Art, and Architecture*

The sounds of a ukulele and a slack-key guitar are identified with only one place on Earth: Hawai'i. Like so many other aspects of Hawai'i's culture, its modern music is a mix of imported instruments and ethnic styles, including American folk songs, hymns, pop, jazz, and South American rhythms.

The ukulele was brought to the islands by Portuguese immigrants. The Hawai'ians thought its rapid plucking noise sounded like fleas jumping, so they named it "leaping flea" or ukulele.

The steel guitar was invented by a Hawai'ian schoolboy in the 1890s. He slid a steel bar along the guitar strings to make a crooning sound that ushered in what might be called the modern era of Hawai'ian music. Singers also sometimes sing in a slack-key style, sliding from note to note.

*Petroglyphs, pictures carved into rock by Stone Age artists, are found on every island in Hawai'i. Heiau, or stone temples, are also found throughout the islands.*

Ancient Hawai'ian music was, along with the hula dance, a means of worshipping, communicating, and recording history. Since Hawai'ians had no written language, their history, genealogies, values, religion, legends, and myths were all passed down orally. The *mele oli* was a chanted poem. Early chants had very little melody or variation in tune.

## *Activities*

1. Investigate the ukulele and the slack-key guitar. How has the music made by the ukulele changed from its original Portuguese version? How is the ukulele like other stringed instruments? Different from them? How is the steel guitar's sound unique?

   ▶ Learn to play a song associated with Hawai'i on the ukulele or steel guitar. Perform the song for the class and share with them what you learned about the ukulele and the steel guitar.

2. Find out about tapa cloth. How is it made? What materials are used? What kinds of designs are used?

   ▶ Create your own tapa cloth by making a geometrical block print on muslin fabric. Use styrofoam or balsa wood to carve out a pattern, then dip it into colored dyes, and color the material.

3. Find recordings of different forms of Hawai'ian music. What is the significance of each? Which types are used for spiritual reasons? Which are used only for entertainment? Can you hear the difference between music made by Hawai'ians for Hawai'ians and music made for tourists?

   ▶ Make a collection of different forms of Hawai'ian music to play for the class. Be sure to include chants with only drums, chants with music, ukulele and slack key guitar.

4. Find out about *kahili*. Why were they used? What is their significance? What colors did the Hawai'ians use to make them?

*This is how to count in Hawai'ian:*

one: *'ekahi;*

two: *'elua;*

three: *'ekolu;*

four: *'eha;*

five: *'elima;*

six: *'eono;*

seven: *'ehiku;*

eight: *'ewalu;*

nine: *'eiwa;*

ten: *'umi.*

▶ Make a kahili. Use an embroidery hoop and cloth to sew feathers on in layers that overlap each layer. Make patterns and pictures as you go.

## *Kaihu's Day*

*Each year, four times as many people visit the islands as live there.*

Aloha. My name is Kaihu. In Hawai'ian that means "light on the ocean." I am eight years old, and I live in Kailua-Kona on the Big Island of Hawai'i. I am an American, but most important to me, I am a native Hawai'ian. That means my ancestors were the first people to call Hawai'i home. My family believes it is very important to preserve our heritage, our language, and our culture, because if we don't, we will lose them and they will be gone forever. We speak the *olelo makuahine,* the mother language, at home. English is actually my second language. My friends and I also speak pidgin.

I live in a new apartment building. My family is on a list to receive land being held in trust for native Hawai'ians. We've been waiting a long time, but someday we will build our own home on the land. We cannot have pets in our apartment complex, but I have made friends with a little mongoose baby, who eats the food scraps I leave outside my door.

I go to Kealekehe Elementary School. I like hot dogs, hamburgers, and French fries. Someday I'd like to go to Disneyland. At school we wear T-shirts, shorts, and rubber sandals called slippers, or no shoes at all—it hardly ever gets cold here.

My dad works in a big tourist hotel, and my mother is a teacher. Sometimes I take my little brother, Kaniau, to our *tutu's* (grandmother's) house, and sometimes he comes to watch me at hula class. Hula is hard work. The men's hula that I am learning has kicks, punches, and jumps like the martial arts. But we also learn to chant the ancient songs, or meles, that tell the history of my people. In ancient times, the hula was a kind of prayer and was performed only by men.

Hula is taught in a *halau* (hula school). My halau has many good dancers, and last year we went to the Merry Monarch Festival in Hilo to see them dance. Halaus from all the islands come to compete. When the men from my halau performed the hula for the hunt, all you could hear was the sound of the *ipu,* their chanting, and their feet pounding the earth. All the people were silent. When the dance ended, the audience clapped so hard we thought Pele would wake up. At first I didn't like hula because my *kumu* (teacher) was so strict. But now I know he just wants us to be proud of who we are. Someday I want to be good enough to wake Madam Pele.

## Activity

What elements in Kaihu's life are traditional? Which are modern? How is his life similar to and different from yours? Who is Pele? What do you think Kaihu means when he says he wants "to be good enough to wake Madam Pele"? Pretend you are inside Kaihu's head as he goes through a day. What are his thoughts when his parents teach him about his ancestors? When he dreams about having a separate home? At school? At hula class?

▶ Write a narrative of Kaihu's thoughts, feelings, and opinions during the day. If you wish, make it into a cartoon that shows and tells his thoughts and actions.

# The Menehunes

## A Hawai'ian Folktale

Long, long ago, the garden island of Kaua'i was covered with a great and ancient forest. Because it had been growing since Pele first made the island, the forest was thick and filled with unknown things. In those old days, it is said, giants walked along the tops

*People use the mountains and the ocean as reference points when giving directions in Hawai'i. Makai means toward the ocean and mauka means toward the mountain. Since mountains form the center of each island and the sea surrounds each, the directions are easy to follow.*

*A ferry provides passage between Mau'i and O'ahu, but the channels between other islands are too rough for anything but large freight or cruise ships. Auto traffic has increased dramatically in recent years on all islands.*

of the great trees. On the forest floor lived a race of little people who came out only at night. While the giants were said to be mean, the little Menehunes were known for their helpfulness. Under cover of darkness, they built many walls and temples that still stand. But some of these structures are not quite finished, for if the Menehunes did not complete their work by sunrise, it would forever be left undone.

One of the Menehunes' greatest deeds was building the Alakoko fish pond. The Menehunes promised to build a pond for a princess and her brother. After sunset, they began to gather from all over the island of Kaua'i, gradually increasing from hundreds to thousands. They stood shoulder to shoulder, in a great double line that stretched for 25 miles. One heavy rock after another was wrestled from the Makaweli quarry and passed hand to hand down to the mouth of the Heleia Stream.

On the banks of the stream, the workers fitted the stones together like a great puzzle. Stone by stone, all night long, they built a wall to dam the fish pond. They were so quiet as they worked one could hear only their footsteps and occasional grunts as they passed the heavy stones.

The princess could hear them. She knew she must not look at them, for no mortal was allowed to see the little people working. Hours passed. The princess could not sleep; she could only listen to the sounds in the darkness and know something wonderful was happening. She had to know what the little people were doing. Most of all, she wanted to know what the Menehunes looked like.

The princess woke her brother, and the two of them crept over to the stream. A sliver of moon glowed with enough light for them to see that the wall of the fish pond was almost done. The two crawled closer to see the little people more clearly, although they knew it was dangerous.

Suddenly the brother and sister could see the Menehunes. The Menehunes were short, less than three feet tall, but strong and thick like ancient tree

stumps. They moved very quickly. They did not talk to each other, but hurried at their work, racing against the dawn.

Just then, one of the workers looked up. He shouted when he saw the royal pair. The prince and princess stood up to run, but at that moment they were turned to pillars of stone.

The time for building was over. There were still two gaps in the wall, but the sun was turning the sky pale blue. When the first ray of light flew like a spear from the sun at the ocean's edge to the beach, the Menehunes vanished. They never let the rays of the sun catch them.

On the beach that morning stood a 900-foot dam of precisely fitted blocks, four feet wide by five feet tall. You can still see the Alakoko fish pond near Lihue on Kauai. Pay particular attention to the two pillars of stone above the pond. They look just like two people looking at the dam.

It is said that the Menehunes celebrated their work with a feast of fish and shrimp. Although no one saw them, their joyful singing and drumming could be heard across the water on O'ahu.

*Everywhere you go in Hawai'i, you are walking on the tops of volcanoes, most of which are currently inactive.*

## Activities

1. Folktales from around the world share many common elements. What are some that came to mind as you read or heard this folktale? Collect another Hawai'ian folktale or a folktale from any of the cultures that inhabit the islands.

   ▶ Present the folktale to the class in a skit or on a filmstrip.

2. Many Irish folktales have "little people" in them. Read some Irish tales to see how Irish little people compare with the Hawai'ian little people in this tale. Choose one Irish folktale.

   ▶ Tell the Irish folktale and the Hawai'ian folktale to an audience. After your presentation, ask

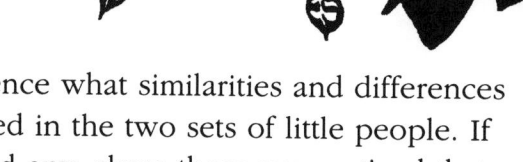

your audience what similarities and differences they noticed in the two sets of little people. If they missed any, share those you noticed that they didn't.

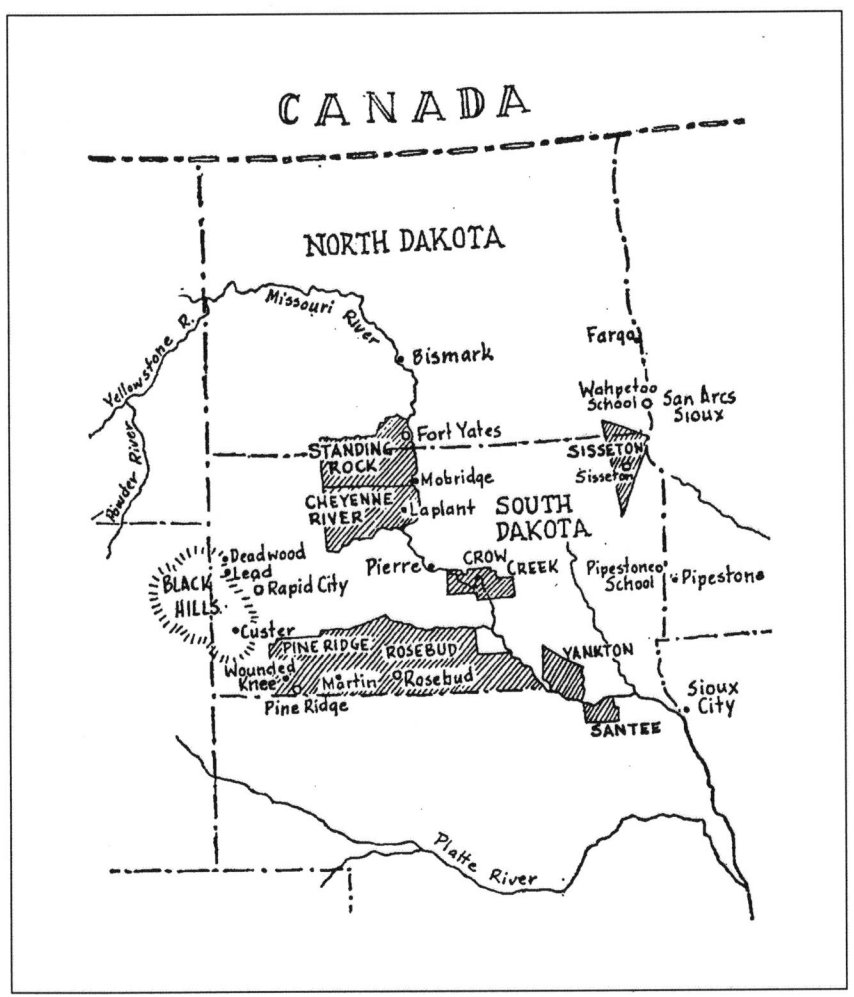

## Overview

**B**efore the 1800s, the Nakota, the Dakota, and the Teton (who called themselves Lakota) lived along the eastern wooded shores of the Missouri River. They were pushed west by European traders and settlers.

The enemies of the tribes called them Sioux, meaning snakes, and the Europeans adopted this name when they arrived. Today many of the

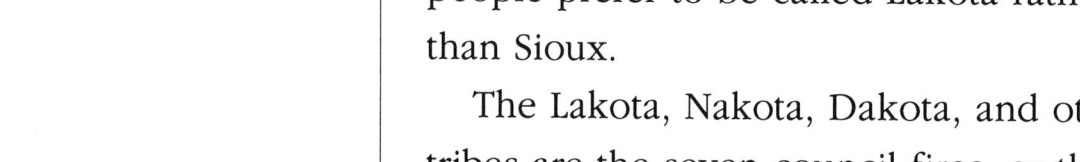

people prefer to be called Lakota rather than Sioux.

The Lakota, Nakota, Dakota, and other tribes are the seven council fires, or the seven western tribes, who refer to themselves as Ikche-Wichasha, which means the Real Natural Human Beings. The seven tribes are culturally and linguistically close, but originally they had only a loose sense of community. They did not come together as a political unit, though they did commune annually during the sacred Sun Dance and discuss common issues.

## Historical Background

Though they once roamed the vast prairie lands as free as the bison, today the Lakota live on reservations throughout North and South Dakota and Nebraska, sharing many of the reservations with other American Indian peoples. Before the fourteenth century, the Lakota lived in present-day Minnesota, Wisconsin, and Manitoba. In the seventeenth and eighteenth centuries, pressure from warring tribes and fur traders pushed them west onto the great plains, primarily the Dakotas.

During the course of their migration, the Lakota divided into three major subgroups. These tribes were close culturally and linguistically, but they had no formal political structure binding them to one another. During the annual Sun Dance, tribes came together to commune and discuss common issues. Each had its own chief and council members who made decisions.

When French fur traders moved into the Missouri River area in the seventeenth century, the Lakota and the traders clashed. The Lakota were pushed west

*Until Europeans introduced horses in the seventeenth century, the Lakota transported supplies using dogs to pull a sledlike travois, a construction of two shafts with material or hide stretched between. When horses replaced the dog, the Lakota called the horses "Spirit Dogs" or "Holy Dogs." Today people drive cars, and horses are used mainly for herding livestock and for pleasure.*

onto the Great Plains, home to the buffalo. The Europeans introduced horses, which replaced the dog-pulled travois as the Lakota's main method of transportation. With horses, the Indians could hunt bison more effectively than before.

Men hunted the bison, usually in one of two ways. The buffalo jumps involved a shaman dressed in a buffalo robe, who would imitate a calf. His behavior would cause the herd to follow him, and he would draw the herd to the edge of a cliff. The rest of the men would then stampede the herd over the cliff, killing many buffalo. At other times, the men would light fires around a herd, trapping the buffalo for the men to kill at will.

The women prepared the meat and the skins, and used every portion of the animal to make food, clothing, tepees, and a host of other useful items. The Lakota still use tepees, but not as their main shelters.

The Lakota raided other Indian encampments and fought against white settlers. The wars against settlers and the U.S. Army lasted thirty-eight years and were the bloodiest of the American Indian wars. Another enemy would also claim the lives of many Lakota in the eighteenth and nineteenth centuries: smallpox.

In the late nineteenth century, a merging of tribes became inevitable. The Black Hills gold rush brought a flood of white pioneers and forced the various Indian tribes to unite as allies against white settlers and the U.S. Army. In June 1876 the Lakota joined with other tribes to fight the battle of the Little Big Horn. The last major Lakota conflict with the U.S. Army was the Wounded Knee Massacre in late 1890, in which about two hundred Indians, including women and children, were killed. (The 1973 Wounded Knee incident was also a political and military confrontation.)

The massacre forced the tribes to surrender to the U.S. government, and they were placed on reservations. The Lakota chiefs and shamans were stripped of power, and the Lakota were forbidden to practice their religion. Starvation, foul water, and disease were just a few of the problems suffered on the reservations. Today's reservations consist of lands depleted

*U.S. schools had forbidden students to speak Siouan in schools and the people have virtually forgotten it; it is now spoken only by the elders. Since the movie* Dances with Wolves, *however, an interest in the language has been renewed in schools and the community.*

*Wounded Knee Creek is eighteen miles northeast of Pine Ridge. The incident began with a misunderstanding of the Wanagi-wachipi, the Ghost Dance.*

*The Ghost Dance is the most rigorous of all Lakota dances. Behind it was the belief that at some time the Earth would be flooded, washing away all white people and the unworthy Indians. The moon and the stars would aid birds in lifting to safety Indians who traveled the red road, the road of correct life that went into the sky, uniting deceased friends and family. When the waters receded, the Indians on the red road would return to a purged Earth and bring peace. The buffalo and deep grasses would be returned. Life would be as it was before the white people came.*

(Continued)

in resources, and the Lakota face increasing government restrictions.

In 1973, armed Lakota warriors waged a protest against governmental restrictions on their religious practices. Under the guidance of medicine men, they took over the Wounded Knee Massacre site and performed many rituals that the U.S. government had long forbidden. They held 250 federal agents hostage for seventy days. Under such pressure and heavy pressure by civil rights groups, in 1978 Congress finally removed bans on almost all Indian spiritual practices. The Lakota retrieved their Sacred Pipe from its hiding place, where it had been kept since the late nineteenth century, and began using it again, along with most of their other ritual objects.

Lakota shamans prophesied that the Dark Night of the Lakota would last 100 years, or seven generations, after 1890, the date of the Wounded Knee Massacre. Only after this one hundred years had passed would the Sacred Hoop, symbol of the Lakota nation's wholeness, be mended. In 1990, on the anniversary of the massacre, 350 Lakota horsemen rode through the battlegrounds in a December blizzard and celebrated their deliverance, which they call Wiping the Tears of the Seventh Generation.

Currently, the adult members of the tribal group elect a council and a tribal chairperson. The council members have the authority to represent the tribe in negotiations with other governments. The Bureau of Indian Affairs (BIA), a federal agency, helps tribal governments, providing technical assistance and striving to help the tribal governments become more self–supporting. The BIA administers and manages the land, including developing and directing water, mineral, and land rights, and developing agricultural and forestry programs.

Much more mending is needed, however, to eliminate alcoholism, diabetes, and tuberculosis, diseases that now plague the Lakota. Perhaps all people can learn from the buffalo, which "faces the wind, no matter if it's hot or cold."

## *Activities*

1. Respond in writing to the quotation of Jenny Leading Cloud (page 118). What do you think it means? How would the beliefs she mentions affect people's behaviors?

   ▶ Develop a similar paragraph that encompasses your beliefs or the worldview of your culture. How does this belief or view affect people's behavior within your culture? Prepare an oral or symbolic visual presentation based on what you have written.

2. Develop a time line that shows the history of the Lakota nation and its struggles with other Plains Indians, white settlers, and the U.S. government. Choose the event you believe had the greatest impact on the Lakota.

   ▶ Prepare a brief oral explanation of this event, its impact, and your beliefs about the importance of this event in Lakota history.

3. Why did the French fur traders "win" when they clashed with the Lakota? How were both groups affected by the conflict and what did they learn from each other?

   ▶ Make a poster that illustrates your responses to these questions. Prepare an oral presentation of your poster for your class.

4. Think about everything that happened in Lakota territory during the 1800s. Research the moving of the Lakota onto reservations. How do you think the Lakota felt about the events? How do you think white settlers felt?

   ▶ Write a diary that might have been kept by a Lakota person or a white settler during the late 1800s. Be sure to include feelings, everyday events, and major events in your diary.

*The Lakota believed that the harder they danced, the sooner the flood would come. They wore blue shirts with red streaks painted on them to symbolize the blue of the great flood with the red road. They also painted on the shirts the stars and birds that would lift the Indians to safety, as well as bullets to protect them from the Army's bullets.*

*Believing the dance to be in preparation for battle, the United States sent the Army to stop the dance from taking place. Among the men sent were those who remained of Custer's last command after the Battle of the Little Big Horn, who were eager to avenge Custer's death. The Army opened fire and killed more than 250 men, women, and children of Chief Big Foot's people.*

*Multiple bands of Lakota are scattered across the vast American prairie. These bands once made up a nation, not only with a common Siouan language but also with a common culture. Now the Lakota share reservations with other tribes, such as the Cheyenne.*

5. Why do you think conquerors usually make the people they conquer give up their religious beliefs? Research the Lakota Sacred Pipe and other religious and ritual objects.

   ▶ Write an essay about the impact on the Lakota of having their religious practices forbidden and having to hide their Sacred Pipe.

6. With one or more classmates, learn as much as you can about alcoholism, diabetes, and tuberculosis on the Lakota reservation. What elements of reservation life lead to these diseases?

   ▶ Formulate a plan to solve one or more of the problems. Develop a presentation to convince others of the importance of solving these problems and of using your solutions.

7. Find out about Lakota history. What do you think were the most significant events? What events changed the course of Lakota history?

   ▶ Make a time line that shows the events and their effects. Illustrate your time line. Present it to your class.

## The People

The nomadic lifestyle of the Lakota evolved as a survival tactic. People traveled to avoid depleting all the resources in one area and because the bison herds roamed and the people followed. At harvest time and through the winter, most bands would return to a main encampment and settle down until spring.

The men of the tribe were responsible for hunting and intertribal raiding. Women were responsible for cooking food and tanning hides for shelter and clothing. To spread out the workload and to maintain population numbers, polygyny (men had more than one wife) was encouraged. The elders of the tribe are respected for their wisdom and well cared for.

Girls married young and helped with the work.

Boys took care of the horses and played games. Boys' sporting contests helped prepare them for adult roles. Running and target shooting developed speed and agility and also improved hunting skills.

Coming-of-age ceremonies included celebrations that involved the whole encampment and vision quests, direct encounters with the Great Mystery Power. In the vision quest, one would leave the village to sit on a hilltop in a vision pit for four days and nights. Visions would come in dreams or voices and would instruct the person about personal medicine. The medicine would be collected items that were placed in a bundle or medicine pouch; only the person who collected the medicine could see the items. There could be many vision quests throughout one's life.

The Lakota had personal guides, known through voices, feelings, and visions, which grew out of the soil. The Lakota faith was closely tied with every aspect of nature. The item that most linked the people to the Great Spirit was the Sacred Pipe. Smoke from the pipe was cleansing and purifying. The values that the Lakota honor and instill in their children are respect for nature, gratitude to the dead, and duty to the unborn.

## Activities

1. How do you think the division of labor between men and women came about?

   ▶ Develop a series of vignettes that illustrates the development of the practices.

2. In what ways does your culture acknowledge coming of age? How are these customs related to adult life in your culture?

   ▶ Make a mural, poster, film strip, or video that illustrates coming of age in Lakota culture and in your culture. Show in what ways, if any, these relate to adult roles in the culture.

*The Lakota believe in personal guides that one knows through voices heard, powers felt, and visions seen. The guide grows out of the soil on which humans walk. The Lakota faith is closely tied with every aspect of nature the people experience.*

*The central element that links the people to the great Spirit is the sacred pipe, believed to be a pathway to the spirit world. Smoke from the pipe is cleansing and purifying.*

*Lakota men could not marry until they had counted coup. Counting coup meant to strike an enemy, but not necessarily to kill that enemy. The phrase was derived from the French word coup, "blow."*

3. Decide what objects are important to you. Close your eyes, clear your mind, and notice what images, thoughts, ideas, or actions come into your mind.

   ▶ Find items that relate to these visions and make a medicine bundle. Keep the items hidden in your bundle. Only you should see your medicine bundle's contents.

4. Why do you think that more men than women are mentioned in many history books, folktales, and myths? Choose one significant Lakota male and research the females that were important in his life. If necessary, create a female personage based on what you find out about the man and the period of history. Or research a female that was important in her own right, as a healer, a leader, or in some other role in Lakota culture.

   ▶ Recognize these important females by creating a song, poem, or dance to tell their story.

5. Explore your town for cultural events related to the Lakota or another American Indian people that live in your region. Attend current American Indian events and report on the powwows, shows, or other events that you attend.

   ▶ Write a short history about the people you study.

6. Find out about some of the symbols the Lakota use to represent themselves and their beliefs. Choose one of the Lakota symbols that you feel represents you in some way.

   ▶ Find a way to use that symbol in a way that would be appropriate within the Lakota culture (paint it on a shirt, make a beaded purse, and so on). In a dance, poem, song, or some other form, show what the symbol means and how it represents you.

7. If you are not Lakota, what are some of the symbols that are important in your culture? What do they represent? What do they say about your

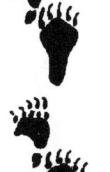

culture? How do these compare with the Lakota symbols? If you are Lakota, compare your symbols with those of another culture.

► Make a chart showing symbols from both cultures and comparing their meanings.

8. With some friends, talk about the qualities each of you has. Then come up with some names that reflect those recognizable characteristics.

► Make name tags with your new names and embellish the tags with geometric designs that you think reflect your name.

9. Find out about Black Elk. Read or have someone read parts of *Black Elk Speaks*.

► Draw a picture of him based on what you learn from the book.

## *Wildlife and the Environment*

The prairie is a vast grassland with very little rainfall. The dry, wind-blown earth discourages farming, except of grasses such as wheat. These grasses are rooted deep in the soil and can soak up the limited moisture. The high grasses are well suited to the grazing needs of bison.

This dry land extends north into Alberta, Canada. To the east, the plains are bordered by woodlands and rivers. More arid land lies to the south, and the foothills of the Rocky Mountains loom to the west. The assortment of flatlands, plateaus, dunes, hills, streams, valleys, and mountains made up a landscape on which the Lakota and other Plains Indians once made a good living.

When the Lakota roamed freely, the rolling plains harbored a variety of creatures. Prairie dogs and meadowlarks were abundant; the occasional majestic eagle flew across the plains; game birds hid in the grasses; waterfowl lived in marsh groves along the banks of the rivers. A wealth of big game—bear,

*The prairies to which the Lakota people moved from along the Missouri River were very windy and had an abundance of grasses. Bison, deer, and antelope thrived there. The bison are almost all gone. The only game animals that remain are deer, antelope, and rabbit. Prairie dogs are abundant and there is a sprinkling of coyotes, black bear, wolves, eagles, hawks, meadowlarks, and prairie snakes.*

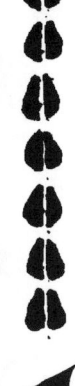

> *"We Indians think of the earth and the whole universe as a never-ending circle, and in this circle man is just another animal. The buffalo and the coyote are our brothers, the birds, our cousins. Even the tiniest ant, even a louse, even the smallest flower you can find— they are all relatives."*
>
> *—Jenny Leading Cloud*

white-tailed deer, pronghorn antelope, and mule deer—found shelter in deep grasses. Predators feasted on a host of smaller animals.

The creature the Lakota prized above others was the honorable bison. Before white people overflowed the land, the bison roamed the plains in great herds. The Lakota hunted the bison and used every part of the animal for food, clothing, tools, and shelter. Railroad owners and the U.S. government contracted hunters to kill off the buffalo, which nearly drove the bison to extinction. Plains Indians began to starve and were forced to surrender to white soldiers.

When people were forced onto reservations, Plains Indian life became a struggle for survival. The U.S. government often promised land in treaties and then later took the land away. Other treaties were never honored. The U.S. government has recently attempted to take water and mineral rights from reservation Indians in order to mine the resources.

One of the main values of the Lakota is respect for nature. Animals are honored and considered medicine that brings personal power, strength, and understanding, as well as healing for the mind, body, and spirit. The majestic eagle, the powerful bear, and brother wolf are a few of the strongest medicine animals. By observing the habits and patterns of their fellow creatures, the Lakota gain wisdom and understanding.

## Activities

1. In what ways are Lakota beliefs about material wealth and the land different from those of the U.S. government? How did these beliefs conflict with those of settlers?

   ▶ Make a large, illustrated chart that shows these beliefs and the conflicts that resulted from differing beliefs.

2. Research some of the environmental movements taking place today.

▶ Write an essay in which you compare and contrast the beliefs behind mainstream environmentalist movements today with the environmental beliefs of the Lakota.

3. Find out about the viewpoints of four to six of the following: Georgia O'Keeffe, Henry David Thoreau, Black Elk, John Muir, Diane Fossey, White Buffalo Woman, and others who have demonstrated a respect for nature. For more interest and variety, you might want to include people such as James Watt or J. P. Morgan on your panel.

▶ Create a round-table discussion in which you and your classmates represent the viewpoints. The discussion should reveal how these people feel about nature, wildlife, and material wealth.

4. Research the life of Crazy Horse.

▶ Tell his life story to the class and explain why he was considered such a great leader.

5. In 1990 bones of a Tyrannosaurus rex dinosaur were found on the property of Maurice Williams, a Lakota living near the Cheyenne River in South Dakota. Learn more about this incident and its importance to the Lakota. Who found the bones? What happened to them? How did the Lakota feel? Where are the bones now?

▶ Write an essay explaining the significance of this event, how you would resolve it, and your reasons for what you would do.

6. Remember an animal you have seen in your dreams and learn about its behavior. How does it protect itself? How does it find food? Where does it live? How might you learn from this animal's behavior, or medicine, as the Lakota would say? What qualities of this animal would be helpful for you to learn?

▶ Prepare a picture of the animal and a description of the essence of the animal and its spirit medicine.

*"These mountains are our temples, our sanctuaries, and our resting places. They are a place of hope, a place of vision, a very special and holy place where the Great Spirit speaks with us. Therefore, these mountains are our sacred places."*
—*Chief John Snow*

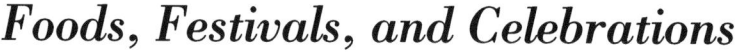

# Foods, Festivals, and Celebrations

Dances were named after the spirit, animal, or person that the dance honored. The Eagle Dance, for example, is a masterful dance. The eagle represents the power of the Great Spirit; the bird is considered a connection to the divine. It symbolizes that relationship of balance between the realm of spirit and the realm of Earth.

The greatest religious ceremony of the Lakota is the sacred Sun Dance, which is an annual summer celebration. All Lakota hunting bands and other Plains tribes commune for twelve days in a gathering called a surround. The Dance-of-Looking-at-the-Sun, or Wiwonyag Wachipi, was traditionally held at the end of the full moon in June or July. It occurred after bison mating season, when the herds were large and the animals' remaining winter coats slowed them. A buffalo hunt was held after the dance.

A special Sun Dance Lodge is built for the ceremony. Twenty-eight lodge poles, one for each day in the lunar cycle, are used to build the lodge. One special tree is placed in the center of the lodge to represent the center of the Earth, uniting it with the sky. The celebrants attach grease to the center pole to symbolize a plentiful life.

In the dance, thongs, usually four, are tied to the trees and the other ends pierce the warrior's body. As he dances, his flesh is torn, symbolizing the spirit's freedom from the bonds of the flesh and the tearing away of ignorance.

After the Indians were moved to reservations, the U.S. government banned the Sun Dance and other traditional rituals. In 1973, Indian rituals were made legal again, and the Sacred Pipe was unearthed. Present-day American Indians come together to celebrate and dance at powwows. Competitions in dress and dance create a magnificent display of pride.

Food and art work are exhibited at these celebrations. The food includes the traditional fry bread, smothered in honey-butter for a special treat. On rare

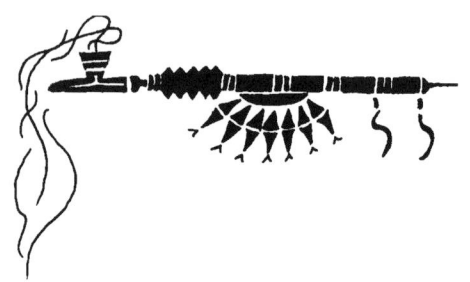

*The Sun Dance lodge is constructed to house the sacred annual Sun Dance. The number 28 is sacred to the Lakota: there are 28 days in the lunar cycle, buffalo have 28 ribs, and so on. The Sun Dance lodge is a huge tent supported by 28 poles made of cottonwood.*

occasions, pemmican, a jerked piece of meat, preferably bison, rubbed with tallow (animal fat) and dried berries, is served.

## Activities

1. Find out more about the Sun Dance. What is its purpose? What does it involve? If you are not Lakota, compare the Sun Dance to some of the rituals in your own religion or belief system. How are they similar? In what ways are they different?

   ▶ With some friends, create a dance (and the music, too, if you can) that symbolizes important elements of your belief system. Perform the dance and provide an explanation of its symbolism.

2. Learn about the Sacred Pipe—its history and its use in rituals. Where is it now, and when and how is it used? Who is responsible for taking care of it? How do young people learn about the Sacred Pipe?

   ▶ Make a narrated filmstrip or video to share what you have learned.

3. Clothing reflects culture and environment.

   ▶ Make Lakota clothes to dress a doll. Prepare a taped explanation of what the clothing tells about Lakota culture and environment.

# Dances, Games, and Sports

In addition to the Sun Dance, the Lakota Indians danced to express their joys and sorrows, to please the spirits, and to ensure the coming of the bison. Usually, only the men danced, making loud noises and wild gestures. Drums, whistles, and rattles would help waken the spirits. The audience's hoots and calls aided the dancers.

Many Lakota games help people improve their hunting skills. These games include archery, foot

---

**Indian Fry Bread**

4 c flour

1 1/2 tsp salt

1 Tbsp baking powder

1 Tbsp sugar or honey

1 c water

Make a sticky dough, adding more water if needed. Let rest for 30 minutes. Drop dough balls in hot grease. Turn to brown both sides.

Top with honey butter: 1/4 cup butter or margarine mixed with 2 tablespoons honey

---

races, horse races, hoop and pole games, snow snake, and lacrosse, with many of the people betting. Lakota women often played the stick game.

## Activities

1. Choose a Lakota game on which to become an expert. In a written, oral, or video presentation, describe the history and development of the game.

   ▶ Teach it to some classmates and play a demonstration game for the rest of your class. Describe its place in Lakota culture.

2. Dances were named after the spirit, animal, or person that the Lakota intended to honor: the eagle, for instance. Find out more about Lakota dances. Find out about songs from some other culture. How do you think the Lakota dance and song compare to that from the other culture as means of expression?

   ▶ Make a chart that compares and contrasts a Lakota dance with a specific song. What is the symbolism of each, who is being honored, and what is the message of each?

3. Find out about the guessing game that Lakota children play indoors. Then collect several sticks and paint one.

   ▶ Close your eyes and divide the sticks equally between a partner and you. Whoever gets the painted stick wins.

4. Find out about Snow Snake, a game Lakota children play during the winter months.

   ▶ Take turns hurling your sticks into the snow to see whose stick travels the farthest.

## Music, Art, and Architecture

Music is an important part of dances, play, and romance for the Lakota people. Traditionally, drums

*The word tepee is broken down in Siouan into ti, meaning dwelling, and pi, meaning used for.*

were made from rotted cottonwood stumps, which were hollowed out by burning. They were then covered on both sides with circles of wet rawhide attached with thongs. When the rawhide dried and shrank, it made a tight drum skin. The people used mallets to beat the drums.

Another loud instrument used for dances was the rattle, usually made from gourds or a rawhide ball tied on a stick. Wood was carved to make flutes for honoring spirits and romancing potential mates. The flute made gentle, birdlike music, whispering its sweet story song in a mystical way.

Clothing was heavily embellished with porcupine quills colored with natural dyes such as berry juice, bark, and other elements. Later, when the fur traders brought glass beads from Europe, the Lakota incorporated beadwork into the geometric emblems on their clothing. Shells were also brought from the northwest coast and were used for decoration.

The Lakota often painted on hides, clothing, and their bodies. Pictograph symbols were used to tell stories and record events and achievements. Paintings were also derived from visions and were believed to have supernatural powers. As a talisman, body paint protected warriors in battle and indicated the society to which a person belonged. Geometric motifs are distinctive symbols of the Lakota. In particular, the five-pointed star, light against a dark background, symbolizes human knowledge lighting up the darkness of ignorance.

## Activities

1. Research Lakota rattles to discover how they are made and used and why they are used.

   ▶ Make a rattle that is similar to a Lakota rattle. Plan a demonstration that includes the how and why of making and using such a rattle.

2. Go to the library and find a recording of traditional Lakota music. Listen to the drumming and

*Lakota*

The Lakota built fires, fueled with wood and buffalo dung, in the centers of their tepees. A hole in the top of the tepee allowed for ventilation. On present-day reservations, homes are heated with wood stoves, electricity, natural gas, and oil furnaces.

The Lakota tepee is still used, but not as a main shelter. Most Lakota currently live in trailers and subsidized government housing.

123

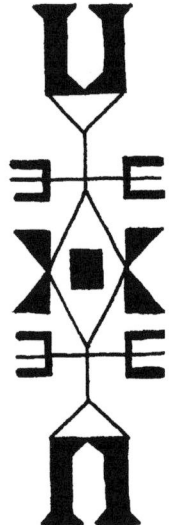

**Siouan words for**

one – *wahn-zhee'-lah*

two – *noo'pah*

three – *ree yah'-mee'-nee*

four – *toh'-pah*

five – *zap'-tah*

I – *Mu-ah*

You – *Nee'ay*

family – *wee-choh'way*

friend – *koo'lah*

dream – *e-hahn-bee-lee*

singing. Have the entire class sing along with a song from the recording. How does singing in this way make you feel?

► Write in a journal what the music brings to your mind.

3. Learn about pictographs. What advantages and disadvantages are associated with using pictographs to communicate?

► Design a bulletin board that illustrates these advantages and disadvantages by comparing a modern billboard to a pictograph.

4. Body painting is part of many cultures. Research the Lakota's use of body paint and that of one other culture. Compare and contrast the cultures' use of body paint in terms of colors and designs used, symbolism, source of colors, and occasions of use.

► Illustrate what you learned on a large, colorful, annotated poster.

# John Running Wolf's Day

John Running Wolf awakens to the smell of the wood-burning stove. His mother, Dorothy Running Wolf, is preparing breakfast before she goes to work. Outside, the sound of Grandfather's chanting blends with the songs of the birds and chickens. Each morning, Grandfather honors his spirit medicine in prayer. John's father died last year of liver failure caused by alcoholism.

After eating breakfast, John puts on a work jacket to face the chilly fall air. Red Cloud, John's horse, greets him at the barn, ready for breakfast. After feeding the chickens, John watches the sun peek out from the horizon.

The school bus honks, and John runs to grab his lunch—a cold Indian taco filled with meat and vegetables. At the reservation school, kids and teachers

alike have few resources, but somehow many students manage to succeed in school and to move on to college. Others must stay at home to help care for the family or get a job.

When John returns from school, he prepares dinner for Grandfather and himself. John's mother isn't home because she works a second job to support the family. Homework comes easily to John, so he finishes his studies, then sets aside a plate of food for Grandfather, who is in the sweat lodge. John must never disturb Grandfather during his purification ritual.

After John finishes the dishes, he and his horse trot off for their evening ride to the plateau. Watching the sunset on the horizon, the pair can hear coyotes yipping after a kill. When John and his horse return, Mother is waiting to kiss him goodnight. He is lucky to have the life he has, to learn from and to dream.

## Activities

1. What elements in John Running Wolf's life are closely related to traditional Lakota life? Which elements are modern?

   ▶ Pretend that you are inside John Running Wolf's head as he goes through a day. Write a narrative of his thoughts. What traditional and modern things does he learn from? What does he learn? Of what does he dream? If you wish, illustrate your narrative, or put it into a cartoon, film strip, video, or comic book that shows or tells his thoughts and actions.

2. Think about your daily life. How would you write a story that, like John's story, tells a lot about your daily life?

   ▶ Use pictographs to tell your story.

*Lakota women make two beaded pouches, one in the shape of a turtle and one in the shape of a sand lizard, for a new grandchild. The child's umbilical cord is put into one to represent longevity, and the other acts as a decoy for evil spirits. The pouch with the umbilical cord is hidden in the cradle board.*

# The Snake Brothers

## A Lakota Folktale

A long time ago, even before the oldest winter count, four young brothers, all good hunters, went scouting for buffalo. They soon came across a lone buffalo, which they killed with their arrows. The buffalo then spoke to them, saying, "Take my meat for nourishment, but leave my skin, head, hooves, and tail together in place."

The youngest brother felt they should do as instructed, but his elder brothers wanted to take the skin home. After a battle of wills, the younger brother persuaded his brothers to give the skin to him to do with as the voice directed them.

While the three older brothers feasted on buffalo hump, the youngest brother spread out the skin, skull, hooves, and tail on top of a hill. He then prayed to the buffalo who had given his flesh for the nourishment of the people. As he prayed, the buffalo parts joined together, bringing the buffalo back to life. The massive creature bellowed, then walked into the hills. The youngest brother watched the buffalo until it disappeared, then he rejoined his brothers.

When he returned, his older brothers laughed at him for missing the best meat. They told their young brother that they planned to take the skin home with them and went to the top of the hill to get it. When they found nothing, they thought the youngest brother was playing a trick on them.

They returned to camp and bedded down. In the middle of the night, the oldest brother awoke to a rattling sound at his feet. The other brothers awoke and the three eldest discovered that their feet had also grown rattles. The youngest brother wept by their sides as he watched his brothers' bodies changing into snakes.

The oldest brothers reassured their young brother that they would always remain his brothers and that they would look after the village. They told him to

*The Great Spirit, Wakan Tanka, was the most honored spirit to the people of the plains.*

return alone to the hole in the hill, which was the entrance to the snakes' home, and they awkwardly slithered into the hole.

The youngest brother took the buffalo meat back to the village and told the story to his people. Four days later, he prepared to go with a war party against the Pahani. He went to the hole and called to his brothers. They came out one by one to hear of his intentions. The eldest brought him a medicine bundle while the other brother-snakes joined in rattling, "This snake medicine will allow you to wiggle out of dangerous situations. The enemy will fear you because the medicine will cause you to strike swiftly with a deadly weapon."

The young brother thanked his brother-snakes and went to war. His snake medicine provided him safety and success. The people of the village were pleased with his performance and wanted to thank the snake brothers. They brought offerings of thanks to the snake hole in the hill with the youngest brother. The older brothers always protected the people with their powerful snake medicine, and the people never killed a rattlesnake after that.

### Activity

The Lakota see the rattlesnake, an animal many people view as evil, as a good friend with powerful medicine. Choose an animal that many people think is dangerous but that you think simply may be misunderstood.

▶ Write a folktale in which you throw a positive light or twist on the "negative" characteristic of the animal you have chosen. How might that characteristic be put to good use if the animal were your friend or a relative?

*The traditional Lakota bands each had a loosely formed government that consisted of a chief and council members, who discussed matters and made decisions for each band. Today a federal agency called the Bureau of Indian Affairs is one of the political voices for the people.*

By
Paula
O'leska

## *Overview*

**P**oland is one of the largest European
countries, approximately the size of
New Mexico. Poland is bordered on
the north by the Baltic Sea, where long sandy
beaches and forested coasts attract tourists.
South of the Baltic there is a lake region with
one thousand lakes, many of them still intact
and surrounded by forests. Then the land
becomes a plain covered with farms, which
occupy the whole central area of Poland. The

plains give way to hills farther south. The hills turn into mountains, culminating with the beautiful, rocky Tatra Mountains that constitute Poland's southern border (with Slovakia). The western border runs along the Nysa and Odra Rivers.

## Historical Background

Since the Iron Age, Poland has served as a crossroads of European trade and a player and sometimes pawn in the struggle for land and power. Originally, central and eastern Europe was inhabited by different Slavic tribes who spoke similar languages. The Holy Roman Empire was spreading Christianity. A Polanie tribal prince, Mieszko I, organized a number of tribes under his own rule. By accepting baptism for his people by the Czech kingdom, he became a sovereign ruler, an equal and ally of the emperor. The year 966 is considered the beginning of the Polish state.

Boleslav the Bold, Mieszko's son, was crowned king of Poland in 1025, thus solidifying the alliance with the western powers and establishing the Piast Dynasty. The Piast Dynasty ruled until 1370, when Casimir III died without a male heir and left the throne to his great niece Jadwiga, who was eleven when she was crowned in 1382. She was married to the Grand Duke of Lithuania, Prince Jagiello, by the Council of Nobles, a rudimentary parliament, and Poland merged with the enormous territory that included most of today's Ukraine and Belarus. Jagiello accepted baptism into the Catholic Church and became Vladislav II, King of Poland. Poland assumed the name of Dual Kingdom of the Crown and Lithuania.

The two hundred years of the Jagellon dynasty were a golden age of peace and prosperity for Poland. Still a forefront of Christianity, Poland was forced to fight to defend western Europe against the numerous

*Seventy percent of Poland's people live in cities and work in industry or services.*

attacks by the Moslem Tartars and Turks, as well as by the Russian Greek Catholics, who had ties to Byzantium.

By the sixteenth century, only 40 percent of the population was ethnically Polish due to the open-door policy of accepting political and religious refugees from the rest of Europe. Literature, arts, and science flourished. The Polish astronomer Copernicus (Mikolaj Kopernik) established the heliocentric theory of planetary motion in 1512.

The last Jagellon king died in 1571 without an heir. The Council of Nobles, which by then had become the parliament (Sejum), declared the monarchy elective. Although this was a gain for democracy, the move to elect kings brought with it the politics of private interest. The effort to restore order and transform Poland into a modern state united all patriotic forces in the Great Diet of 1788–1792. The Great Diet proclaimed a new constitution, modeled after the U.S. Constitution, freeing the serfs and promising equality to all classes. The neighboring absolute monarchies of Russia, Prussia, and Austria felt threatened and encroached on Poland. Despite the heroic uprising in 1794 led by Thaddeus Kosciuszko, famous for his role in the American Revolution, Poland could not reseist the overwhelming forces of the monarchies and was finally partitioned in 1795.

Despite the loss of political independence and the banning of the Polish language, Polish culture continued to evolve. Writers and poets, who endeavored to preserve the language, and other artists fled into exile. Composer Frederick Chopin was one of the more famous of those in exile.

Poland was able to regain its independence in 1918, but in 1939, Hitler invaded the country and war began in Europe. Again, the Polish language and culture were banned, and a widespread underground movement was formed to resist the invaders.

In 1943, the Allies signed the Yalta Agreement, which divided Europe into spheres of influence and gave the Soviet Union opportunity to dominate Poland.

*In western Poland is Biskupin, a site where archaeologists have discovered layers of cultures going back to the late Neolithic period of about 3500 years ago. A village with houses joined together dating from around 550 B.C.E. has been reconstructed at this site. It represents a community of approximately one thousand people living in an egalitarian system.*

*Poland is the site of several German extermination centers used in the late 1930s and early 1940s. Auschwitz-Birkenau is the most famous. With grass growing over the crumbling masonry of the former crematories, the uncompleted boiling-down works, and the pyre pits, it is hard to realize that four million people died here. But visitors can still see the double fence of posts curved like hockey sticks, the empty cylinders of the swift-acting Cyclon B gas that was used to asphyxiate masses of people, and the piles of human hair, clothes, and eyeglasses that the Nazis salvaged from the dead.*

Communists took hold of Poland. Their control was to last for forty years.

Despite repression and censorship under Communist rule, Polish culture and political resistance continued. Years of unrest culminated in the Gdansk shipyard strikes of August 1980. Solidarity trade unions, under the leadership of Lech Walesa, challenged the government of General Jaruzelski. Although the opposition leaders were arrested and martial law imposed for five years, the government was finally forced to accept the trade unions as partners. In 1989, Poland held the first free elections in the eastern bloc countries, ensuring a peaceful transition to democracy and a market economy.

## Activities

1.  From the mid-1800s until the present, Poland has struggled against foreign invasion and political upheaval. Choose an invasion or a political movement that occurred during this time period about which to learn. Why did it occur? Who was the leader? The opposition? What was the main issue? How was the conflict resolved? What were important short- and long-term effects?

    ▶ Make a large chart that illustrates your understanding of the conflict, its resolution, and the effects of the resolution.

2.  Learn about Solidarity. How did it begin? How did Lech Walesa come to be involved with it? What important events are related to the Solidarity movement? What has the movement accomplished?

    ▶ Make an illustrated time line of Solidarity's history to the present.
    *– or –*
    ▶ Make a large chart comparing Polish Solidarity to the U.S. trade unions.

3.  In historical times, kings and queens were often teenagers or younger, such as Polish Queen Jadwiga.

Find out what education Jadwiga had to have to be ruler. How does her education compare to your own?

▶ Write an essay about what you would do if you were the queen or king of your school, town, county, or state.

4. Poland has experienced communist, monarchist, and democratic governments. Find out about these systems of government. Who has the power under each system? How is the power divided?

▶ Chart the social, political, and economic differences in the three systems. Discuss the positive points and drawbacks of each.

5. Find out about communism and capitalism. What are characteristics of lifestyles in both systems? Why did communism fail in Poland and other Eastern Bloc countries.

▶ Create a board game that teaches others about the two philosophies and lifestyles. Be sure to include positive and negative aspects of both.

6. Find a recent newspaper or magazine article about Poland's government. How is the newly formed democracy working? What problems is Poland having.

▶ Present your findings to the class in the form of a television newscast.

7. Research the boundary shifts that have occurred in Poland over its history. When did each shift occur? Why did it occur?

▶ Make a series of maps showing the boundary changes. Label each map to include the dates and reasons for a boundary shift.

8. Find out about Polish history. What do you think were the most significant events? What events changed the course of Polish history?

▶ Make a time line that shows the events and their effects. Illustrate your time line. Present it to your class.

**Famous Polish people**

**Mikolaj Kopernik (Copernicus):**
*(1473–1543)*
*astronomer who established the theory that the Earth orbits the sun*

**Josef Koreniowsky (Joseph Conrad):**
*(1857–1934)*
*author of* Lord Jim, Heart of Darkness, *and other works*

**Marja Sklodowska Curie:**
*(1867–1934)*
*Nobel Prize–winning physicist*

**Karol Wojtyla:**
*(1920– )*
*first Polish Pope, Pope John Paul II*

*The Polish language is a branch of the western Slavic group of languages, but over the centuries it has absorbed a large number of Latin, French, German, and recently, English words.*

# The People

Polish people consider themselves warm, friendly, and hospitable, as well as independently minded and rebellious. They love foreigners. Many a tourist has found a new family in Poland, either figuratively or by marriage. Once they make friends with someone, that person becomes family, which means they will go out of their way (sometimes overbearingly so) to take care of him or her.

Family is very important to the Polish people. Families often stay in one location throughout their lives, so there is an extended support network with grandparents and friends contributing to household chores and childcare. In most families, both parents have to work, but daycare centers are readily available. If children go to college, they typically choose one close to home. Most children live with their parents until they marry, sometimes even afterwards, often in very crowded conditions because of the shortage of housing created by the Communist government.

The Polish version of "Blood is thicker than water" is "Closer is the shirt to the body than the overcoat." The phrase means that people take care of their own, but the phrase also applies to neighbors and community. It is common for people to "just pop in" for a chat, a cup of tea, or a glass of vodka.

Because of the advent of capitalism, people are currently forced to work harder and they have less time to spend at home. The people's values are also changing: traditional caring is often replaced by cutthroat competition.

Education starts at age 6 and is compulsory until age 16. In first grade, children are divided into classes of twenty to forty students and will spend the rest of grade school with the same class. This approach provides small children with a sense of stability they need and allows strong bonds of friendship to develop; these bonds often last a lifetime.

Through the first three grades there is only one teacher for all the subjects. Beginning in fourth grade, however, specialists come in and the teacher remains as class mentor or tutor, leading special periods for general subjects or special interests.

Beginning in the fifth grade, foreign language is compulsory. Almost everyone speaks at least a little bit of English, German, or French. English is extremely popular and many stores or products have English names, regardless of people's ability to pronounce them.

School begins at 8:00 A.M. Lessons are forty-five minutes long, with five- to fifteen-minute breaks between. Children go to school only for the time they have lessons, so the lower grades may be done as early as 10:30 in the morning. All schools have playrooms for children whose parents work.

At 15, grade-school graduates choose either *lyceum*, a program in humanities and the sciences, or *technikum*, a technical program that prepares students for a specific profession. Both programs have competitive entry examinations, fixed curricula with few electives, and the *matura*, a graduation examination that qualifies students to take entrance examinations to universities. The students who do not pass the entrance examinations to secondary schools are funnelled into narrowly specialized vocational schools of generally lower quality; these students do not receive a high school diploma. This policy has created a mass of undereducated workers, mostly from working class and peasant backgrounds, who are hard to retrain and cannot pursue further education easily.

Before the fall of communism in 1989, the schools were run by the government, but since then there has been a growing number of private schools with more flexible and alternative curricula.

There are about ten universities in Poland, which have a curriculum of liberal arts, humanities, and theoretical sciences. Technical science, medicine, arts, and economics are taught in separate institutions of higher learning. Most of the universities are located

*In Poland, children have to learn at least one Western language in school. By now, almost everyone speaks at least some English.*

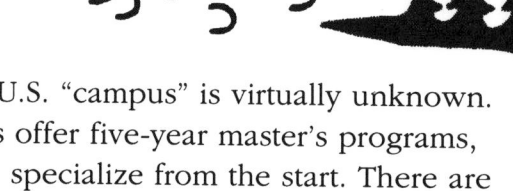

*The Catholic Church has played a major role in uniting the Polish people. Ninety-three percent of Poland's people are Catholic,*

within cities; the U.S. "campus" is virtually unknown. Polish universities offer five-year master's programs, in which students specialize from the start. There are no bachelor's programs.

Traditionally, teachers, especially university professors, have enjoyed very high prestige. The poorest families often aspired to have one or more of their children become teachers. The prestige has gradually eroded, however, due to the Communist government, which fostered anti-intellectualism, paid low salaries, trained teachers inadequately, and used the schools for indoctrination. Capitalism has brought its own problems, however; the focus on money and material success is rapidly replacing the old respect for learning.

Polish people have an indomitable spirit that manifests itself in fierce attachment to Poland's independence and many sacrifices to attain it. The spirit also manifests itself in a great sense of humor, which produced many jokes and much comedy, even during the most tragic periods of history, such as World War II and martial law in 1981. Communist humor was quite primitive and mostly aimed at ridiculing capitalists. Because of communist censorship, the Polish people turned to sophisticated humor and raised the art of allusion and irony to new heights. Everyone knew how to read between the lines, and even classical texts could be interpreted in a new way, as a comment on some absurd aspect of reality. With the fall of communism, both art and humor have to find new forms of expression. The Polish people, however, do not often laugh at themselves.

Communism is a totalitarian system introduced to Russia in 1917 through the Bolshevik Revolution headed by Lenin. Lenin claimed to be putting into action principles of Karl Marx's philosophy. This philosophy proclaimed "dictatorship by the proletariat," with the workers owning the means of production. It banned all religion, which Marx had called the "opiate of the poor." It taught that, in order to create the "new, communist man," it had to abolish capitalism, which is based on exploitation, and replace it with communal living. What the philosophy meant in practice was that the government became the sole owner of all land and factories. Of course, such ownership meant that the private property of millions of people was confiscated. The Soviet government did not allow any private property, but the Polish government had to grant concessions by allowing some peasants to own small farms, since confiscating them would have led to an uprising. In the U.S.S.R., collectivism resulted in widespread famine that killed an estimated two to three million people. Because Polish agriculture survived, however, Poland managed to produce excess produce to export.

In Communist Poland, all power rested with the Communist party, which controlled the government. All democratic institutions were just farces. Government planned everything, beginning with which industries were allowed to exist and ending with what plays small-town theaters could produce. The government established a huge bureaucracy that enjoyed immense privileges such as expensive cars, private villas, travel, and special goods stores, while the rest of the country struggled with shortages of everything from meat to shoes to housing to toilet paper. Individuality, creativity, and initiative were punished or at least discouraged, or had to be channelled through official government venues.

Even though Poland was a predominantly agricultural country, when the Communists took over in 1945, they forced it to industrialize in order to change the bourgeois mentality and produce a larger working class. Thus, inefficient steel mills and other heavy factories were built around large old cities such as Cracow, which caused serious environmental damage. The shortage of housing became so acute that parents would begin saving for children's apartments as soon as they were born. Everyone had to register their permanent address with the Communist police, which, ironically, was called the "citizen's militia," and carry an identification card at all times. People were not allowed to move to a big city unless they had an

*During World War II, one of every nineteen Polish people, totalling six million, were killed. Half of these people were Jewish. Three million Jews lived in Poland before World War II; about five thousand live there today.*

137

apartment, which often was only possible through marriage or, occasionally, through a job.

In addition to free health care, free education, and affordable housing, communism promised full employment (except, of course, if one was blackballed), which meant overemployment almost everywhere. The wages were low, so most people had second jobs. It was a common practice in many jobs, especially white collar jobs, for people to arrive at 8:00 A.M., do a little work, leave at 11:00 A.M. for a few hours to do some shopping (called "hunting" in those days) because the shortage of all goods often made it impossible to buy anything after work. The common saying was, "They pretend to pay us and we pretend to work." Over the years, the situation produced widespread contempt for work and a lack of self-discipline, which makes it very hard for many individuals to adjust to the demands of the current capitalistic society. This phenomenon is common to all of Central Europe. Even though communism turned equality into "equal poverty for all," a whole generation brought up under such conditions found it better than the uncertainty that came with democratic forms of government. Many Polish individuals, however, are taking full advantage of current opportunities, which is causing Poland to have the fastest economic growth index among post-Communist countries.

Living for two hundred years under domination, including communism and Germany's occupation during World War II, has resulted in another unfortunate phenomenon: contempt for authority. During those years, it was a virtue to disrespect and disobey the government. One could get almost nothing done without cheating or lying. Taking advantage of all institutions was something of which to be proud. Suddenly, there is a democracy, with a parliament, a president, and other government officials being chosen in free elections; the old attitude of distrust, however, cannot be changed so rapidly. Most observers predict that it will take at least one generation to

*Beneath the town of Wieliczka is one of Europe's largest and oldest salt mines. The mine has twenty chambers. The chamber called the Chapel of St. Kinga is 180 feet long.*

*Statues carved from salt are everywhere. Pictures are carved in the wall and a salt crystal chandelier that works hangs from the ceiling.*

*This chamber is also used as a place for children with respiratory problems to heal by breathing in the highly mineralized air.*

develop the respect for and ability to work within the democratic system.

## Activities

1. Choose a period in Poland's history to research. Find out about the people who settled the country, their customs and culture.

   ▶ With several others who have chosen different periods about which to learn, develop a progressive story of Poland's history. Present the story to your class.

2. Find out how many Nobel Prize winners in the twentieth century were Polish. In what categories did they win the prize? Which of them are still alive? Choose one that interests you and find out more about that person. What personal or professional qualities made that person your favorite?

   ▶ With the rest of your class, combine everyone's research and make a large poster of the Polish Nobel Prize winners.

3. Find out about the Black Madonna. What is she? Why is she significant to the Polish people? What are two or three of the legends surrounding her?

   ▶ Tell one of the legends to the class. Be sure that you choose one that illustrates her importance.

4. Think about the importance of national independence. Compare Polish values of independence with those of U.S. citizens. What would you do if you had to live under foreign occupation and were threatened with punishment for using your own language and following other aspects of your culture?

   ▶ Present a play to your class in which you show the importance of national independence to yourself and to Polish citizens.

> *"Nothing in life is to be feared. It is only to be understood."*
> — Marie Curie

*Poland has a variety of landforms. At the southern border are high mountains, including the steep, rocky Tatra Mountains that are comparable to the Alps. Smaller mountains rise to the north, and in the center of the country are plains. Further north is a lake region, and beyond that, the Baltic Sea lies at Poland's northern border. The main river of Poland is the Vistula, a source of many Polish legends.*

5. Research the role of the Catholic Church and Catholicism thoroughout the political and cultural development of Poland and other parts of Europe. Is there separation of church and state, or does the Catholic Church still have a say in Polish politics? What issues regarding such separation arose in the United States in the last few years? What issues arose in Poland? How were they resolved in both countries?

   ▶ Prepare a debate about the merits of a religious state vs. the merits of a secular state.

6. Find out more about the Polish educational system. How is it similar to the U.S. system? What extracurricular activities are offered in the Polish system? What do students study?

   ▶ Make a chart illustrating the differences.

7. Find out if there are any Polish societies or Polish immigrants in your community. Invite a person to speak to your class.

   ▶ As a class, come up with a set of at least fifteen questions to ask your guest. Discuss what you learned after your guest has made his or her presentation.

## Wildlife and the Environment

Poland has very colorful wildlife. Its many lakes, flat plains, and mountainous areas attract large numbers of beaver, swans, cormorants, geese, heron, eagles, elk, deer, and wolves. Three of Poland's not-so-common animals are the European buffalo, the wild Przewalski's horse, and the wild boar.

The European buffalo, also called the wisent, once roamed the continent. It is a cousin to the American bison but has a smaller head higher up on its body. By the early 1900s, only a few of these giant animals existed. In 1919, the last wisent in the Bialowieza Forest was killed by a poacher. Britain, Germany, Poland,

and Sweden joined efforts to find captive animals that had come from this same forest. Two cows were found in Sweden and a bull in Germany. They were brought to the Bialowieza Forest to be raised in captivity. Ten years later, the herd had increased to fourteen. In 1952, the buffalo were released into the wild. A record of every newborn bison has been kept and a name is given to each. The Bialowieza and the adjoining Russian forest now share the world's largest herd of these animals.

The tarpan, or Przewalski's horse, is the only true wild horse that exists today. Like the wisent, the tarpan has had to be rescued from near extinction. Other wild horses, similar to those found in the United States, are really descendants of runaway domestic horses. The Przewalski's horse is related to the domestic horse but looks more like a donkey. It has a grayish brown coat, a brown mane, and a black streak down its back. Faint bars appear on the upper part of its legs and its lower legs are black. The tarpan stands 53 inches tall.

Wild boars are very strong and ferocious. They are about three feet tall but do not grow as heavy and fat as a domestic hog. The boar's lower jaw has two powerful tusks used for fighting. The wild boar lives in dense forests, where it hides from danger.

The major environmental problem facing Poland today is air pollution. The poisonous gases from industry combine with the noxious waste of the coal burned to produce energy to run factories. Pollution carried by winds from other countries adds to Poland's environmental problems. Acid rain, caused primarily by sulfur dioxide emissions, can cause trees to die and it is estimated that two-thirds of Poland's forests have been seriously damaged from air pollution. Added to this problem is the Chernobyl nuclear disaster that has affected many eastern European countries in ways that even time may not heal.

Water pollution is Poland's second leading environmental problem. Coal has been mined from deep mines surrounded by salt deposits that produce huge

*In the Holy Cross Forest in central Poland there is a 1200-year-old oak tree called Bartek (Bart).*

*The massive tree is considered a nature monument and it takes eight people holding hands to reach around it.*

volumes of saltwater. Seven thousand tons of this waste water get pumped daily into Poland's two main rivers, the Vistula and the Odra. With the discovery of more efficient ways to use coal, however, the deep mines are closing one by one. Great amounts of human sewage are dumped into the Vistula River and the river's ecosystem is dying.

Poland's people suffer from this pollution. Human life expectancy is becoming shorter, disease in children is increasing, and diseases caused by industry are also increasing. Katowice, a city in industrial Poland, is reputed to be the most polluted city in all of Europe. Concerned parents send their children to relatively unpolluted areas of the mountains for holidays so their bodies may rest from the pollution of the cities.

There is good news, though. Since the collapse of communism, pollution has been reduced by 50 percent. Old plants and inefficient systems are being closed down. As Poland became involved in world trade, industry was forced to raise the quality of its production and add preventive equipment to factories, which improved some of the problems.

The problem with burning coal is not improving as quickly. Poland's greatest mineral wealth lies in her coal fields, and 4.2 million tons of sulfur gas is spewed into Poland's air each year as a result of coal burning. Poland is currently looking into new ways to burn coal more efficiently and cleanly.

As in much of eastern Europe, few natural ecosystems have survived the long history of development by various groups. In Poland, national parks cover only 4 percent of the forested mountain areas. Some less-disturbed lowland areas have also been taken into protection, increasing the total amount of protected land in Poland to 9 percent. There are plans to increase protected habitats in Poland to 28 percent by the year 2000.

The meandering Biebrza River in northeast Poland is internationally important because of the unique meadow and peat bog habitats that surround it. These

*A traditional Polish activity in the fall used to be picking wild mushrooms, but now radiation from the Chernobyl nuclear accident has polluted large areas of Polish soil and made eating wild mushrooms unsafe.*

meadows and peat bogs cover 200,000 acres and are actually maintained in part through the farming methods that have been a part of Poland's tradition in this area. Small, private landowners have for many years produced their own hay and grazed small herds of livestock, using very low-impact farming methods. Terns, ducks, and birds of prey live in or migrate to the Biebrza River valley in impressive numbers. A few unique species rely on this land, as well. Eastern Europe's first private nature reserve is in the Biebrza in a six-acre plot of marsh that has been privately purchased to protect land used by the great snipe.

Eastern Europe countries have been taking steps to preserve the beauty and health of their land. Hungary, Poland, and Bulgaria recently created new ministries for environmental affairs. Since eastern European ecosystems are greatly affected by the actions of each other's people these countries have begun to act cooperatively to assist one another in preserving ecological balance. The cost of cleaning up previous damage, however, is high. The cost of stopping the pollution caused by industry is also high and relies on advanced scientific and technological solutions, which may not be readily available or may cost too much. Here again, the people must make choices and sometimes they choose hardship.

In some ways, eastern Europe has been a leader in conservation. These countries have been among the first in Europe to develop national conservation programs and to create protected areas that cross country boundaries. Poland shares the Tatra/Tatransky National park with other countries. Two alpine plant species in the Tatra Mountains were given protection four years before the United States created the world's first national park, Yellowstone.

The Bialowieza National Park in Poland near the Russian border is called the "green lung" of the country. Although it covers only 13,300 acres, it is in the center of a 470-square-mile forest. The Bialowieza is unique because it is the last surviving fragment of a primeval lowland forest in Europe. This special forest

*Coal has been an important natural resource for Poland.*

143

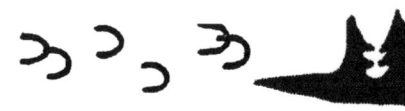

has great species diversity with 113 different plant communities. One-fourth of Poland's flowers, more than 550 species, are here. In open spaces of the forest are peat bogs, meadows, and marshes. Trees in this virgin forest may be between 250 and 400 years old and more than 100 feet tall. It was here that Napoleon's troops hid, and this land has been ruled by kings and tsars. Today, the Bialowieza Forest is a national park, a United Nations Biosphere Reserve, and a World Heritage site.

## Activities

1. Research the wisent and the American buffalo. Learn about their body structures, diets, habitats, and their common predicament of facing near extinction.

   ▶ Make two scale models, one of each type of buffalo in its native habitat. The models should illustrate the similarities and differences you have learned about these animals.

2. Learn about the tarpan: its origin, history, and habitat. Research the herds of horses that are called wild in the United States: their origins, histories, and habitats.

   ▶ Make a filmstrip and write or record a narration that will share what you learned with others.

3. Learn more about Katowice, Poland, which is considered to be the most polluted city in Europe. What types of pollution does it have? Why is it so polluted? What effects does the pollution have on the people, plant and animal life, and buildings? What steps are being taken to reduce the pollution? How successful do you think these steps will be?

   ▶ Write an essay that traces the history of the Katowice pollution. In the concluding paragraph, state clearly your opinion about the possible success of cleanup, and give reasons to support your opinion.

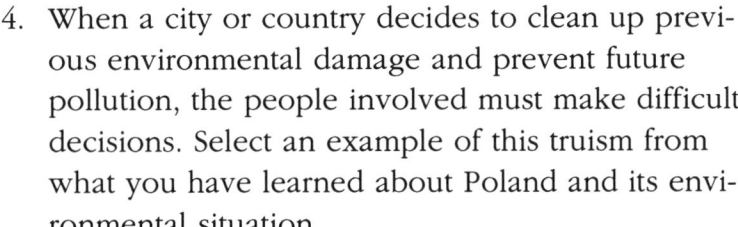

4. When a city or country decides to clean up previous environmental damage and prevent future pollution, the people involved must make difficult decisions. Select an example of this truism from what you have learned about Poland and its environmental situation.

   ▶ With some friends, develop and present a simulated town meeting that focuses on an ecological issue. Be sure to include the viewpoints of a variety of people. Consider as well their views of the short- and long-term effects related to this issue.

5. Find out about the lakes in Poland. How many are there? Are they concentrated in one area, or are they spread out across the country?

   ▶ Make a large, mural size map of Poland that shows where all the lakes are.

6. Research Przewalski's horse. How did it get its name? Has it ever been domesticated?

   ▶ Give a presentation on the horse to your class. Include illustrations, a brief history, and a note on how it was named.

7. Find out how coal processing and burning create air and water pollution. Then find out the extent of these problems in Poland. Finally, find out whether air and water pollution have improved or worsened during the last twenty years.

   ▶ Make a chart that shows your findings.

8. Research peat bogs. How do they form? How long does it take one to form? Where are they located around the world? Where are they the most common? Then find out the many different ways in which people use peat.

   ▶ List the ways in which people use peat. Then do a demonstration of one of the ways for your class.

*Poppies are abundant in Poland and poppyseeds are often used in cooking and baking. Poppyseed streudel and kutia, a Christmas delicacy made of soaked wheat berries, poppyseeds, and honey, are two favorites.*

## Foods, Festivals, and Celebrations

**Kisiel**

*1 pound fresh cranberries, strained, with skins discarded*

*potato starch*

*sugar*

*Sweeten the cranberries to taste and boil with potato starch until the liquid thickens. Kisiel is usually served cool with a dash of sour or whipped cream.*

In Poland, the main daily meal is eaten in the afternoon and usually consists of two or three dishes. A light supper follows in the evening. Traditional Polish cooking was quite heavy, with rich sauces and overcooked vegetables, but within the last two generations, nutritional awareness has made raw vegetable salads very popular. People also eat traditional pirogis, blintzes with cheese or fruit, potato dumplings, and grains. Polish people eat many soups, including potato, sauerkraut, tomato, krupnik (wild mushroom with barley), and borscht, both the traditional Polish kind and the Ukrainian kind, which has vegetables and beans. Pork is the meat of preference, though it is quite a bit more expensive than beef. Potatoes are always served with the main meal. Buckwheat and barley are popular grains; a favorite summer meal is buttermilk served with buckwheat. The most popular desserts are fruit compote, seasonal fresh fruit, and *kisiel* (pronounced "kishel"). Almost all women take pride in serving their home-baked cakes, especially apple and plum. At Easter, *baba,* raised yeast cake, is obligatory.

In winter months, no vegetables can be grown in Poland and the people store root vegetables for winter staples. They also pickle many vegetables. The Polish people pickle cucumbers in their own juice; they do not use vinegar. In the last years of the Communist regime, food was so scarce or expensive that pickling became a necessity.

A very popular party and tourist dish is hunter's stew, called *bigos,* which is made of sauerkraut slowly stewed with pieces of meat and spices. It is said that the longer it is cooked, the better. Poland also produces excellent German-style beer called Zywiec, which is often exported.

One of Poland's fun festivals is Juvenalia, a two-and-a-half-day festival for students. The students dress up in costumes and wander or dance through the streets. Adults, including the police, turn the town over to the students. The whistles, horns, bells, costumes, and songs about politicians don't seem to bother adults.

Christmas is a major celebration in Poland. Trees are not put up until Christmas Eve and are decorated with sweets and paper toys. People put hay under their tablecloths for Christmas Eve dinner, and before they eat, they reach under the cloth and grab a straw with which to tell their fortunes. Christmas dinner consists of twelve meatless courses. After dinner, the family goes to midnight mass. Pets and livestock all receive Christmas wafers and pieces of bread for their Christmas celebration. A traditional legend says that when midnight comes, the animals are able to speak. Christmas is still largely a religious holiday and, although everyone receives a present under the tree, the presents are often small or symbolic; they are not the main focus of the holiday.

In the Polish calendar, as in the calendars of many Catholic nations, each day is named after a saint or patron. Everyone has a name day, which is celebrated more than birthdays. November 30 is St. Andrew's day, and it is a folk custom on the eve of St. Andrew's day to pour melted wax on cold water and forecast the future from the shapes the wax takes. This process is called Andrzejki. New Year's eve is called Sylvester's.

The Thursday before Ash Wednesday is called Fat Thursday. People everywhere in Poland, even in schools and offices, eat large quantities of *paczki*, raised yeast doughnuts with sugar icing.

## Activities

1. Visit a local supermarket and find some foods imported from Poland (often ham or jam). Find out more about how they were made and how they got to the store. Then choose one or more of the foods imported from Poland.

### *Pirogi*

wonton-type wrappers
1/2 pound cottage cheese, drained
1 egg yolk
1 tsp butter
pinch of salt

*To make filling, mix everything but the wrappers together. Wet two edges of the wrappers. Place a teaspoon of filling in the center. Fold the wrappers over and press out all air. Pinch the edges together to seal. Boil the pirogis in salted water. When they float, cook them five minutes longer. Top with butter and bread crumbs to serve.*

*Millions of people make a pilgrimage to the monastery on the mountain Jasna Gora in Scestochowas each year to visit and honor the painting of the Black Madonna.*

*The 600-year-old Black Madonna has been considered the queen of Poland since the beginning of the fifteenth century and was officially crowned in the seventeenth century after the miraculous rescue of the monastery from a Swedish invasion.*

▶ Make a chart that compares the ingredients and methods of the food you chose with those involved in making that same food in the United States.

2. Juvenalia is an interesting and unusual Polish celebration. Learn as much as you can about Juvenalia, including its origins and history.

   ▶ Plan and present a skit that shares the history and spirit of Juvenalia. Include costumes in your skit, if possible.

3. Find out about Polish foods. What foods do Polish farmers typically grow? How are some of them prepared?

   ▶ With several friends, plan a Polish picnic for your class. Prepare many of the foods you have researched. Include the recipes and a short description with each.

4. Obtain a Polish calender and find out when your name day is. Find out when some of your friends' and family members' name days are. Then choose someone whose name day is coming up soon.

   ▶ Plan and hold a celebration for that person in honor of his or her name day.

## *Dances, Games, and Sports*

Poland is a country of a thousand lakes as well as high rugged mountains. In this inspiring atmosphere, many sports and recreational activities take place. Fishing, sailing, swimming, hiking, and skiing are all favorite pastimes. The Polish people excel at soccer, cycling, and track and field. Children and adults can join sports organizations and compete in team and individual events during the warm-weather months.

Folk music and dance festivals are very popular with tourists and citizens alike. The Polish national dance is the mazur, a very vigorous dance from central Poland. Fredric Chopin, inspired by the dance,

created a new, softer form he called mazurka and wrote more than fifty of them. Some of Poland's other folk dances include the *krakowiak* (from Crakow), the *kujaviak*, a slow dance, and the *oberek*, a fast dance. The one that is still danced outside of folk festivals is the *polonez*, a stately walking dance used now to open official balls. The polonez also inspired Chopin, who wrote many piano works called polonaises. Originally, each dance came from a different region and was performed in a colorful costume from that part of the country. In some regions, the dance traditions still exist, although the authentic customs are quickly dying out.

## Activities

1. The climate and topography (land forms) of a country dictate the sports and other recreational activities in which the inhabitants will engage. Research the topography of Poland and its recreational activities to find how the former has influenced the latter.

   ▶ Alone or with a friend, create a mural of Polish sports that also illustrates its weather and natural features.

2. The national dance of Poland is mazur, but many people associate only the polka with that country. Learn about these dances. How are the different? Similar?

   ▶ With a friend or alone, demonstrate one or both dances for your class to appropriate music.

# Music, Art, and Architecture

The Communist government put tight controls on the music and art of Poland. In the 1950s, jazz was illegal and was labeled a "degenerate Western influence." Literature, the fine arts, and film were supposed to glorify communism and its achievements. These

*Poland has a 300-year-old organ located in Oliva. It has eight thousand pipes. It is decorated with wooden angels, which ring bells and blow trumpets. As the organ plays, a wooden star cimbs into a wooden sky to announce the birth of Christ.*

*People must wear soft felt slippers in all Polish museums to protect the expensive marble or inlaid wood floors.*

restrictions resulted in socrealism, or socialist realism, which was designed to promote the Communist philosophy and to discourage capitalism. The heroes and heroines of these socrealism stories were morally upright bricklayers and tractor drivers engaged in building a "glorious future" and uncovering subversive activities of the nasty capitalists who were bent on destroying the workers' paradise.

The Communist government replaced authentic folk customs with highly stylized versions of dances and songs performed by professional, subsidized companies. Some of these troupes have toured the United States many times. The Communists also replaced authentic artists with professionals in the traditional arts such as tapestry, woodcarving, pottery, and silversmithing. The artists were controlled through state-run stores. Two original folk arts survived, however. One is painting on glass, called *górale*, which is native to the Tetra Mountain highlanders. The other is paper cuts, made by using large sheep shears to create complex and delicate designs on paper.

Despite years of government censorship, Polish artists did not give up. The art of poster design flourished. Tapestry weaving has been elevated to a new level by Magdalena Abakanowics, an internationally known artist who creates highly original sculptures from wool and nontraditional materials. Jazz, initially embraced by young people as a sign of rebellion, has become a well-established and beloved form of expression. Poland has produced some outstanding jazz artists, some of whom now live in New York; pianist Adam Makowicz and violinist Michael Urbaniak are two. Annual jazz festivals are held in Warsaw and Wroclaw and jazz singer Basia has won hearts in Warsaw, London, and New York. The classical music of Krysztof Penderecki gained international acclaim and Henryk Gorecki's third symphony topped the charts.

In the late 1950s, after the initial loosening of government controls, Polish filmmakers burst onto the movie scene and have become known for their daring and honest handling of subjects previously prohibited by the government, as well as for their innovative style that blends symbolism and realism. The best known of this wave is Andrzej Wajda. His pupil, Agnieszka Holland, now working in Hollywood, recently made an award-winning film of the children's book *The Secret Garden*. Polish director Krzysztof Kieslowski, who now works in France, has been winning awards, and Roman Polanski is famous in the United States for producing films such as *Rosemary's Baby* and *Chinatown*. Jerzy Toeplitz, who ran a film school in Lodz, moved to Australia in 1968 because of government repression and has instructed a number of award-winning Australian directors. Jerzy Grotowski, an outstanding theater director, is considered the father of contemporary avant-garde theater and has inspired many European as well as American directors.

Polish culture is thriving and contributing to the world culture in many ways. Because of the current financial crisis, however, the culture is going through hard times.

*The emblem of Warsaw is the mermaid holding a shield and a sword. The emblem is related to a legend that says she emerged from the Vistula River to protect the country. There are statues of the mermaid in Warsaw.*

## Activities

1. The *kobza* is an unusual Polish musical instrument. Learn about the kobza. Who first made one? Of what is it made? How is the sound produced? How has it changed over the years? If you can, locate someone who plays a kobza or a recording of someone playing one.

   ▶ Make a chart that illustrates what you learned about the kabza.

2. Frederic Chopin was a great Polish composer. Research Chopin's life and his music. For what instruments did he compose? What is unique about his music? What else was happening in the Polish culture at the time he was composing? What is this period called? Choose a specific period of his life on which to focus.

*Religious festivals, holidays, and rituals play a large part in most Polish lives.*

> ▶ With one or more friends, present "A Day in the Life of Frederich Chopin." Be sure the narrator tells the audience the who, where, why, and when of Chopin's life so they will understand the skit.

3.  With some friends, divide into several groups. Each group will choose a dance to learn, research the part of the country from which the dance came, and find out what costumes are worn when performing it.

> ▶ Perform your dance for and share your information with the other groups.

4.  Watch Agnieszka Holland's production of *The Secret Garden*. Find out why she chose to make a film of this particular book. Find out more about her life and career. What other films has she made?

> ▶ Make a video about her, or write an article for your school or local paper.

## Piotrek's Day

Piotrek, 9, is a third grader in Warsaw. Today he gets up late because his class in on the second shift, and he will go to school from 11:00 A.M. until 2:00 P.M. His parents started work at 8:00 A.M., and his sister Ania is already in school, so Piotrek makes his favorite breakfast, cornflakes with milk and a cheese sandwich.

Piotrek gets ready for school, dressing quickly and carelessly combing his hair—something his mother doesn't let him get away with on mornings she is here. His school is only a few blocks from his house. Today will be an easy day; he has two periods of Polish language, one of math, and one of religion, which nobody takes very seriously. Between lessons everyone has ten minutes to run around on the playground and sometimes Piotrek even manages a few soccer moves with his buddies.

When lunch break comes, Piotrek rushes to the lunchroom so he can be first in line. Today the menu is vegetable soup, boiled beef, mashed potatoes, and string beans, all of which Piotrek eats hungrily. Piotrek makes bets with his friends Janek and Tadek about who will be able to get second helpings, but Mr. Kowalski, who has prepared the food, will not let them have seconds and chases them away.

After school, Piotrek runs home because it is his turn to help clean the house. The cleaning takes only half an hour, so Piotrek has time to watch cartoons on television while his mother prepares dinner. Ania and her girlfriend Misia watch, too. Piotrek tries to ignore Ania as she teases him about his huge appetite in the lunchroom today.

When Piotrek's father comes home at 4:30, the family sits down to a dinner of borscht and cheese blintzes, with apple cake for dessert. Father and Mother ask how school was, and everyone talks and laughs during the meal. After dinner, Father takes Piotrek to his weekly soccer practice at the district sports club. Piotrek loves soccer. Ania spends this time practicing her flute and doing her homework. She is in the fourth grade and has more subjects and homework than does Piotrek.

When Piotrek returns home, he must also do his homework, but he preferes playing games on his computer. When his mother calls the family for supper, he quickly finishes his work. This meal is light and offers another opportunity for the family to get together. Father has had to go back to the office to finish a project, so Mother, Ania, and Piotrek discuss their upcoming visit to their grandparent's house on Sunday.

At 8:00, Ania and Piotrek watch "Night-Night," a children's television program, and then it is time for Piotrek to go to bed, as tomorrow his class is on the first shift and he must be at school by 8:00. Piotrek asks his mother to read to him, and he falls asleep, content with the day.

*The word Poland is derived from the word pole, which means "field."*

## *Activity*

Think about Piotrek's day. How is it like a day you might have? How is it different?

▶ Write a letter to a pen pal in Poland. Tell him or her about your life at home and school.

*– or –*

▶ Write a letter to Piotrek, telling him how your life is similar to and different from his. Then imagine that you are Piotrek and write a letter back to yourself.

# A Nest of Eagles

### *A Polish Folktale*

Once long ago, three brothers lived together in a northern land. Their names were Czech, Lech, and Rus (pronounced Cheh, Leh, and Roos). The brothers loved their home. Its land was rich and green and watered by a silver river. Huge trees stood like sentinels all around.

After a while, each brother had prospered so much in their homeland that there wasn't enough room for them all to live. One day, they went for a walk and Lech climbed a huge tree to see what he could see. He looked to the south and saw tall mountains, gleaming lakes and rivers, and warm, gentle sunlight. He called down to his brothers and told them what he had seen. "Fine!" said his brother Czech. "I will go to that land and make it my home." And he did. Next, Lech looked to the east. There he saw endless miles of land, vast prairies, and broad river valleys filled with animals and birds. He told his brother Rus. "Fine!" said Rus, "I will go and make it my home." And he did.

Lech looked to the north and there was the sea. He looked west. He saw a thick forest with wild animals. "I cannot make my home in either of these places," he thought. "What shall I do?" Then Lech looked in the tree in which he sat. Beside him was a nest, an eagle's nest with three white eaglets. "Of course, now I know what I must do," said Lech. "I must stay here and make this my home."

Lech built a town and called it Gniezo, which means "nest". It became the first town of Poland. A white eagle has been a part of Poland's coat of arms ever since.

## Activities

1. Folktales and legends may be based on fact or may serve to explain events or phenomena. What facts about Poland are included in "A Nest of Eagles"? Who is symbolic? Fictional?

   ▶ Write a folktale that explains something about your community. Include symbolism, fiction, or exaggeration to make your tale more interesting.

2. Find out about the Polish coat of arms. Find a picture of it. What does each symbol mean?

   ▶ Invent symbols to represent your name or some aspect of your family history and design your own coat of arms.

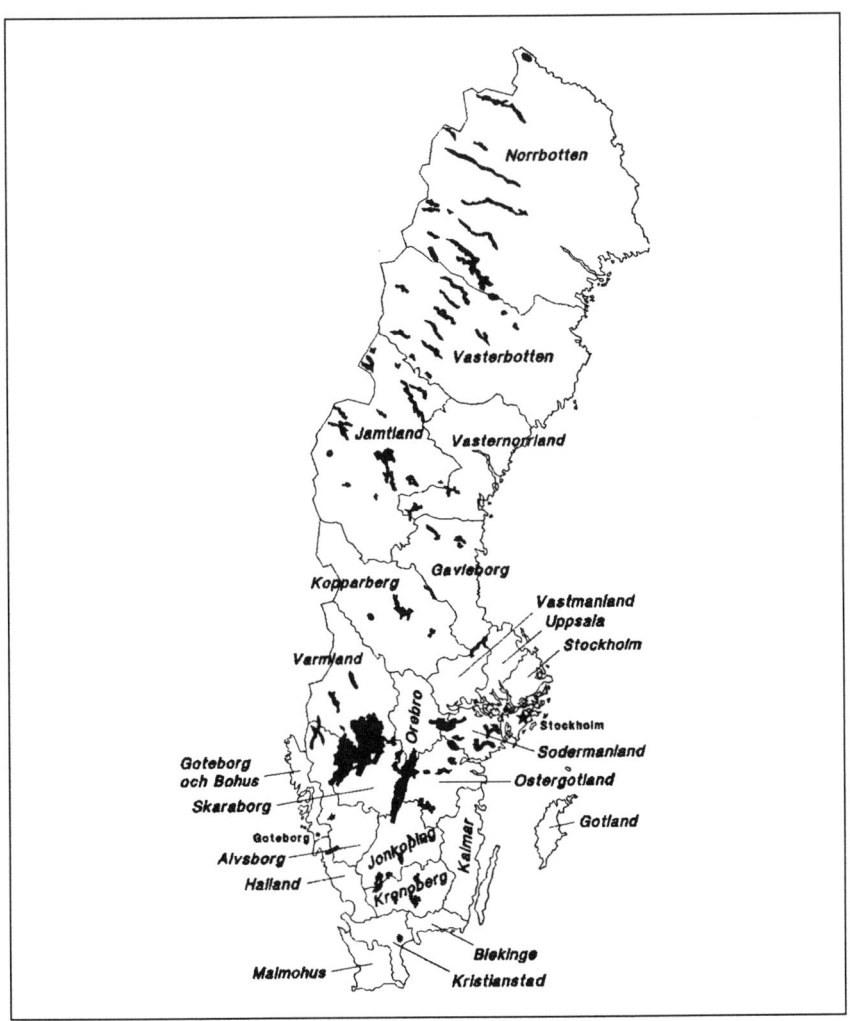

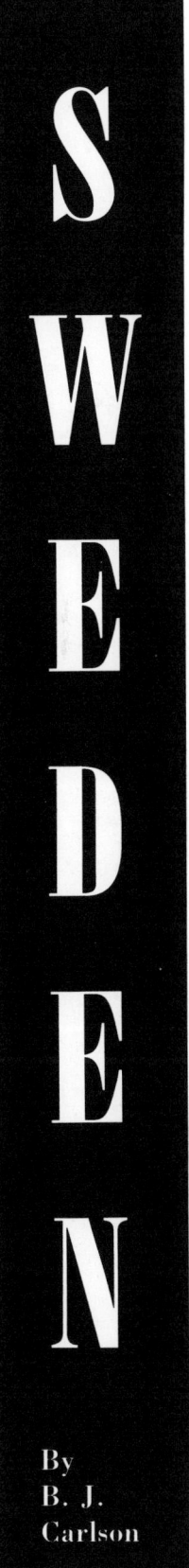

## Overview

S tark and stunning, conservative but
controversial, Sweden is a land that
boasts nearly 100,000 lakes, majestic
mountains, many natural resources, and many
creative inventors. Sweden is bounded on the
west by Norway and on the east by Finland
and the Baltic Sea. The northern part of the
country reaches into the Arctic Circle. The web

157

*In the late second or early third century, Scandinavian people began to produce runes, stones with carved characters. Runic characters are made up almost entirely of straight strokes, which are easily carved on wood and stone. Runes are thought to have magical powers and were used in Scandinavia for 1,000 years.*

of lakes, rivers, canals, and locks in Sweden is so intricate that you can cross the country from Stockholm to Gothenburg by boat. Stockholm, the capital, is built on fourteen islands that are connected by fifty bridges.

## Historical Background

The first written accounts of Sweden come from the Roman historian Tacitus in the first century. Tacitus talked about a warlike people he called the Suiones and others have called the Svears. These people clashed with and conquered their southern neighbors, the Goths. The resulting merger of these two groups produced the Vikings, a people well known for their far-reaching ocean explorations and for their brave but fierce warriors. The Vikings were remarkably skilled sailors and traveled as far as Iceland, Greenland, Spain, and North America. The Russian city of Novgorod was founded by a Swedish Viking named Rurik in 862. Some Vikings traveled as far as Turkey and Arabia and became guards for the royal courts there.

The Viking religion was based on a complex mythology, which has been used as the basis for operas, folktales, and artwork. Some Viking traditions also have become an integral part of Swedish culture.

In the 800s, Saint Ansgar attempted to Christianize the Swedes, but it was not until the 1100s that the Swedes were converted to Christianity under Eric IX, who became the patron saint of Sweden. A period of relative calm followed Eric's reign, and Sweden was governed by a number of kings who were not interested in the outside world. For a while, the Catholic Church provided the only source of outside information to Sweden.

In the 1200s, Sweden became involved in boundary conflicts with other Scandinavian and European countries. The wars to resolve such conflicts continued for 600 years.

One of the most significant changes in Sweden's history came in the 1500s, when Gustavus Vasa introduced Lutheran Christianity to the nation. In 1604 the Catholic religion was banned, and Sweden has remained Lutheran ever since.

During the Thirty Years' War (1618–1648), which devastated Europe, Sweden emerged as one of the victors and established a great northern empire. During Sweden's "Age of Freedom" (1718–1773), a time of relative peace, the Royal Opera, the Royal Ballet, the Swedish Academy, and the Drottingholm Theater were established. When the Swedes joined other European nations in a successful campaign against Napoleon in 1813, they were rewarded with dominion over Norway. Norway gained its independence from Sweden in 1904, and the current boundaries between the two countries were established.

In 1435 Sweden formed the first parliament in Europe, the Riksdag, which still exists. In the last 100 years, the Swedish government has become a model of innovation and cooperation. The country is run as a democracy, but it still has a king who performs mostly ceremonial duties. Riksdag members are elected for three-year terms, and a high percentage of the 349 members are women. All Swedish citizens 18 and older may vote, and 90 percent of the population does so. Women have been able to vote in Sweden since 1914.

Sweden was one of the last European countries to industrialize, in the late nineteenth and early twentieth centuries. At the turn of the century, 90 percent of Swedes lived in the countryside, but today 80 percent of the people live in the cities and more than half live in apartments. In 1900 three out of every four people earned a living from the land, but by 1970 the number was down to one out of every eight.

*The southernmost tip of Sweden is north of Juneau, Alaska.*

*To maintain the social welfare state in Sweden, taxes are high*

*Sweden's system of government emphasizes equality and responsibility; the system provides for people from the cradle to the grave.*

The Swedish welfare system is a comprehensive program designed to narrow the gap between the rich and the poor. Swedish people have a very high standard of living, and, in fact, no one is extremely poor. Two-thirds of the government's annual budget is spent on social assistance programs such as medical and dental care, child care, prenatal care, and programs for the sick and disabled. Swedish people are guaranteed a minimum of four weeks' paid vacation each year. The Swedes believe that art is as important as economic and social equality, and the government financially supports arts organizations.

The attitude of cooperation that has developed in Sweden is evident in the association the Swedes have formed with Norway, Iceland, Denmark, and Finland. These five countries, which once vigorously and regularly fought over boundaries, now have created common postage rates, a common passport area, and almost as much freedom for people to move between countries as people in the United States have to move between states.

## Activities

1. The ancient Vikings have captured the interest and imagination of people today. Become an expert on one Viking or the Vikings of one period of time. Where did they live? How did they support themselves? What explorations and discoveries did they accomplish?

   ▶ Draw a large map that shows where the person or people you chose to study lived, as well as the Viking exploration of that time. On a map of the world, indicate the areas known to have been reached by Vikings. Compute the distances they traveled.

2. King Gustav Adolphus's daughter became "King Christina." Learn about her life and her reign. What was she like as a person and as a ruler?

What things happened in Sweden during her reign? Why did she give up her throne?

▶ Based on your information, develop a skit about King Christina. Use a narrator if that helps you tell a better story.

3. Research Sweden's "Age of Freedom." When was it? Why was it called that? What significant events occurred during this time? What were the effects of these events?

▶ With friends create a mural that illustrates the richness of this time, as well as showing specific people and events.

4. Learn about the Swedish welfare system. What benefits does it offer? What problems does it cause or include? Would the system work in other countries? Why or why not? After you learn about the system, decide whether or not it would work in our country.

▶ Write a letter to the editor of your local newspaper stating your belief and providing reasons and examples to support your belief.

5. Find out about Swedish history. What do you think were the most significant events? What events changed the course of Swedish history?

▶ Make a time line that shows the events and their effects. Illustrate your time line. Present it to your class.

6. The statement is made that the Swedish educational system stresses uniformity. How is uniformity stressed? In what ways are students and their learning or work expected to be uniform? How is this approach different from or similar to that in the school you attend? How do you think uniformity in school will affect students when they are adults?

▶ Based on your research and your thoughts, make a large Venn diagram that illustrates the similarities and differences between your

*The money in Sweden is called krona, plural kronor. One krona is divided into 100 ore. One hundred kronor is written 100 SEK. Coins come in denominations of 1, 5, 10, and 50 SEK. Paper money is made in 10, 50, 100, 500, 1,000, and 10,000 SEK.*

*At an excavation of a small Stone Age community outside Ellos in western Sweden, archaeologists found chewing gum believed to be 9,000 years old. The gum is tooth-marked and is believed to have been chewed by a Stone Age teenager. The dark-colored gum was made of resin sweetened with honey.*

school and Swedish schools. Use arrows going out of the circles to show what effects the various practices will have when the students are adults.

7. Learn about the wars in which Sweden has been involved over its history. How often has Sweden been involved in wars in the last century? What influenced Sweden to decide to get involved in or stay out of wars? To what kinds of pressure did the Swedes respond?

▶ Paint a large mural in which you show the progression of Sweden's attitude toward war and the European community.

## The People

Stark and stunning, precise yet creative, conservative but controversial—these descriptions reflect the richness of Sweden and its people, many of whom feel a close bond with the United States because most Swedish families have relatives there. The first Swedish settlers to North America came in 1638, led by Peter Minuit. They settled in what is now Delaware and lived peacefully with the Delaware Indians. Eventually, more than 1.5 million Swedes, nearly 25 percent of the Swedish population, left their homeland for America.

In general, Swedes are law-abiding people, and lawbreakers receive stiff penalties. For instance, drunk drivers receive an automatic year in jail. This conservative bent is also seen in the educational system, which stresses uniformity.

The Swedes express their care for the land by practicing forest conservation (every tree that is cut down is replaced by another), through cleanliness (in general, litter is not a problem), and by decorating simply.

Most Swedish people have televisions, watch the same movies and TV programs that are seen in the United States, and enjoy the same music. Except for cable TV, Swedish television and radio don't broadcast advertisements.

# The Sami

In a rocky, wooded region of far northern Europe live a unique group of people who call themselves the Sami (Laplanders). These people live close to nature, following time-tried traditions that have helped them survive for more than 8,000 years. The origin of the Sami is a topic for academic debate. The Sami are shorter and darker in appearance than the Swedes, and anthropologists have theorized that Sami long ago migrated to Scandinavia from Siberia, Mongolia, or Asia. These brown-eyed, dark-haired people, with small hands and feet, have long been recognized as exceptionally fit and healthy. Disease is rare among the Sami, and their strength is legendary. They are especially famous for their skiing ability.

Throughout Lapland, a region with no fixed boundaries, migrating reindeer herds have given life to the land's human inhabitants, who eat the animal's meat, drink its milk, and use its sinew, fur, hides, bones, and antlers for clothing, homes, and tools. The Sami have domesticated the reindeer, using the animals to pull heavy loads; they even race reindeer. Of 32,000 Sami, about 1,500 live as nomadic reindeer herders, and in the northern woodlands, many Sami are reindeer breeders.

The Sami language has many elements of Finnish and Hungarian, but also resembles languages spoken in northwestern Siberia. The Sami also use many Swedish and Norwegian words, including some from an obsolete Old Norse language. Sami from different areas speak different dialects.

The traditional Sami religion is based largely on the natural world. Religious leaders, or shamans, were reportedly able to tell the future, and Swedish peasants sometimes hired them to predict the sex of their future children. Personal Sami shrines, or *seides,* are made from a ring of antlers or an odd-shaped stone surrounded by twigs.

Lutheran missionaries in the twelfth century discouraged the Sami culture and tried to convert the

*The Swedish regard for sharing is carried into daily life and is expressed by their belief in "everyman's right." This practice allows all people to pick berries and mushrooms, to fish, and to hunt on private property, as long as they do not vandalize, invade other people's privacy, or litter.*

*In Boden a line of white stones marks the rim of the Arctic Circle. In this region, sometimes called "the land of the midnight sun," the sun does not set for two months in summer, and residents may not see a sunrise for two months in winter.*

*Although communities thrive in the Arctic, 85 percent of Sweden's 8.6 million people live in the warmer southern half of the country.*

Sami to Christianity, but the Sami resisted these efforts. Eventually, Sweden took control of Lapland's resources, which include mineral ores, timber, and sources of hydroelectric power. Although the Sami have won confirmation of their ancestral rights to hunt, fish, and herd in Lapland, these rights were given only to those who herd reindeer (about 15 percent of the Sami population). The same rights were given to a million or more Swedish sportsmen, which may deplete the resources the Sami need to survive. A recent Swedish law gives the Sami a separate parliament, however, which may improve the political power of these people who follow traditional ways.

Although the Sami have adopted many new technologies, a movement to preserve traditional Sami culture blossomed in the 1940s. Today, newspapers, radio programs, and special schools promote Sami traditions. Like so many indigenous cultures around the world, the Sami have had to balance their traditional ways with the ways of the modern technological world.

## Activities

1. Research the life of one of these people: Jenny Lind, Dag Hammarskjold, or Raoul Wallenberg.

   ▶ Create a filmstrip or report your findings in a way that you choose.

2. Locate someone from your community who is of Swedish descent. Ask if you can make an appointment to interview the person. Prepare at least eight questions to ask in the interview. For example, you might find out where in Sweden this person or his or her ancestors came from, what the land and climate there are like, why the person left Sweden, what Swedish customs the person keeps, and what the person's favorite things about Sweden are.

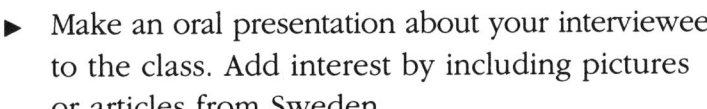

▶ Make an oral presentation about your interviewee to the class. Add interest by including pictures or articles from Sweden.

3. Make a list of ten people who have been Nobel Prize winners and include their accomplishments.

▶ Write a one-page biography about one of them, describing the work for which he or she was awarded the prize.

4. Find out about the Sami. Learn about their beliefs, way of life, and values. Find out how the Sami used reindeer in the past. Compare that with how the Sami people use reindeer now.

▶ Write a story set in Lapland with Sami characters. Be sure your setting and action are rooted in fact.

5. Find cultures other than the Sami who live in bear habitat and have stories about bears.

▶ In an essay or other product of your choice, compare these stories to Sami beliefs about bears.

6. Ninety percent of Swedish people vote in the general elections. What percentage of Americans vote in the national elections? What percent of the people in your town, city, or state vote? Why do you think there is such a difference?

▶ Make a case for your reasons and present them to the class.

7. Find out how population statistics of the United States compare with those of Sweden. Compare the population density and percentage of foreign-born citizens in both countries.

▶ Make a chart that shows your results.

8. Sami are noted as fit and healthy people. Research the Sami lifestyle. What elements or aspects of their lives might account for their good health? How does their lifestyle compare with yours?

▶ Make a large chart that illustrates your comparison and contrast of the two lifestyles.

> *"What is hidden in the snow comes forth in the thaw."*
> —*Swedish saying*

*Moose are plentiful
in Sweden.*

*There is a red climbing
rose that is found only
in Sweden, on the
island of Gotland.*

# *Wildlife and the Environment*

Many animals are indigenous to Sweden, though there are few reptiles or amphibians. Each year, millions of waterfowl and other birds migrate to the pristine lakes of northern Sweden. The Sami revere the bear because they believe it has near-human intelligence and can understand their language.

Also found in Sweden are lemmings, small hamsterlike rodents, whose behavior is puzzling to humans. Every four years or so they fight with each other and then rush off to the sea. Along the way many of them die.

Sweden, like many other European countries, is facing environmental damage from acid rain—rain that carries pollution. Sulfur dioxide, released from factories and cars in Germany and England, blows into Sweden. Acid accumulates in the snow, and when it melts into rivers and lakes in the spring, the acid kills fish eggs and fry, as well as insects and algae. Many lakes have become lifeless as a result. The nuclear power industry has affected Sweden's water quality as well. At Forsmark, about 50 miles northeast of Uppsala, seals, fish, and other inhabitants of the Baltic Sea are dying because of pollutants dumped from nuclear power plants.

Air and water quality have been improving, however. Sulfur dioxide emissions have fallen by 75 percent since the late 1960s, the release of mercury into the environment has dropped 100 percent, and emissions of carbon monoxide have been reduced by 34 percent.

Green issues have a high political priority in Sweden. In 1909 the Swedes established the first nine national parks in Europe. Sweden now has about one thousand nature reserves and about twenty national parks.

The Nature Resources Act protects several Swedish river systems from hydroelectric power development and preserves twelve large, uninhabited, and roadless mountain areas from industrial development. Sweden

also has twenty sites dedicated to preservation of wetland habitats.

Sweden's determination to improve environmental conditions is evident in a national program called the Natural Step. Instituted in 1989, this program aims to promote natural steps to stop practices that endanger Earth. The program also sponsors a competition that recognizes positive environmental programs. In 1992 the winner was Borlange, a city in which 90 percent of the homes are heated with renewable sources of energy.

*Sixty percent of Sweden's forest products are exported.*

## Activities

1. Research acid rain—its causes and effects. After you learn about acid rain, focus on its effects on Sweden's environment and efforts to clean it up.

   ▶ Make a filmstrip that illustrates what you learned. Tape record the narration or present it "live" to your class.

2. Learn as much as you can about the Natural Step program. Of what does it consist? How widespread is it? How successful? How well might it work in other countries?

   ▶ Using what you learned, design a Natural Step program for your community. Plan and present live or on videotape a commercial to encourage others to participate in the program.

3. Compare the length of daylight hours in Sweden from mid-summer through mid-winter. Research Seasonal Affective Disorder (SAD) and find out how the long days of summer and the short days of winter affect the lives of people in Sweden.

   ▶ Present an illustrated report to your class in which you elaborate on the problems caused by the seasonal changes.

4. Find out about the geographic elements of Sweden. Compare them to those of the United States.

▶ Make a relief map of Sweden. Paint all the lakes blue. Compare your map to a U.S. map to see if there is a place in the United States that has as many lakes as Sweden.

5. Choose three birds that migrate to Sweden and learn about them. What are their mating and nesting habits? Why do they choose Sweden? What animals prey on them? What, if any, environmental problems threaten them?

▶ Write a proposal in which you suggest ways to overcome or change the environmental threats to your three chosen birds.

## Foods, Festivals, and Celebrations

Most Americans have heard the word *smorgasbord*, which means literally a meal of sandwiches but is actually a table loaded with as many as forty different foods. The most popular Swedish foods are *lutefisk* (codfish soaked in lye and then boiled), *kottbullar* (spicy meatballs in a cream gravy), *getost* (goat cheese), cookies (called biscuits in Sweden), and coffee. Swedes eat fish of some kind nearly every day.

The Swedes hold many celebrations throughout the year, and no month goes by without one. Santa Lucia, the queen of light, is remembered on December 13. On Santa Lucia Day, the oldest girl of the house dresses in a white robe and wears a crown of candles on her head. The other girls also dress in white robes and carry candles. Boys dress in long white shirts and pointed hats. Together the children go to their parents' bedroom, with coffee and special rolls, and serve them breakfast in bed.

Christmas is a major holiday in Sweden and begins with a thorough cleaning of the house. On Christmas Eve, the elf called Father Christmas distributes gifts. A big Christmas dinner is served, and children sing and dance around the Christmas tree. A very common Christmas ornament is the goat, representing the old Viking god Thor.

---

**Tjack Pannkaka (egg pancake)**

*(serves 6)*

*4 eggs*

*1 1/2 c flour*

*1/2 tsp salt*

*1–1/2 c milk*

*1/4 c butter*

*Beat the eggs lightly; add flour and salt and stir in the milk a little at a time. Put the butter in a 9" x 12" cake pan and place it over heat until the butter melts. Pour the batter into the pan. Bake the pancake at 400°F for 30 minutes. Remove it from the pan and let it stand for a few minutes. Serve it with jelly, sauce, or berries and sausages.*

The Midsummer Festival is a major summer holiday that honors the longest day of the year. People dance around the Maypole all night and go to church the next day. Boat racing is often part of the celebration, and many people wear their best traditional clothes for the festival.

## Activities

1. Become an expert on the Swedish celebration of Santa Lucia Day. Why would Swedes be especially aware of and grateful for light? When was this day first celebrated? How was it celebrated? How has the celebration changed over the years?

   ▶ Use poster board to make a family of Swedish paper dolls. Make the traditional Santa Lucia Day costumes in which to dress the family. Make a bulletin board display that centers on the paper dolls and tells about this special day.

2. Christmas is a major holiday in Sweden. What winter holiday does your family celebrate? How? Learn as much as you can about the Swedish Christmas celebrations.

   ▶ Pretend you are a Swede, and keep a diary from two weeks before Christmas until one week after.

# Dances, Games, and Sports

In Swedish, *loppet* means ski race. Each year on the first Sunday in March, Swedes hold the Vasa Loppet, a ski race to honor Gustavus Vasa. In 1523 Gustavus offered to help the Swedish people overthrow the ruling Danish king, a cruel monarch. But the people were afraid and refused Gustavus's offer. So Gustavus left the town of Mora and headed out in the cold and snow to Salun. After Gustavus had gone, the people of Mora changed their minds and sent two of their best skiers to catch up with him and bring him back.

---

**Kottbullar
(Swedish meatballs)**

*Swedish meatballs, called kottbullar, are often served at midday, the main meal of the day. (serves 6)*

*1/2 c bread crumbs or stuffing mix*

*1 c canned milk*

*1 pound ground beef*

*1/4 c chopped onion*

*1 egg*

*1/2 tsp nutmeg or allspice*

*2 tsp salt*

*1/8 tsp pepper*

*2 tsp flour*

*1 c hot water*

*Soak the bread crumbs in 1/2 cup of canned milk. Mix the ground beef, onion, egg, nutmeg, salt, and pepper into the crumbs. Shape this mixture into small balls no larger than walnuts. Fry the balls in butter until they are browned on all sides. Take them out of the pan and stir the flour into the juice that remains. Add the other 1/2 cup of the canned milk and the cup of hot water. Heat this mixture until it is a thick sauce. Put the meatballs and sauce into a baking dish and cover the dish. Bake the meatballs at 350°F for 15 minutes. Remove and serve.*

*Swedish contributions to technology include the cream separator, the screw propeller, the computer mouse, and our plant classification system.*

๊ะ ๊ะ ๊ะ ๊ะ ๊ะ

*Alfred Nobel, who invented dynamite, left nine million dollars in his will to establish the Nobel Prizes, which are awarded for contributions to humanity. First awarded in 1901, the Nobel Prizes are still given every year in Stockholm on December 10 in the fields of physics, chemistry, medicine, physiology, and literature. On the same day, the Nobel Peace Prize is awarded in Oslo, Norway.*

Gustavus returned to lead the people in driving the Danes out of Sweden. The trail to Salun that the skiers used to catch up with Gustavus Vasa is still used in the race today. About 12,000 skiers participate each year in the 55-mile race.

Skiing was originally a means of transportation for Swedes. Ski jumping began as a way to navigate cliffs and crevasses. Sweden has produced many ski champions.

Tennis is also very popular in Sweden. There are more tennis players per person in Sweden than in any other country. Another popular Swedish sport is orienteering, which involves navigating with a compass and map.

## Activities

1. Learn as much as you can about Gustavus Vasa. What was his early life like? What experiences and personal qualities helped make him an effective leader?

   ▶ With friends prepare and present a skit based on what you learned and focusing on the day the two skiers went after him to bring him back to Mora. Be sure your skit presents historical information to your audience.

2. The sports of a country are frequently related to its climate and landforms. What geographic and climatic characteristics of Sweden might make orienteering popular?

   ▶ Learn about orienteering and, when you have become an expert, give a demonstration of orienteering to the class. Include equipment or large drawings of the things orienteers use.

3. Find out how one of the Swedish tennis champions got started playing tennis and what kind of training he or she had in Sweden.

   ▶ Share your findings in some way with the class.

# *Music, Art, and Architecture*

Music is such an integral part of Swedish life that one of every ten people sings in a choir. Folk songs and *viso* (ballads) are very popular in Sweden. The viso tells a story in poetic language and is usually accompanied by a guitar or lute.

The traditional Sami song is made up of a series of simple phrases, linked together by rhythmic humming. Called *juoigos,* these songs have been passed down through generations, despite the discouragement of Christian church leaders. Sami have always created new songs spontaneously as well.

The drum is a sacred instrument to the Sami and was used by shamans in important rituals. The traditional Sami drum was hollowed out of a piece of wood and was made in an oval shape resembling a bowl. The drumhead, made of animal skin, was painted in red with pictures of Sami gods, animals, and runic symbols. A reindeer horn was used to beat the drum. Christian missionaries felt the drum was a symbol of Sami paganism and ordered the drums to be burned at churches in huge public bonfires. About eighty of these traditional drums were saved from the flames.

Sweden is also known for its glass-making, and Swedish glass is shipped all over the world. Glassmakers produce a wide variety of art objects, vases, and plates, using a procedure that hasn't changed much in 2,000 years.

Swedes are proud of their *hemslojd,* which are homemade crafts. These include beautiful rya rugs, carved and colorfully painted wooden Dala horses, and dainty lace.

*Stockholm's sport and concert hall, the Globe Arena, is the world's largest indoor multipurpose arena and dominates the city skyline.*

## Activities

1. Research Sami music. Obtain and analyze a recording of one or more Sami songs. How is it similar to and different from your favorite kind of music? What instruments are used in each, and how are they similar and different?

► Present your analysis to the class, using recordings to illustrate your points and conclusions.

2. Learn about Swedish glass-making. What processes are used? How are the processes and products unique to Swedish glass-making? What do you find most beautiful about Swedish glass? Find out about one other culture in which glass-making is an important craft. What processes are used in this culture? How are they different from the processes used in Swedish glass-making?

► With pictures or the products themselves, give a presentation to your class on Swedish glass-making. Show the differences and similarities between Swedish glass and the other glass you have chosen.

3. Read a Swedish myth. What is its significance? What information about the world does it give the Swedes?

► Create a short play based on the myth you chose. Make a filmstrip or overhead transparencies that illustrate what you learned. Present your knowledge to the class using the filmstrip or transparencies as visual aids.

## Kirsten's Day

My name is Kirsten and I am seven years old. I have an older sister, Klara, who is 10 years old. We live in an apartment in the city of Uppsala. The city has a very old and famous university, founded in 1477. My father is a schoolteacher and my mother is a lawyer.

Each morning during the school year, I get up early to get ready for school. I like school, so I don't mind getting up early, even in the winter when it is very dark and cold. For breakfast I eat my favorite food—*filbunke*—which my American uncle says is like yogurt. I put cinnamon sugar on my filbunke and usually have hardtack (biscuits) also. At school we get a big lunch, provided by the government.

**Swedish Days of the Week**

| | |
|---|---|
| Sunday | *sondag* |
| Monday | *mondag* |
| Tuesday | *tisdag* |
| Wednesday | *onsdag* |
| Thursday | *torsdag* |
| Friday | *fredag* |
| Saturday | *lordag* |

Hello in the Swedish language is *Goddag*.

I am looking forward to the third grade, when I will study English. When I know English I can visit my uncle in the United States. He lives in a very big city called Los Angeles.

In the winter, I like to go skating or skiing after school. If the weather is too cold, I read books at home. Sometimes Klara teaches me English words. I already know how to count to ten in English and to say the days of the week.

Klara and I have jobs to do around the house. I make my bed every day and set the table for dinner. Klara does the vacuuming every week and helps with the cooking. Both of us love Christmas, when we help cook special foods and decorate the house. I especially like to help make *pepparkakor,* spicy gingerbread cookies cut in shapes such as stars, hearts, people, and goats.

In the summertime, our whole family goes to our *stuga* on the island of Gotland. Our summer home is very near the city of Visby, where there is an old city wall and many beautiful churches. We swim and enjoy the summer sun, which lasts well into the night. My parents let us stay up late, but not as late as we do during the big Midsummer Festival. That is a special day, the longest day of the year. We dress up in traditional clothes and dance all night long. Part of the celebration is the dance around the *majstang,* or maypole, a tree trunk decorated with flowers and streamers.

My dream is to travel and to see as many countries in the world as I can. When I grow up, I want to be a schoolteacher like my father.

## Activity

Find out about the Midsummer Festival. Why and how is it celebrated? How is it like and not like something you celebrate?

▶ With your class create a midsummer or midwinter festival that celebrates the season and the area where you live.

*So many people in Sweden have the same first and last names that phone books list people's occupations along with their names.*

*Traditional stuga, country houses, are built of wood and are usually painted with red paint from the copper mine in Falun.*

*Mountains cover nearly one-fourth of Sweden. The highest peak in Sweden is Kebnekaise, which rises nearly 7,000 feet at the edge of the tundra, just north of the Arctic Circle. This majestic mountain is located within the city of Kiruna, which, covering 8,700 square miles, is the world's largest town by area.*

❧ ❧ ❧ ❧ ❧

*Within Kiruna is yet another mountain, Kiirunavaara, the Iron Mountain. Lying beneath its surface are an estimated three billion tons of iron ore, one of the largest concentrations of high-quality ore in the world.*

# Odin and the Giants

Odin was the father of the early Scandinavian gods. He was an old man with a beard and only one eye. The legends tell that he traded his other eye for the gift of wisdom.

Odin had 12 sons, the eldest of whom—Thor—was constantly battling with giants. The giants were very jealous of the gods and wanted their possessions. It was Thor's job to protect the gods' home, Asgard, from the giants.

One day a giant offered to build a wall around Asgard so that it would always be protected from its enemies. In payment for building the wall, the gods said they would give the giant the sun, the moon, and the goddess Freyja—but he would have to complete the wall in just one winter. The gods thought they wouldn't have to pay the giant, because they thought the task would be impossible. But what the gods didn't know was that the giant had a helper, the stallion Svaoilfar, who moved twice as many stones each night as the giant did by day. Three days before the wall was to be done, it looked as if the giant would have to be paid. What were the gods going to do?

Loki, the son of a giant, was very handsome but also very evil. He sometimes aided the gods and sometimes opposed them. Loki came up with the solution. He turned himself into a mare and wooed the stallion Svaolifar away from the job of building the wall. The giant was not able to finish the wall in time and was slain by Thor. A colt born to the mare and Svaolifar became a magical eight-legged horse, named Sleipner, which Odin rode.

## *Activity*

Giants appear frequently in folklore. Choose a giant from each of two other folktales to compare and contrast with the giant who was going to build a wall around Asgard.

▶ On a large piece of poster board, make a Venn diagram of the giants' similarities and differences.

## Overview

Isolation has long been a condition of the Tibetan people, and for many years the world has been intrigued by the mystery of this difficult-to-reach land. It is the gateway to the world's highest peak, Miyolangsangma, or Mount Everest. On the vast Tibetan Plateau, nestled amongst the K'un-lun Himalayan ranges, the Tibetan

By
Johanna
Bangeman

*The Himalayas are not only the world's highest mountains, they are also the youngest, having been formed by the collision of the Indian and Asian continental plates only 50 million years ago.*

ৎ ৎ ৎ ৎ

*The Himalayas have more than 17,000 glaciers.*

people are surrounded by great mountain peaks. The average Tibetan land is 15,000 feet above sea level, and it is the lowland area (13,000 feet) in the center of the country that supports most of the population.

In this land sometimes called the "Rooftop of the World," the Tibetan people have lived for thousands of years, surrounded by some of the highest mountain peaks on Earth. Many mountains rise above 20,000 feet. The vast Tibetan Plateau stretches for miles in the center of the country. The remaining magnificent mountains and harsh deserts are mostly wild and undeveloped. In the valley areas one can find wildflowers and rhododendrons. The plateau is filled with many lakes and salt marshes and is the source of great Asian rivers including the Brahmaputra, Indus, Mekong, Salween, and Yangtze.

Mount Kailas is one of the most sacred mountains to the people of Tibet, Nepal, Bhutan, and India. Called the "Precious One of Glacial Snow" by Tibetans, Kailas rises in splendor near the source of four major rivers. Tibetans often compare the peak to the palace of a deity. The mountain is an important figure in one of the most widely read and beautiful stories of

Tibetan literature, *The Hundred Thousand Songs of Milarepa*.

Most Tibetans dream of seeing Kailas for themselves during their lifetime, but as few as 200 pilgrims a year realize this goal. Those who make the pilgrimage to Kailas may travel for weeks or even months to experience its power and revelations. Upon arrival, the dedicated pilgrims will circle the entire mountain or do prostrations to show respect and to accumulate merit. The 19,000-foot Drolma La Pass on the northeast side of Kailas is festively marked with prayer flags strung between rocks and boulders. Before reaching this pass, Tibetans leave a lock of hair or a tooth to symbolize their death and rebirth to a new and more spiritual life.

*The base of Mount Everest is higher than the highest summit of the Alps.*

❦ ❦ ❦ ❦ ❦

*Even today, there are mountains and valleys in Tibet that have not yet been explored or mapped.*

## Historical Background

Tibet has been inhabited for centuries by rugged people whose lives have been inseparable from their religion and their natural environment. Buddhist monasteries are the foundation of Tibetan culture and have political, economic, and educational importance. The Chinese have destroyed thousands of these religious centers during their occupation and only six are still functioning. To become a monk today, one must be approved by the Chinese government.

Tibet's history has been linked for centuries with the history of China and India. Boundaries and control of the land have shifted many times between

> *"We are visitors on this planet. We are here for ninety or one hundred years at the very most. During that period, we must try to do something good, something useful, with our lives. Try to be at peace with yourself, and help others share that peace. If you contribute to other people's happiness, you will find the true goal, the true meaning of life."*
>
> —His Holiness,
> the 14th Dalai Lama

these countries. Though the people of these three regions have often fought savagely, they have exchanged many aspects of their cultures. The land disputes continue to have an impact on the Tibetan people.

Prior to the fifth century, most of Tibet's history was passed down through legends and mythology. In the seventh century, Tibet was a powerful Asian nation under the rule of King Srong-tsen Gampo, who conquered the neighboring regions of Burma and western China. As part of the Chinese emperor's tribute to Srong-tsen Gampo, the Tibetan king was given the emperor's daughter in marriage. Srong-tsen Gampo also extended Tibet's boundaries across the Indian border, and he took a princess from Nepal as a wife, as well. Both queens were Buddhists and converted their husband to their faith. Under Srong-tsen Gampo's influence, the Buddhist religion spread throughout Tibet. Lamaism, a sect of Buddhism, has since become the primary religion of Tibet. It was Buddhism that brought about the development of a written Tibetan language.

Tibet continued to grow in power and size throughout the eighth century. After many border changes, China and Tibet signed a peace treaty in the ninth century. At one time, the Tibetans had 10,000 monasteries. Then, in the thirteenth century, the Mongols, under the leadership of Genghis Khan, overpowered the Tibetans. Later, Kublai Khan appointed a favorite Tibetan priest as priest-king of Tibet, with dominion over its lands and people.

Tibet was independent of Chinese domination for several centuries. In the late 1300s, the first Dalai Lama—the highest spiritual leader in Tibet—was born. By the 1600s, Tibet had formed a theocratic government, headed by the Dalai Lama, who ruled by divine guidance. Each Dalai Lama is thought to be a reincarnation of Chenrezi, the Buddha of Compassion.

In the 1700s, the Chinese military helped rid Tibet of Mongol domination, and the Chinese emperor then appointed the seventh Dalai Lama. A new boundary

between China and Tibet was marked by a pillar erected in 1727, southwest of Batang. In the 1860s, war broke out between tribal people in eastern Tibet. The tribal people appealed to both the Chinese and Tibetan governments for help. The Dalai Lama sent troops to end the fighting and successfully regained control of these eastern lands, but disputes with China continued over the boundaries and control of Tibetan land.

In an attempt to settle the disputes, a conference was held in Simla in 1913, with representatives from China, Tibet, and India. The countries agreed to divide Tibet into Outer Tibet and Inner Tibet and settled upon boundaries. Chinese dominion over Tibet was recognized, but it was agreed that China should not convert Tibet into a Chinese province. Two days after the Chinese government signed the agreement, they rejected it.

In 1949, Peking radio broadcasts announced the "liberation" of Tibet, and the Chinese mounted a military campaign to control the country. Tibet's appeal to the United Nations, Great Britain, the United States, and India did not bring military support or peace-making efforts. In 1951 the Chinese government and a Tibetan delegation signed an agreement allowing the Chinese takeover. Hundreds of thousands of Chinese settlers were sent to colonize Tibet, and food shortages became drastic. Tibetan revolts and demonstrations led to a national uprising. When fighting broke out in Lhasa in 1959, the Dalai Lama and members of his government fled the country. He now resides in Dharam Sala as a guest of the Indian government. An estimated 120,000 Tibetans escaped from Tibet. Claiming the 1951 agreement was signed under pressure, the Dalai Lama revealed the methods the Chinese government had used. As many as a million Tibetans are thought to have been killed since the takeover. A protest in 1987 resulted in the deaths of many more Tibetan people in Lhasa.

The Chinese have formally dismissed the Dalai Lama from his official roles in Tibetan government.

> *"If we ourselves remain always angry and then sing world peace, it has little meaning. So, you see, first our individual self must learn peace. This we can practice. Then we can teach the rest of the world."*
>
> *—His Holiness, the 14th Dalai Lama*

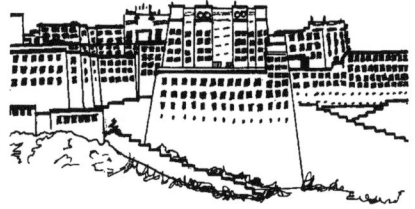

*Of the hundreds of monasteries that existed before the Chinese takeover, only six remain.*

Tens of thousands of lamas (monks) and priests have been sent to forced labor camps, and religious symbols have been removed from Tibetan monasteries. The six remaining Tibetan monasteries are under Chinese control.

The future of the Tibetan culture remains uncertain. The Dalai Lama, however, continues to serve as a revered spiritual leader. He has sent delegations to Jewish communities to explore ways of maintaining a culture far from one's homeland, and Tibetan communities have begun to form in various parts of the world. Both the Chinese and Tibetan people have difficult times ahead in the quest to resolve age-old disputes.

Though Tibetans are dispersed throughout the world, and those who have stayed in Tibet are under strong Chinese control and influence, they still maintain a sense of unity, held together by their devout belief in Buddhist Lamaism. Religion is such a central part of Tibetans' lives that the Dalai Lama, even in his exile, acts as a spiritual and temporal leader of the Tibetan people. Although he must live outside his former country, he works hard to keep Tibetan culture alive and he has dedicated his life to peace, not revenge. He was awarded the Nobel Peace Prize in 1989.

Under a new economic plan, the Chinese have reorganized the farmland into communes, developed Tibetan resources, and created military sites to protect the Chinese regime. There are an estimated eight million Chinese now living in Tibet and only six million Tibetans. By continuing to send Chinese people to Tibet, the Chinese government hopes to weaken the Tibetan culture and prevent any Tibetan attempt to return to power. The Dalai Lama is willing to let China control Tibet's foreign policy as long as Tibetans are allowed to manage their own internal affairs.

Instead of being discouraged by the Chinese attempts to destroy their religion and culture, the Tibetan people have maintained a calm intensity. Their faith seems only to be strengthened in the face

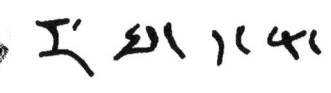

of continuing repression. Even those in exile keep their culture alive, promoting compassion and universal responsibility for human rights.

## Activities

1. Find out about the geographical elements of Tibet. Where is the Tibetan Plateau? Where are all the mountain ranges?

   ▶ Make a relief map of Tibet. Draw the map on a large sheet of poster board. Draw the Tibetan Plateau and all the mountain ranges. Using a scale of 1/2 inch = 10,000 feet above sea level, make physical features out of papier-mâché, modeling clay, or dough. Be sure to include your scale in the map key.

2. Have your class prepare at least five questions each about the Buddhist religion and culture, including the basic Buddhist beliefs and how followers practice their religion. Then find a Buddhist who lives in your community. Invite the Buddhist to your class.

   ▶ Conduct a question and answer session in which your classmates ask your Buddhist guest the questions they wrote.

3. Research the 1949 Chinese invasion of Tibet. Why is Tibet important to China? What events led up to the invasion? What important events have occurred since?

   ▶ Draw a time line of events. Mark the invasion in red. When you present your time line to the class, explain what you have learned.

4. On a globe, trace Tibetan immigration patterns since the 1950 Chinese invasion. Put markers in the places where the Dalai Lama has lived in exile. Mark in a different way where the greatest concentration of Tibetan people resides outside Tibet.

*Because of Tibet's high altitude, visitors may suffer from acute mountain sickness (AMS), which in extreme cases can be fatal. Headaches, weakness, breathing problems, nausea, a cough, dizziness, and loss of appetite are some of the symptoms. The body may take as long as a month to build up enough red blood cells to provide a person with the oxygen needed at such high altitudes.*

*Tibet has few roads and people travel on foot, with carts and donkeys, with carts and tractors, and on horseback. Some people travel by bus or jeep.*

ॐ ॐ ॐ ॐ

*The village of Jiachan is believed to be the highest inhabited town on Earth. It is located at 15,870 feet above sea level.*

▶ Show your markings to your class. Conduct a discussion in which you investigate how you think the exiled Tibetans feel.

5. Learn about the Dalai Lama.

▶ With one or more friends, paint a mural that describes his life—birth, childhood activities, and flight from Tibet. Be prepared to explain your mural to viewers.

6. With several friends, become experts on the relationship between Tibet and China. When each of you has a significant level of expertise, divide the group into even numbers.

▶ Prepare a panel discussion or debate in which one team defends China's position and the other defends Tibet's. Following the discussion, poll the audience as to who they think is right.

7. Research King Srong-tsen, who ruled Tibet in the seventh century. How was he able to conquer Burma and western China? What changes did his conversion to Buddhism bring about? What personal qualities do you think he had? Choose a period of his life that seems most important to you.

▶ Write diary entries he might have made during this time, including events and his ideas and emotions.

8. Find out about the people surrounding King Srong-tsen. Who were his advisors? Who were his family?

▶ Prepare a skit that informs viewers about the king, events, and his ideas and emotions during the period of time that interests you.

9. Become knowledgeable about the 1913 conference held by China, Tibet, and India in Simla.

▶ With friends, re-create one or more discussions that might have led to the signing of the agreement. Present the discussions to the class, being sure that each country's interests and views are included.

10. Find out about Tibetan history. What do you think were the most significant events? What events changed the course of Tibetan history?

   ▶ Make a time line that shows the events and their effects. Illustrate your time line. Present it to your class.

## *The People*

The Tibetans are a rugged people. Although Tibet has very little wood with which to build fires, Tibetans still do not have central heating in their homes. People cook over small open fires, burning pieces of juniper or yak dung. To preserve heat, they build houses without chimneys, so their homes are often smoky.

A land with an average elevation among the highest in the world, Tibet can be very cold. Tibetans wear many layers of clothing and sheepskin coats to protect them from the weather. Over thousands of years, their bodies have adapted to the cold and high altitude. They now have increased blood flow to their extremities, a high metabolism, and an insulating layer of fat. For centuries, Tibetan hermits have used a method for keeping warm at high altitudes called *thumo reskiang,* which involves mental control of bodily functions.

Survival for Tibetans is hard work. Life expectancy in this harsh world is between 50 and 65 years, and people marry at a young age. Their homes have no running water, and they do most work by hand—from farming to road building to making cloth. Many Tibetans live in large extended families, where everyone helps with the work. Tibetan nomads live in tents made from yak skins. Other people live in flat-roofed, one- or two-story houses. Monks and nuns live in monasteries built high in the mountains.

Nonviolence is a basic premise of the Tibetan religion. Under Chinese rule, practice of Buddhism is forbidden in Tibet, so some parents send their children

*Sherpas are people of Tibetan origin who make their living accompanying mountaineering expeditions to Mount Everest. They generally live above 9,000 feet and seldom venture below the malaria line, around 4,000 feet.*

on the difficult trek over the Himalayas to India, where they can grow up in freedom and can practice Buddhism. Those who complete the trip are taken care of by Tibetans living in India.

## Activities

1. Learn as much as you can about the everyday life of Tibetan people. Choose one activity that is part of everyday life.

    ▶ Make a filmstrip or create a play that shares what you learned. Be sure to include what you learned about the way in which Tibetans greet each other.

2. Become an expert on the effects of very high altitude—on the human body, on cooking, on plants, and on animals.

    ▶ Make a large chart, filmstrip, or a series of overhead transparencies that illustrate the effects you learned. Provide narration when you present the chart or transparencies.

3. Research the Tibetan religion. What principles besides nonviolence are important in this religion? Pretend you are a Tibetan who believes the family yak has been stolen by a neighbor. How, as a religious Tibetan, can you get it back?

    ▶ Present a monologue or skit that includes your nonviolent solution to the problem.

4. Learn about how Tibetans dress. How is every article related to where they live and their culture? How does the dress of children differ from that of adults? Men from women? Why do you think that is so?

    ▶ Illustrate what you learned in one of these ways:

    *Make a collage of pictures of Tibetan dress cut from magazines*

    *Draw pictures of Tibetan dress*

    *Make a Tibetan outfit for one or more dolls*

    *Make a Tibetan outfit for yourself or a friend*

*A typical Tibetan greeting is "Tashi delek," which means something like "Live long, prosper, and be happy."*

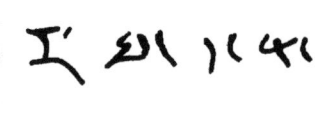
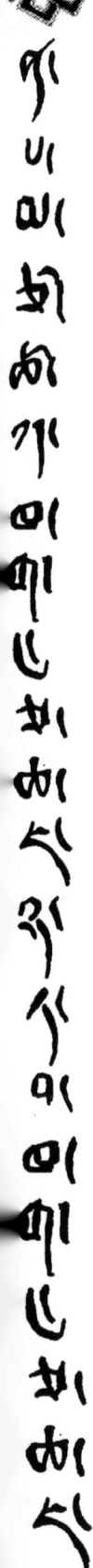

5. Research the practice of Tibetan Buddhists sending their children to India to learn about and practice Buddhism.

   ▶ Write a story based on your research that tells about one or more such children. Include the difficult journey, the children's feelings about the situation, and the differences in life style.

6. Find out about the Seven Stages of Birth (pre-conception, conception, gestation, birth, bonding, infancy, and childhood). Then think about the ideas about birth your own culture holds. How many stages are there? How important is each stage? Do the stages correspond in any way to the Tibetan stages?

   ▶ Choose one of the Tibetan stages and a corresponding stage from your own culture. Write an essay in which you compare and contrast the two. Be sure to include in your essay your opinions on the benefits and drawbacks of each belief.

7. Learn as much as you can about the pilgrimage to Kailas. Why do people want to make such a pilgrimage? How long might it take to circle Kailas? What weather is common in this area? What do Tibetans believe about Kailas—how is it related to their culture and religious beliefs?

   ▶ Pretend you are a pilgrim to Kailas, and keep a diary of your journey from home and the pilgrimage experiences.

8. Find out how the recent building of roads has affected the Tibetan people and their environment. What long-term effects do you believe the roads will have?

   ▶ After researching and thinking, write an editorial on this topic. Remember, an editorial conveys an opinion as well as factual information. Be sure to support your opinion with reasons.

*Tibet has the world's largest lithium mine, with a lithium deposit equaling half the world's known total.*

9. Locate a Tibetan who lives in your community and who is willing to be interviewed. Develop at least ten questions before the interview. What was life like in Tibet? Why did he or she leave? What was the journey like? How, if at all, does Buddhist Lamaism affect her or his daily life? What is the most difficult thing about living in this country?

▶ Present the information you gather to the class in an interesting way. Invite the Tibetan to speak to the class.

## Wildlife and the Environment

Wild animals used to be plentiful in the high plateau region of Tibet. Buddhists believe that sentient (conscious) beings should not be killed, and under Buddhist rule animals freely roamed the country. Since the Chinese invasion, animal herds have been depleted by hunting.

Kiangs, antelopes, and yaks are common in Tibet, which also has gazelles, snow leopards, lynx, wolves, brown bears, huge-horned argali sheep, blue sheep, musk deer, woolly hares, black-lipped pikas, saber falcons, upland hawks, lammergeier, black-necked cranes, sand grouse, eagle owls, gulls, and ground jays. The plateau has many lakes and salt marshes, which are wintering grounds for the rare black-necked cranes. In the alpine zone, lichen, marmot, ibex, brown bears, and snow grouse survive the cold weather.

The yak is very important to all aspects of Tibetan life. It can weigh a ton, have 30-inch horns, and long hair. People use the yak's coat and skin to make boots, homes, clothes, and even boats. Rugs are woven from its hair. From its body comes meat, and from the *dzo* (female), milk, cheese, and butter. Dzo butter is burned in lamps, and dried yak dung is used for cooking. The yak is usually black in color, but occasionally a wild golden one can be seen. The wild yak is considered an endangered species.

*Lichens are able to survive the extreme Tibetan climates. Lichens may grow only an inch in 25 years, but some are as old as 4,500 years.*

*Yaks can survive at altitudes above 10,000 feet, but below that they begin to die.*

*A female yak is called a dzo or dri. A male is called a yak.*

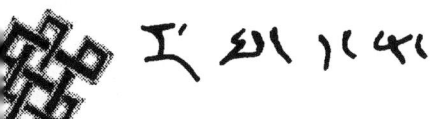

For centuries the Tibetans have lived in harmony with their environment and wildlife. Now hunting for fun and profit threatens the balance of nature. The Chinese have built many roads in Tibet, destroying natural resources in the process. Forestry and mining have followed the roads, also destroying the beauty of the land.

The Dalai Lama has said that he would like the entire Tibetan Plateau to become a peace sanctuary and the world's largest natural park. Recently China established the Chang Tang, a desolate northern sector of Tibet, as the second-largest nature preserve in the world. This act resulted from a collaborative effort between Western naturalists George and Kay Schaller and their Tibetan and Chinese colleagues, who laid the groundwork with their research from 1988 through 1992.

## Activities

1. Research an animal native to Tibet. Learn about its habitat, ecosystem, food sources, environmental dangers, and life cycle.

   ▶ Write a story about the animal and illustrate the story. If you wish, make a book to contain the story.

2. Find as much information as you can about the yak and the ways it is used by Tibetans. What, if anything, is wasted?

   ▶ Draw a large labeled diagram of a yak, showing how its products and body parts are used.

3. Learn about the Chang Tang and how it came to be. Who opposed its establishment? Why? Who supported its establishment? Why? Take a stand as to whether the Chang Tang is good or bad for Tibet.

   ▶ Write a persuasive essay based on your belief and your research.

*A special Tibetan creature is the aweto, a brownish caterpillar that looks like a silkworm and produces a tonic good for coughs, lumbago, and other problems.*

*Sky burial is the most common form of Tibetan burial. After death, a body is blessed, tied up in a cloth, and taken to a mountainside site. The body is then cut up, the bones are pounded, and the body is mixed with tsampa so the birds will eat it, taking the body into the sky.*

# Food, Festivals, and Celebrations

Tea with dzo butter is a common Tibetan drink. *Tsampa* is a staple food. It is made of roasted barley, formed into balls and mixed with dzo butter, tea or hot water, and sugar or salt.

Tibetan festivals and celebrations revolve around the Buddhist holidays, bringing in the new year, the seasons, or Buddha's birthday. Hardly a month passes without a celebration. During the Incense Festival, evil ghosts prowl the country looking for a human spirit to take over. But if the spirit of a person is very happy, the ghosts cannot take possession. So the Tibetans dress up and celebrate their happiness!

The Washing Festival lasts about a week, during which people go to the river and wash themselves and their clothes. Legend tells that this bathing can cure all kinds of sickness. During Tsong-ka-pa's Festival, people celebrate the anniversary of the death of Tsong-ka-pa by lighting butter lamps and placing them on window sills and rooftops.

## Activities

1. Learn about Tsong-ka-pa's Festival. Who was Tsong-ka-pa? What did he accomplish during his lifetime? Why is his death celebrated? How is it celebrated?

   ▶ Make one or more butter candles by pressing softened butter and a wick into a clay bowl or vigil light container. Light the candle(s), and darken the room. What is the light like? How long does a candle last? What effects would this type of light have on life after dark? Demonstrate a butter candle and share your thoughts with the class.

2. The Tibetans celebrate many interesting festivals. Choose one on which to become an expert. Learn how it is celebrated. What foods, customs, and garments are associated with the festival? Why is it celebrated? Pretend you are a Tibetan.

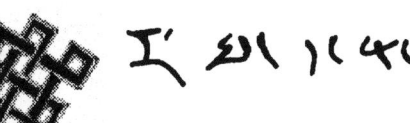

► Write diary entries before, during, and after the festival. Include facts, thoughts, ideas, and emotions in the entries.

# Dances, Games, and Sports

The most important Tibetan dances are the Cham dances, performed at special times by monks wearing masks and beautiful brocaded costumes. Masks are usually made of wood, metal, or leather. The dances tell a story in pantomime, often honoring a saint or religious person. They may include the appearance of terrifying deities. Cham dances take place at New Year, at solstices, and on birthdays. Some of the dances include a dialogue, such as "The Conversion of the Hunter by Milarepa."

## Activities

1. Find out more about Cham. What deities are honored most often? How are the costumes made? What or whom do the masks depict? Then choose a Buddhist saint or religious person.

   ► Make a mask that one might use in a Cham dance. Show it to your classmates and ask them to guess the characteristics of the saint or religious person whom it honors.

2. Find out about one other dance, game, or sport that the Tibetans enjoy. What are the rules, if any? How is it done? What is the purpose or significance of the activity?

   ► Demonstrate how to dance or play the activity you have chosen.

# Music, Art, and Architecture

Tibetan chanting is a deeply religious and difficult practice. It sounds unusual to Western ears. The deep, guttural sounds produce unique overtone harmonics,

*Monasteries, mani stones (dome-shaped shrines), and prayer wheels all are visible expressions of Buddhist culture. Pilgrimages to sacred places are also common to Tibetan religious practices.*

**Numbers in Tibetan language:**

| | |
|---|---|
| *1* | *cheek* |
| *2* | *nyee* |
| *3* | *soum* |
| *4* | *shee* |
| *5* | *nga* |
| *6* | *drouk* |
| *7* | *dun* |
| *8* | *giay* |
| *9* | *gou* |
| *10* | *choo* |

**Days of the week:**

| | |
|---|---|
| *Monday* | *Dawa* |
| *Tuesday* | *Mikma* |
| *Wednesday* | *Lhakpa* |
| *Thursday* | *Purbu* |
| *Friday* | *Pasang* |
| *Saturday* | *Pemba* |
| *Sunday* | *Yima* |

**Other Tibetan words:**

| | |
|---|---|
| *mother* | *amalag* |
| *father* | *pulag* |
| *boy* | *bou* |
| *girl* | *boumo* |
| *thank you* | *touk-jay chay* |

which are believed to aid the worshippers in prayer.

One kind of Tibetan drum, the *damaru,* has skins on both sides. Drummers turn the instrument from side to side with a handle and strike it with balls tied to strings. The drums are often decorated with beautiful cloth banners.

Another interesting Tibetan instrument is the eight-foot-long brass trumpet. During religious ceremonies, trumpeters sit upon stools and hold the instruments so the far ends rest upon the ground. Drums and cymbals usually accompany the trumpets. In old Tibet, trumpets were made of human or tiger thigh bones and were used to get rid of demons. In Tibet you may sometimes also hear a shepherd boy's flute as he keeps track of his charges.

Art and religion are inseparable in Tibet. *Tangka* (pronounced "tanka") are colorful religious paintings. Elaborately detailed and brightly colored, they often contain references to Buddhist mythology. Inside monasteries, bright wall murals tell stories and history. Gold statues and jewel-encrusted objects glow by the light of butter lamps. Tibetans weave rugs, aprons, and blankets that feature religious symbols and designs. Colorful prayer flags are thought to carry prayers to Buddha.

Tibetan art is beautifully integrated into everyday items. Turquoise, coral, and silver are used as jewelry and to decorate common objects. In Tibetan homes, you may see silverwork on tea cups or a flint strap. Tibetan women wear colorful felt and wool boots, brightly colored blouses, and multicolored aprons. Even horse bridles are brightly colored. Men sometimes wear red yarn in their hair, and women may braid their hair into 108 braids, a sacred number in Tibetan religious beliefs.

The *mandala,* a Sanskrit word meaning "circle," is a common pattern in Tibetan art. It shows the universe as a circle of mountains, oceans, and continents, with a mythical mountain at the very center—reaching from the depths of hell to the wonders of heaven.

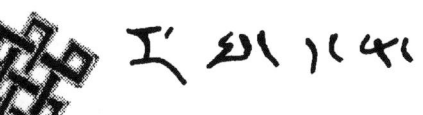

## Activities

1. Read some Tibetan myths. Choose one to illustrate.

   ▶ With one or more friends, make a brightly colored mural that tells the story of the myth.

2. Research Tibetan musical instruments. Obtain a recording of Tibetan music, and learn to identify the instruments. If the music tells a story, learn that, too.

   ▶ Play the recording for the class and share what you learned.

3. Find out the significance of Buddhist prayer flags. In what ways are they use? Of what are they constructed? What colors, if any, are used?

   ▶ Make a prayer flag. Create a symbol for a quality you value: gentleness, honesty, or friendliness, for example. Block print or paint your symbol on fabric.

4. Find out about the Tibetan practice of braiding their hair into 108 braids. What significance does this practice hold for Tibetans?

   ▶ Braid someone's hair into 108 braids, or with yarn, make 108 braids to put on the head of a student or doll. Show your project to your class and tell them of the significance.

*"If you cultivate love, compassion, and so forth for your own welfare, seeking happiness for yourself, you are bound within a selfish viewpoint which will not lead to good results. Rather, you should have an attitude of altruism, seeking the welfare of others from the very depths of your heart."*

*—His Holiness, the 14th Dalai Lama*

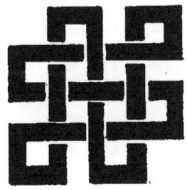

## Tenzin's Day

Tenzin is a six-year-old girl who herds sheep to high pasture and watches her two-year-old brother. Tenzin takes tsampa and tea with her for lunch. As Tenzin watches the herd, she sees a lot of wild animals, feels the wind on her rosy cheeks, and watches the powerful, silent mountains in the distance.

Upland hawks hunt the small pikas (similar to rabbits) that scurry through the grasses to their holes. Tenzin respects the beauty of the many forms of life around her, and she feels most peaceful when her little brother is napping and the animals are grazing.

After working all day, Tenzin and her little brother bring the herd back. Now she must help haul water, grind barley for more tsampa, and gather yak dung, which she throws on the wall of the family's yak-hair tent to dry and to use later for a cooking fire. Tenzin's family will move with the herd, looking for good grazing land, so she won't stay in one place very long.

*Sometimes Tibetans braid their hair into 108 braids—a sacred number.*

## Activity

Tsampa is a staple in the Tibetan diet. Try this Americanized version of tsampa, substituting cow's butter for yak's butter.

▶ Roast barley in a pan or in the oven. Grind the barley with a mortar and pestle. Take some of the barley flour, mix it with softened butter and salt, and add enough hot water or tea to shape the dough into little balls. Eat it for a snack.

# Uncle Tompa Paints a Bull

## A Tibetan Folktale

One day Uncle Tompa was walking through the fields. He saw a man plowing. His plow was being pulled by a pair of bulls. Uncle saw that one of the bulls was black, while the other had black and white spots.

So Uncle sat down near the man. "Hello!" he said. "You have a very healthy pair of bulls. It is too bad they are an unmatched pair."

"Why is that?" the man asked.

"Because one is black and the other is spotted."

"I cannot do anything about that."

"Sure you can! You can make the spotted one into a black one."

"Could you do that for me, then?"

"Yes, yes, and it will cost you only one cup of beer," Uncle replied.

They both agreed on the price. Uncle then untied the spotted bull from the plow. He took some black mud and rubbed it all over the bull's body. Finally, the white spots were all covered with mud. The spotted bull looked as black as the other one. Uncle gave it to the owner and said, "After three days, give him a bath, and then all the spots will turn as black as they are now."

The man continued his plowing and said, "You can go to my house for the beer." Uncle went to the house, which was not too far from where the man was plowing.

Uncle met the owner's wife and said, "I just sold a black bull to your husband. He told me to get the money from you. If you don't trust me, you can look out the window and see for yourself." She looked down from her window and saw the pair of black bulls. So she gave Uncle the cost of one bull, and Uncle went off with the money.

## Activity

Uncle Tompa is a trickster. Many cultures have tales about tricksters—coyote, Br'er Rabbit, and Anansi, for example. Read trickster tales from several cultures. Choose two to compare and contrast (using Uncle Tompa as one if you wish).

► Tell both stories to the class, then point out their differences and similarities.

For a thousand years the Tibetan people have believed in the kingdom of Shambhala, believed to be a hidden earthly paradise.

One Tibetan story tells of a young man's journey across the central Asian mountains to search for Shambhala. After a long trek across deserts and mountains, he reaches a cave inhabited by an old hermit.

The sage asks him why he is traveling across the wastes of snow. "To find Shambhala," he says, to which the sage replies, "Ah, then, you need not travel far, for the kingdom of Shambhala is in your own heart."

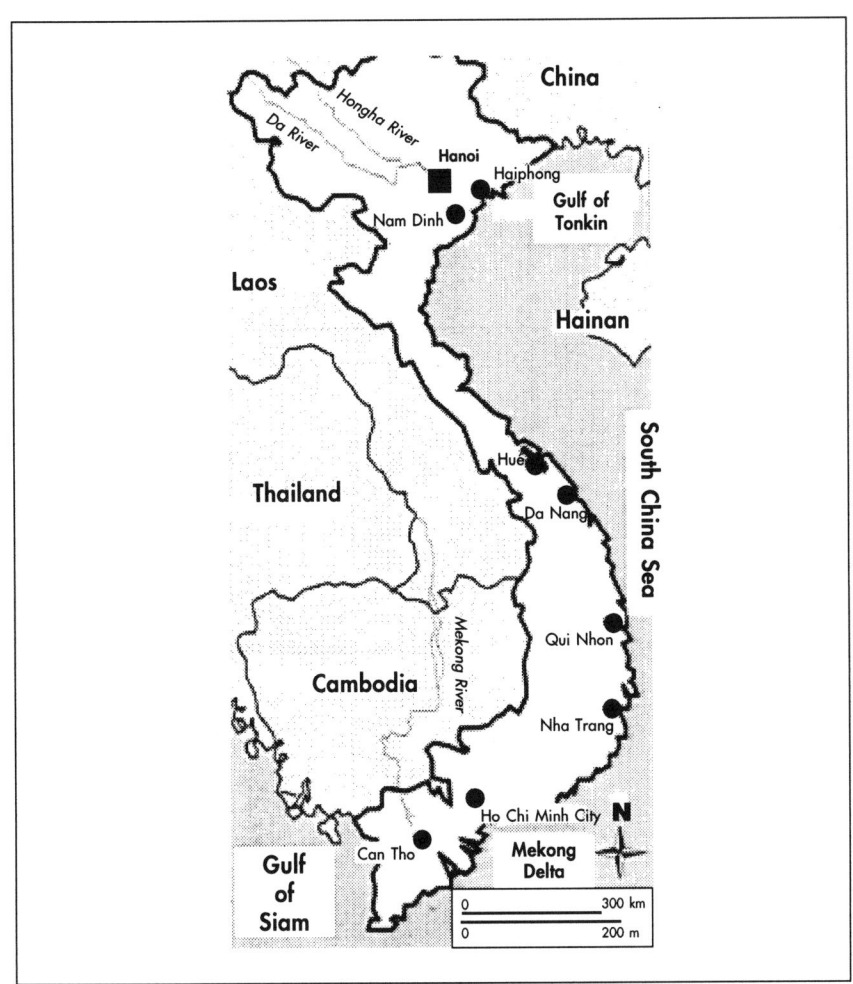

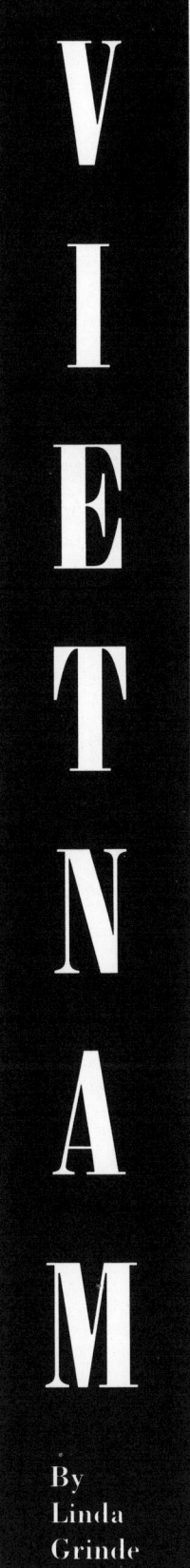

## Overview

Vietnam, situated on the eastern shores of the Indochinese peninsula, is bordered by a continuous range of mountains and hills on the west and the South China Sea to the east. This long, narrow country is little more than 30 miles wide in some places. More than 200 rivers cut through the mountains, which are marked at the lower altitudes by dense tropical rain forests. In contrast, the

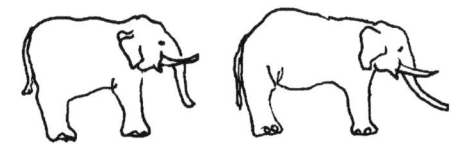

central highland region experiences a long dry season. Coastal Vietnam is quite varied with its peaceful bays, jutting limestone walls, sand dunes, and farm areas.

## Historical Background

Before Europeans arrived in the sixteenth century, Vietnam's long history was one of conflict. The people we call Vietnamese are descended from natives of southern China, who fled south in about 3000 B.C.E. to avoid being absorbed by the Chinese. These early Vietnamese moved into Tonkin, then further south to Champa. They drove the indigenous people they encountered into the jungles of the central highlands. Native Cambodians were pushed westward.

Over the centuries, the Vietnamese fought with the Chinese, with local minority groups, and with each other. From 111 B.C.E. until the revolt that gained them independence in 938 C.E., the Vietnamese struggled against Chinese occupation. Although the Vietnamese then ruled themselves for nearly 600 years, this was not a peaceful time. Invasions occurred regularly and the Vietnamese struggled to protect their borders. In 1288, in a notable battle, they defeated Kublai Khan.

The first Europeans arrived in the 1500s. The Vietnamese defended themselves against Portuguese, British, Dutch, and French colonists. The French persisted and in 1858 invaded Vietnam in force. In 1884 Vietnam was declared a French protectorate.

The French held Vietnam until World War II, when the Japanese invaded and occupied the country until 1945. Although the French returned, Ho Chi Minh and the Vietminh independence movement resisted French control. The fighting continued from 1946 until the bloody defeat of the French at Dien Bien Phu in May 1954.

A cease-fire agreement signed in Paris in July 1954 divided Vietnam along the Ben Hai River. All land north of the 17th parallel became a socialist nation,

*Vietnam's location on the South China Sea provides excellent opportunity for trade.*

with Ho Chi Minh as president. The French withdrew from the north and 900,000 pro-French Vietnamese fled to South Vietnam. In the south, Ngo Dinh Diem was selected premier of the interim government. He proclaimed the south the Republic of Vietnam and became its first president.

In 1959 North Vietnam adopted a socialist constitution that called for the reunification of Vietnam. North Vietnam began sending troops into South Vietnam in 1964, with the Soviet Union and China providing arms assistance. The United States, fearing that South Vietnam would lose to North Vietnamese forces, began air strikes in the north in 1964 and sent the first ground troops to South Vietnam in 1965. For the next 10 years, the United States fought an undeclared war in Vietnam. U.S. troop withdrawal began in 1969.

The United States, North Vietnam, South Vietnam, and the Viet Cong (South Vietnamese rebels) signed a cease-fire agreement in Paris in January 1973, but the fighting continued. By April 1975 Saigon had surrendered to the North Vietnamese, and the country was officially reunited in July 1976. South Vietnam was essentially absorbed by the North.

Fighting with Cambodia escalated in 1977, however, and Vietnamese forces had pushed the Khmer Rouge Cambodians into Thailand by 1980. The Chinese attacked and occupied the Vietnamese border for a short period in 1979. Peace with China is still uneasy and the borders remain heavily guarded.

In 1993 the United States ended the trade embargo against Vietnam. New political tolerance and private business ownership have allowed the Vietnamese economy to become more stable. Foreign investors are pouring new money into the economic system as Vietnam prepares to play a new part in the world order. It appears that after centuries of fighting, Vietnam may be able to call itself an independent and self-sufficient nation.

*About 24 percent of the land is readily arable, including the densely settled Red River valley in the north, narrow coastal plains in the center, and the wide, often marshy Mekong River delta in the south. The rest of the land is made up of semiarid plateaus, barren mountains, and rain forests.*

*In spite of adversity, the Vietnamese people maintain a very high literacy level.*

～ ～ ～ ～ ～

*Vietnamese children write their family name first, their middle name next, and their first name last.*

## Activities

1. Become an expert on Vietnam's history. Based on the information you gather, think about these questions:

   *What are the reasons that the Vietnamese people have been in conflict with others and each other throughout history?*

   *What effects have geography and climate had on Vietnam?*

   *What do you think the future holds for Vietnam?*

   ▶ Using what you have learned and thought about, make a filmstrip that focuses on the conflicts in Vietnam over time.

2. In the 1500s several groups of Europeans attempted to colonize Vietnam. What made Vietnam attractive to them? What would they gain if their efforts were successful? Learn as much as you can about a specific group of colonists. Pretend that you were their leader.

   ▶ Write diary entries from the time you left your homeland until you were driven out or established a colony in Vietnam.

3. Ho Chi Minh is an important person in modern Vietnamese history. Learn as much as you can about him, his successes and his failures. Choose a significant event or time in his life.

   ▶ Develop a scene that you and some friends will present. Be sure the audience learns about Ho Chi Minh and Vietnam from watching the scene.

4. The United States fought an undeclared war for more than ten years in Vietnam. Research this time—1964 to 1976. What did U.S. troops do? How was this conflict different from a declared war? What were the effects on the Vietnamese of the U.S. actions? On the United States? Pretend that you lived in South Vietnam during this time.

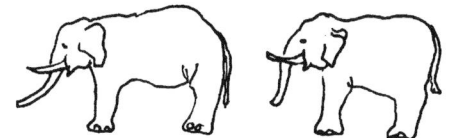

▶ Write an essay that tells the Vietnamese side of the story and that includes conclusions and recommendations.

5. Learn about the Khmer Rouge Cambodians. Why did they begin to fight against the Vietnamese in 1977? Who was their leader? What did they want to accomplish? How did the Vietnamese troops force the Khmer Rouge into Thailand in 1980? Take the perspective of a Vietnamese person

▶ Create a docudrama of important events between 1977 and 1980. Videotape your production or present it live. Be sure people will learn from viewing it.

6. Find out about North Vietnam and South Vietnam during the war. Where were the countries divided? What forests were defoliated? Who defoliated the forests? What were the major waterways?

▶ Make a relief map of Vietnam. Mark the elements mentioned, plus any others that you think are important. Present your map to the class.

7. Invite someone who has lived in Vietnam and someone who fought in the Vietnam conflict to come to your classroom and speak to your class on different days. Discuss the viewpoints of the two visitors. On what points did they agree? Disagree?

▶ If your two visitors disagree with each other, set up a debate with half the class taking the Vietnamese person's point of view and the other half taking the soldier's point of view. If they agree with each other, set up a panel discussion of the various reasons each feels as she or he does.

8. Alone or with some friends, research the differences in the houses built in South Vietnam and those built in North Vietnam.

*It is estimated that one-half of the boat people, 1.4 million Vietnamese and 300,000 Chinese, died before reaching their new land.*

► Build a scale model of a South Vietnamese village and one of a North Vietnamese village using as much as possible materials that the people themselves would use.

9. Research the Vietnamese flag and the coat of arms. When were the designs adopted? What do the symbols mean?

► Make a chart with the images drawn separately and an explanation beside each one.

10. Find out about Vietnamese history. What do you think were the most significant events? What events changed the course of Vietnamese history?

► Make a time line that shows the events and their effects. Illustrate your time line. Present it to your class.

## The People

In many ways, over hundreds of years, life has changed little for the people of Vietnam. The economy is basically agricultural, and the real heart of the country is in its thousands of tiny, rural villages.

People wear lightweight, cone-shaped hats as a shield against the sun. Clothing is loose fitting and made of thin cotton or hemp. When they are not doing hard physical labor, women wear a traditional costume called an *ao dai* (pronounced "ow die"), a tight-fitting tunic with long silky panels in the front and back, over loose-fitting pants.

Chinese and French influences are evident in language, art, literature, music, theater, and architecture. Almost everyone with a high school education studies French literature, and books written in French are common.

Less than 1 percent of the people own automobiles. The bicycle is the most popular method of transportation. It is also possible to travel by boat on Vietnam's many small canals and waterways.

*The population is 84 percent Vietnamese, 2 percent Chinese, and 2 percent Cambodian. The rest are mountain people, called Montagnards by the French. These are tribal people, indigenous groups who were forced into the mountains when the land was first invaded and developed their nomadic culture in isolation.*

A village or country home is a simple structure made of bamboo, wood, straw, or mud, with palm leaves for a roof. For privacy and to keep the dwelling cool, the home might be surrounded by a wall of banana, guava, or mango trees. In the cities, many people live in Chinese-style shophouses, with a store on the ground floor and living quarters behind and above. Homes in both the cities and rural areas include a central area for honoring ancestors.

On family-owned farms, family members work seven days a week tending rice paddies. The growing of rice is a year-round vocation, involving cultivating, harvesting, tending, and transplanting. In the cities, people manufacture and process cement, fertilizers, iron and steel, paper products, and textiles. They also dig ditches, carry concrete blocks, or construct buildings. Men and women work as welders, help in medical clinics, and work in canneries preparing food. Many international companies are currently building offices in the major cities, which creates construction and service industry jobs.

The government provides twelve years of schooling for children. Many young people go to eastern Europe, Russia, or other countries to study. Vietnam has two universities and more than forty colleges and specialty schools.

## Activities

1.  Learn about everyday life in Vietnam. Where and at what do adults work? Who takes care of small children? What is the family structure? What are meals like? What do people do for recreation?

    ▶ Create several puppets and present a puppet show about life in a Vietnamese village.

2.  Learn as much as you can about Vietnamese clothing. How does the clothing typically worn in North Vietnam differ from that worn in South Vietnam?

*Buddhism, Taoism, and Confucianism all have contributed to Vietnamese philosophy and culture.*

∾ ∾ ∾ ∾ ∾

*Vietnamese Catholics were openly opposed to the socialist government in North Vietnam. Many of the boat people who fled or were forced to leave Vietnam after the war were Catholic Vietnamese.*

▶ Make a male and a female paper doll with clothing representative of both North and South Vietnam. Dress the dolls in the clothing. Present the dolls to the class and point out how each item of clothing is appropriate to the Vietnamese climate and lifestyle.

3. Choose a specific region of Vietnam on which to become an expert.

   ▶ Make a diorama or a model of the landscape, a typical home, and vegetation of this region. Be prepared to present your model and explain its elements.

4. Learn as much as you can about growing rice.

   ▶ Create a miniature rice paddy and sprout rice. Make a filmstrip that tells about rice cultivation in Vietnam. Tape record or present the narrative for your filmstrip.

5. Learn about the ceremonies and the reasons the Vietnamese pay honor to their ancestors. What similarities and differences do you see between the way families you know think about their ancestors and the way the Vietnamese do?

   ▶ Write an essay in which you examine the similarities and differences you discovered.

6. Research the mountain people (*Montagnards* to the French). Why do they look and speak differently than do other Vietnamese people?

   ▶ Draw pictures of the mountain people in their traditional dress. Use the drawings to illustrate a report.

7. Compare the beliefs of Buddhists, Confucianists, and Taoists. Where do these beliefs conflict? Where do they agree?

   ▶ Write a play with three characters, each representing one belief. In your play, present a problem that the characters will solve using their different belief systems.

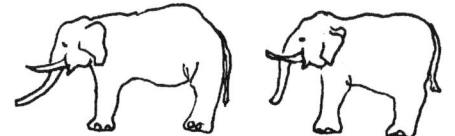

# *Wildlife and the Environment*

Vietnam has a variety of interesting wildlife from myriad small insects and birds to tigers and elephants. Smaller than the African elephant, the elephant in Vietnam is an intelligent animal that can be trained easily.

Water covers parts of Vietnam. There are also mountains, plains, plateaus, and jungles. In the waters live leeches, mosquitoes, crocodiles, and a number of fish species. The jungles hum with the calls of a variety of insects and with the pleasant songs of brilliant birds. Chattering monkeys, languors, macaques, and gibbons add to the din of Vietnam's jungle.

Aggressive agriculture and overpopulation threaten an already unstable environmental situation. Although it has been twenty years since the Vietnam War, the country is still struggling with the environmental destruction it endured during that war. U.S. armed forces dumped twelve million gallons of Agent Orange, a defoliating chemical, on South Vietnam between 1962 and 1970. According to U.S. records, Agent Orange was spread over an area the size of the state of Connecticut to eliminate the foliage that provided hiding places for the Viet Cong. As a result, more than 10 percent of Vietnam was defoliated. Thousands of Vietnamese and American veterans who were exposed to Agent Orange have suffered from a variety of illnesses, including cancer, as a result of their exposure. Agent Orange has also caused birth defects in the descendants of those same populations. The poisonous herbicide destroyed an estimated 29 percent of Vietnam's forest land and drove to near extinction 77 species of mammals. The Douc Langur monkey, for example, lost its habitat in the chemical rain and was also eaten by hungry soldiers. It is on the brink of extinction.

Efforts are being made to end the ecological crisis. In the Mekong River Delta, for example, people are helping to restore the habitat of the Eastern Sarus

*Most farmers in Vietnam plow with wooden plows and water buffalo.*

crane, a bird that symbolizes new life to the Vietnamese. During the war, the wetlands that were its habitat were drained and denuded.

*Rice, the primary crop in Vietnam, is commonly eaten at every meal. The shape of the country is said to be like two rice bowls on the ends of a pole.*

## Activities

1. Investigate Vietnamese insects. Choose five types on which to focus. Learn about their habitats, their food sources, and their life cycles.

   ▶ Draw these insects to scale against a realistic background. Be prepared to present an oral explanation of your drawing.

2. Become an expert on the impact of the U. S. military on Vietnam during the Vietnam War.

   ▶ Develop and videotape a docudrama that presents what you learned.

3. Learn about the Douc Langur monkey. How many were there before the Vietnam War? What happened to them during the war? What is happening to them now?

   ▶ Write a story about these monkeys that reflects what you have learned.

4. Find out more about Agent Orange. What is it? Why was it developed? Is it in use today? What effects is it having on the Vietnamese population and U.S. soldiers who were exposed to it? Has the U.S. government done anything to help people who were exposed to the chemical? What?

   ▶ Write a proposal to present to the Senate in which you suggest compensating those who were affected by the chemical or in which you suggest not compensating those affected. Support your suggestions.

5. Find out more about the elephant in Vietnam. In what ways do the people use the animal? How do they treat elephants? Then find out about the African elephant. What are some of the similarities? Differences?

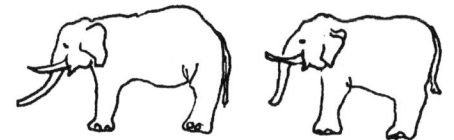

▶ Write a visualization in which the reader or listener imagines himself or herself as an elephant in Vietnam. Be sure to include a warm-up, the actual visualization, and a process by which you bring the person gently out of the visualization.

## *Food, Festivals, and Celebrations*

Rice is the dietary mainstay of Vietnam, which is one of the top five rice-producing countries in the world. In addition to rice, a typical Vietnamese meal consists of foods such as corn, sweet potatoes, yams, arrow-root, and soybeans. Duck, chicken, and pork are considered luxuries, but fresh and dried fish are common. *Nuoc mam,* a fermented fish sauce, is used as a dip and provides an important source of protein. Tea is almost a national drink.

Everyone in Vietnam celebrates Tet, Nguyen-De, the lunar new year. It is Christmas, Easter, Fourth of July, Mardi Gras, and everyone's birthday all rolled into one holiday. For a week in late January and early February people return to their parents' homes, bringing food and gifts. It is a time to review the past, enjoy the present, and plan the future. Debts are repaid, mistakes corrected, and wrongdoings forgiven.

Tet is a time for new clothes, fancy foods, and fireworks. It is an occasion for honoring the ancestors, whose spirits are believed to visit during the celebrations. Food is offered and incense burned.

On the night before the New Year, people stay up until midnight to do a good deed. It is thought that a protective spirit of the household will report in heaven on the deeds of each family member. The first visitor to the house the next day is very important, as this person can bring good luck in the new year.

Other important holidays include the Children's Festival and government holidays such as Unification Day.

---

### *PHO BO*
### *(Beef with Noodle Soup)*

*4 to 6 beef soup bones*

*2 lbs. beef roast*

*2 medium onions*

*1 3" piece of ginger root*

*1/3 cup star aniseed*

*1/2 tsp. MSG*

*2 Tbs. salt*

*1/2 tsp. sugar*

*3 green onions, chopped*

*cilantro, chopped*

*1 package Pho rice noodles, cooked and drained*

*Place the bones and meat in a large pot of water and bring to a heavy boil. Skim off the foam as it rises. When the soup remains clear, about 30 minutes, add the rest of the seasonings. Simmer another 30—45 minutes. Slice the roast very thin and prepare the noodles. When ready half-fill soup bowls with cooked Pho noodles and thin slices of meat. Ladle soup over meat and garnish with green onions and cilantro.*

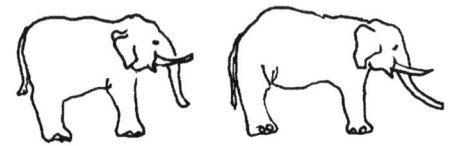

*Each person celebrates his or her birthday twice each year, once on the day of birth and again on Tet, the lunar New Year.*

## Activities

1. Investigate Tet, Nhuyen-De. What holiday that you celebrate is it most like? Most unlike?

   ▶ With one or more friends, create a mural that illustrates the customs and reflects the meaning of this celebration.

2. Focus your attention on the 36 hours that comprise the Vietnamese New Year celebration.

   ▶ With friends, develop and present a skit based on the night before and day of this New Year. Be sure the audience learns from watching your skit.

3. Research typical Vietnamese food. Find out what the staples of the diet are and find some recipes.

   ▶ Make the recipes and serve them to your class.

# Dances, Games, and Sports

Throughout Asia kite flying is a popular activity, and children and adults enjoy making their own kites. Some are quite beautiful and intricate. Some games, such as soccer, hopscotch, and card games, are as familiar in Vietnam as they are in the United States.

A favorite game during the New Year celebration is *Bao-cu-ca-cop* (squash-crab-fish-tiger). A cloth is divided into six squares, and pictures of these animals and two more are put in the squares. Coins are placed on the squares, and children take turns rolling a die that has pictures of the animals on its sides. If a child rolls an animal that has coins on it, the child keeps the money.

Another child's game is Bite the Carp's Tail. Six or more children form a line, each holding on to the waist of the person ahead in line. The child at the front is the "head" of the carp and the last is the "tail." The challenge is for the head to catch the tail. Throughout the wiggling chase, the line must not

break. When the head finally bites the tail, the head goes to the end of the line, and the game begins again.

## Activities

1. Become an expert on Vietnamese kites and kite flying.

   ▶ Make a kite in the Vietnamese style. Show your kite to the class and share what you have learned. If the wind is right, fly your kite for all to see.

2. Learn about the carp in Vietnam. What is a carp? Why might Vietnamese children play a game based on a carp?

   ▶ Draw a labeled diagram of a carp. Organize and play a game of Bite the Carp's Tail with some friends.

# Music, Art, and Architecture

*Vong-co,* the traditional music of Vietnam, is heard everywhere, and the *Non-ka* dance is performed to the Vong-co music. The Non-ka is the wide-brimmed hat worn for protection against the tropical sun. The Non-ka dancer does a slow, balancing dance, moving the hat in a free-flowing style to the music.

The strong Chinese influence on Vietnamese culture is evident in language, art, music, theater, and architecture. The French influence is also strongly felt. Poetry is very important to the Vietnamese people. Long epic poems are memorized, lovers speak to each other in poetic verse, and all people write poems about their life experiences.

Block prints are for sale all over the country, as is high-quality lacquerware. In the highlands, women weave blankets, skirts, blouses, and loincloths, and men weave baskets and mats. Embroidery is another Vietnamese art form.

*Vietnam's most famous epic poem is* Kim Van Kieu, *the story of a girl's struggle to maintain the honor of her family. The plot is long and involved, yet many Vietnamese have memorized the entire poem.*

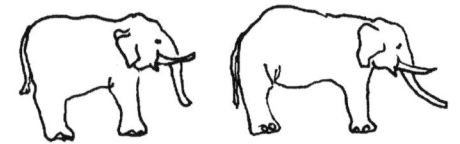

*Many Asians take two-hour naps at noon when the temperatures are too high to work.*

In recent years, people have returned to traditional music and arts. The gong is the most common musical instrument.

## Activities

1. Learn about and listen to Vietnamese music, especially gong music. Find metal objects that resonate, and learn to "play" them Vietnamese style.

   ▶ Make a presentation that includes information and gong music.

2. Investigate Vietnamese blockprints. What do they depict? What colors are used? How are they made?

   ▶ Use a styrofoam block or cut a potato to make a Vietnamese-style block print on paper or fabric. Display your block print in the classroom.

3. Research Chinese opera. What stories do the operas tell? What do the costumes look like? How is the stage space used? Why is Chinese opera important to the Vietnamese?

   ▶ Find a videocassette of a Chinese opera at your local library or rental store. Present it to your class. Be sure you can explain to your classmates what is happening in the opera.

4. Investigate the embroidery worked in Vietnam. Who does the embroidery? What colors are used most frequently? What subjects do the Vietnamese most often embroider? For what purpose do they use the finished pieces?

   ▶ Do your own embroidery project. Choose a subject or create your own, and work the embroidery using the same colors and materials a Vietnamese person might use.

5. Find out about lacquer. What is it? Where does it come from? How is it used?

   ▶ Create your own piece of lacquerware using the Vietnamese pieces as models.

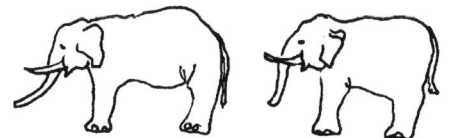

# Ngay's Day

In a small Vietnamese village, eight-year-old Ngay and his family arise as the sunlight begins to slip through the bamboo walls of their home. Ngay rolls up his sleeping pallet and joins his parents, grandmother, and sister for a breakfast of rice and fruit. After breakfast, Grandmother lights the incense on the altar, where pictures of the family's ancestors are displayed. Each family member leaves a small offering of food, tea, or flowers.

Ngay's father puts out the monkey bridge, a bamboo stick used to span the trench he has dug around the house to keep small animals and intruders away. The planting of the year's rice has been done and now the family must watch the water buffalo herd to keep them from eating the new sprouts.

Putting on his straw hat, Ngay mounts one of the buffalo and takes the herd to a place safely away from the new rice. While the herd grazes, Ngay fishes and watches the playful otters and the lazy crocodiles. At lunchtime, Ngay ties the herd to trees, gathers his day's catch, and returns home.

As the family eats soup together, Ngay's father talks about the village plans to plant *melaleuca*. These fast-growing trees, he says, can be used for firewood and will be a cash crop because of their medicinal value. They will disrupt the land less than does the traditional rice crop. Ngay's father explains that their family would be involved in the planting.

Then it is time for Ngay and his father to go to the village schoolhouse. Ngay's father has a college degree, so he teaches the children in the afternoons. Ngay has learned to read and is proud of his ability to add and subtract.

After school Ngay runs to the village well and helps his grandmother bring water home. Before dinner he has time to play soccer with the other children. Then he joins his family for rice and vegetables with fish sauce, tea, and coconut cookies.

*It is common for all family members to work seven days a week on the farms.*

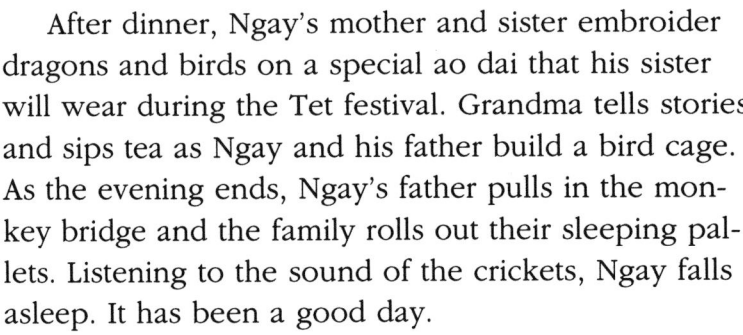

After dinner, Ngay's mother and sister embroider dragons and birds on a special ao dai that his sister will wear during the Tet festival. Grandma tells stories and sips tea as Ngay and his father build a bird cage. As the evening ends, Ngay's father pulls in the monkey bridge and the family rolls out their sleeping pallets. Listening to the sound of the crickets, Ngay falls asleep. It has been a good day.

*Most Vietnamese believe in reincarnation, the idea that one is reborn as another physical being after death.*

### Activity

Where in Vietnam might Ngay live? How can you tell where he might live? Do you think this story takes place before, during, or after the Vietnam War? Why?

▶ Write "A Day in the Life of" a Vietnamese child who lives in an area that was sprayed with Agent Orange during the war. Include the child's thoughts, feelings, and observations.

# The Farmer, the Buffalo, and the Tiger

One day a farmer was plowing a field with his water buffalo. They had been working hard since dawn, but the farmer did not want to quit until he had finished the whole field. As the buffalo became tired and hungry, he began to slow down. The farmer picked up a stick and hit the buffalo to make him move faster. Every time the buffalo slowed down the farmer whacked him with the stick. Neither the farmer nor the buffalo noticed a large yellow tiger sitting in the shade of the trees watching them work.

Finally the field was finished and the farmer let the water buffalo loose to graze. When the farmer had disappeared into his hut, the tiger approached the buffalo.

"Poor buffalo," said the tiger. "Why do you let the man beat you? You are big and strong and could easily get away."

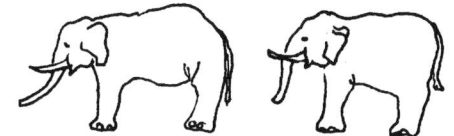

"Ah, great tiger," groaned the buffalo, "the man looks small and weak, but he is king of all the creatures because of his intelligence."

"Intelligence?" the tiger frowned. "What does it look like? I want to see this intelligence."

When the farmer returned, he saw the tiger and wanted to kill him. The water buffalo told his master the tiger meant no harm and only wanted to ask him a question. The man listened.

"I have heard about how your intelligence makes you greater than anything under the sun," said the tiger. "What does it look like? Would you show me your intelligence?"

"I would be glad to show you, but it is at home in a bag," replied the man as he began leading the buffalo back to his hut.

"Wait," cried the tiger. "Don't go away."

"You are clever, tiger," the farmer laughed. "If I leave my buffalo here with you, you will kill him and eat him. I will show you my intelligence only if you will let me tie you up until I get back."

"If this intelligence is so great," said the tiger, "I must see it." And he agreed to be tied up.

The farmer took the rope from the plow and tied the tiger tightly to a tree. Then he took the plow and hit the tiger over the head and killed him.

"See, I told you," laughed the water buffalo. In fact, he laughed so hard that he hit his teeth on a rock and knocked them right out. That is why water buffalo have no teeth to this day.

## Activity

This folktale contains elements typically Vietnamese—water buffalo, tiger, and farmer—and it explains a natural phenomenon—the water buffalo has no teeth.

▶ Create a tale set in your environment with elements from your culture that explains a natural phenomenon. Share your tale with the class.

> *"Even a long ladder can never reach the sky. Even a self-sufficient person needs the help of others."*
>
> —*Southeast Asian Proverb*

# Appendix

## *Biomes*

Biomes are living communities of plants and animals. More than one system of categorizing biomes exists. The UNESCO Man and Biosphere Program uses Miklos Udvardy's classification system, which divides the globe into fourteen biomes. Udvardy's divisions are used throughout *Many People, Many Ways*.

tropical humid forest
subtropical and temperate rain forest
coniferous forest
tropical dry forest
temperate broadleaf forest
evergreen forest and scrubland
warm desert and semidesert
cold winter desert and semidesert
arctic desert and tundra
tropical grassland and savannah
temperate grassland
mountain and highland system
island system
lake system

**Tropical rain forest biomes** occur in equatorial regions and are the most complex systems in the world. The rain forest has many layers of canopy that act as different habitat zones and create great diversity in species. The soil and air are moist, the temperatures are stable and warm. Minerals cycle quickly through the soil and exist primarily in the biomass.

**Coniferous forests** exist primarily in the Northern Hemisphere, north of temperate woodlands. Winters in these areas can be severe, and the areas have short growing seasons. Evergreen coniferous trees predominate and there is little or no shrub layer. In the far north, the *taiga*, or boreal, forests contain birch, willow, alder, and aspen. Food webs are complex. These forests often have wetlands.

**Tropical dry forests** have an annual rainfall of less than seventy–eight inches per year. There is no precipitation for part of the year, and many trees drop their leaves seasonally. These areas include the monsoon forests of tropical Asia. There are fewer species in tropical dry forests than in the rain forests.

**Temperate broadleaf forests** are warm and wet, and they are most often near the ocean. In such areas, deciduous plants thrive. Temperate forests have a shrub layer and ground cover, and the mild temperatures allow organic matter to build up, making the soil very rich. Many animal species live in these areas, and complex food webs exist.

**Evergreen forests and scrubland** have hot, dry summers and cool, wet winters. The plants in these areas are drought resistant. Because there are many fires in such areas, many of the plants are also fire resistant, and some depend on fire to release their seeds. The trees are either deciduous or evergreen.

**Deserts and semideserts** occur where less than 10 inches of rain falls each year. Some desert areas have regular seasonal rainfall, some have sporadic rainfall, and still others may not receive moisture for years. Most of these desert areas are hot. The lack of water restricts plant and animal life to only a few species highly adapted to the necessary survival strategies of drought conditions. These are the only biomes that are spreading, encroaching on the savannas and steppes that surround them.

**Cold winter desert and semidesert** areas have cold winter temperatures and warmer summer seasons. Rainfall is sporadic and snow is not as severe as in arctic desert regions. In some cases drought conditions exist. Plant and animal species are more varied than in the arctic or hot desert regions.

**Arctic desert and tundra** areas are cold, have little rain, and experience long periods with no precipitation. The plants which survive in these regions are typically small, long-lived plants that can survive beneath snow. Lichens and mosses are often prevalent as well as low-growing shrubs. Small rodents, predators, and herbivorous mammals can be found. The long summer days with warmer temperatures bring on high biological activity for a short time period. Insects and migrating birds may be plentiful in the summer season.

**Tropical grasslands and savannas** form the edges of the great tropical forests. Such areas are too dry to support the closed canopy that make up tropical forests. These areas generally have one or two dry seasons, and the annual rainfall can be from ten to fifty inches. The highly productive grasses of these areas are often five or six feet tall, and patches of scrub and trees may dot the landscape. Many species of large herbivorous and carnivorous animals have evolved in these areas. Migrating birds are plentiful during the wet season.

**Temperate grasslands** occur in the continental interiors of temperate areas. Cold winters and summer droughts restrict trees to the wetter areas near rivers. Annual rainfall is generally ten to thirty inches. Grasses predominate, making the habitat ideal for herbivores. These areas are called prairies, steppes, and pampas. The majority of temperate grasslands have been disrupted by agriculture and the resulting severe soil erosion.

**Mountain biomes** generally have temperatures that fall as the altitude rises, and the temperatures may have great fluctuations. Warm, moist air currents shed water as they cool at the higher elevations. Mountain regions often have distinct species, in much the same way as island biomes, because of the natural isolation. The elevation determines the species that will occur. At different elevations, one mountain biome may have vegetation zones that correspond to tundra, grasslands, scrublands, coniferous or broadleaf forests, and subtropical forests. Insect populations are often varied and various animals species exist at different elevations.

**Islands** generally have only a few plant and animal species. These may be relics of once widespread forms of ancient species, or they may be relatively new species that evolved in the isolation of the system. Islands that were at one point part of a larger land mass may have species with characteristics similar to the species on the larger land mass. The islands that were formed in the middle of the ocean as the result of volcanic activity may have species evolved from chance arrivals of various species. All island species are vulnerable to outside influence because they often have small populations and few safeguards against predators.

**Lakes and wetlands** vary greatly depending on the availability of oxygen, the amount of water, the size, the depth, and the temperature. The wetland ecosystems include rivers, lakes, marshes, fens, swamps, bogs, salt marshes, mangrove swamps, and estuaries. The wetland areas are generally in a stage of the natural progression from an aquatic to a terrestrial habitat. Lakes and wetland areas are generally rich in wildlife and plant species.

# References

Burton, Robert, ed. 1991. *Nature's Last Stronghold.* New York: Oxford University Press.

Tudge, Colin. 1988. *The Environment of Life.* New York: Oxford University Press.

# Bibliography

## General

Bernbaum, Edwin. 1990. *Sacred Mountains of the World*. San Francisco: Sierra Club.

Burton, Robert, ed. 1991. *Nature's Last Strongholds*. New York: Oxford University Press.

Davis, Kenneth C. 1992. *Don't Know Much about Geography*. New York: William Morrow.

Demko, George K. 1992. *Why in the World: Adventures in Geography*. New York: Doubleday.

Enloe, Walter, and Ken Simon. 1993. *Linking through Diversity: Practical Classroom Methods for Experiencing and Understanding Culture*. Tucson, Ariz.: Zephyr Press.

Fowler, Virginia. 1981. *Folk Art around the World*. Englewood Cliffs, N.J.: Prentice Hall.

Grosvenor, Melville, ed. 1973. *Primitive Worlds: People Lost in Time*. Washington, D.C.: National Geographic Society.

———. 1971. *Vanishing Peoples of the Earth*. Washington, D.C.: National Geographic Society.

*The How and Why Library: Holidays and Birthdays*. 1982. Chicago: World Book-Childcraft.

*The How and Why Library: Stories and Fables*. 1982. Chicago: World Book-Childcraft.

King, Laurie. 1994. *Hear My Voice Bibliography: An Annotated Guide to Multicultural Literature from the United States*. New York: Addison-Wesley.

King, Laurie, ed. 1994. *Hear My Voice: A Multicultural Anthology of Literature from the United States*. New York: Addison-Wesley.

———. 1994. *Hear My Voice: A Multicultural Anthology of Literature from the United States*. Teacher's Guide. New York: Addison-Wesley.

Kovacs, Edna. 1994. *Writing across Cultures: A Handbook on Writing Poetry and Lyrical Prose*. Hillsboro, Ore.: Blue Heron.

Miller, G. Tyler, ed. 1975. *Living in the Environment: Concepts, Problems, and Alternatives.* Belmont, Calif.: Wadsworth.

Severin, Timothy. 1973. *Vanishing Primitive Man.* New York: American Heritage.

Singer, Andre, and Leslie Woodhead. 1988. *Disappearing World.* London: Boxtree.

Tudge, Colin. 1988. *The Environment of Life.* New York: Oxford University.

Wright, John W. 1993. *The Universal Almanac* 1994. New York: Universal Press.

# *Brazil*

## Video Recordings

Boorman, John. 1985. *The Emerald Forest.* Embassy Home Entertainment. 113 mins.

> Rated R for nudity, suggested sex, and violence, but has sections depicting Amazon Indian life that are valuable for the classroom.

The Kayapo. 1987. *The Disappearing World Series.* Terrence Turner. 58 mins.

Kroyer, Bill. 1992. *Fern Gully.* Twentieth Century Fox. 75 mins. Animated.

The Mehinacu. 1987. *The Disappearing World Series.* Terrence Turner. 58 mins.

The Umbanda. 1987. *The Disappearing World Series.* Terrence Turner.

## Recordings

Brazilliance! *The Music of Rhythm.* 1990. Rykodisc.

> A compilation of various artists' songs that together provide a detailed history and examples of the samba. With twenty-two songs from slow to festive, this recording is an excellent educational tool.

*Canta Brasil: The Great Brazilian Songbook.* 1990. Polygram Records.

> *Canta Brasil* (Sing Brazil) is an extensive collection of Brazilian music intended to display the popular traditions rising from the samba. A wonderful collection with great liner notes.

Crutcher, Rusty. 1987. *Amazon Song.* Emerald Green Sound Production.

> Recordings of sounds from the Amazon jungle in Peru weave with quiet musical sounds.

*Egypt: Al-hadra-Insad.* Sufi Music, Lark in the Morning. vol. 4.

> The Al-hadra-Insad Sufi order was formed in Egypt between 1867 and 1939. The recording is a recitation of poems.

Machado, Edi. *Edi.* BNS 102.

> A Brazilian-born singer who combines the Afro-Brazilian beat of the samba, Latin and American funk, reggae, and jazz scat. High energy!

Parahyba, Joao. *The New Lambada.* 1990. Happy Hour Music.

> The northeastern Brazilian dance, the lambada, has been popular since the 1930's in Brazil and around the world. Parahyba is a Brazilian percussionist well versed in Afro-Brazilian rhythms.

Rabello, Raphael, and Dino. *7 Cordas.* 1991. Caju Music.

> Popular Brazilian guitar music performed by Dino and Raphael.

Robison, Paula. 1993. *Brasileirinho.* Omega Record Group.

> A unique fusion of classical and Brazilian music performed by classical flautist Paula Robison and an ensemble of renowned Brazilian musicians. Includes popular Brazilian music from choros to bossa nova plus traditional classical pieces played in a Brazilian style.

## Books

### Juvenile

Bailey, Donna. 1991. *Brazil.* Madison, N.J.: Raintree Steck-Vaughn.

Bender, Evelyn. 1990. *Brazil.* New York: Chelsea House.

Carwading, Mark. 1988. *The Illustrated World of Wild Animals.* New York: Simon and Schuster.

Cross, Wilbur, and Susanna Cross. 1984. *Brazil.* Chicago: Children's Press.

Gerson, Mary-Joan, and Carla Golembe. 1994. *How Night Came from the Sea: A Story from Brazil.* Boston: Joy Street.

Haverstock, Nathan. 1987. *Brazil in Pictures.* Minneapolis, Minn.: Lerner Publications.

Henley, Paul. 1980. *Amazon Indians.* Englewood Cliffs, N.J.: Silver Burdett Press.

Morrison, Marion. 1989. *Indians of the Amazon.* Vero Beach, Fla.: Rourke.

Perry, Ritchie. 1992. *Brazil.* rev. ed. Englewood Cliffs, N.J.: Silver Burdett.

Waterlow, Julia, and Peter Bull. 1992. *Brazil.* Wautoma, Wis.: Bookwright Press, E. B. Houchin.

Winter, Jane Kohen. 1993. *Brazil.* North Bellmore, N.J.: Marshall Cavenish.

### Teacher

Belting, Natalia M. 1992. *Moon Was Tired of Walking on Air.* New York: Houghton Mifflin.
    A beautiful collection of South American Indian folktales based on creation stories and myths of the Ancestors.

Bensusan, Susan, ed. 1973. *Latin American Cooking: A Treasury of Recipes from the South American Countries, Mexico, and the Caribbean.* New York: Galahad Books.

Caulfield, Catherine. 1984. *In the Rainforest.* Chicago: University of Chicago Press.

The Cousteau Society. 1992. *An Adventure in the Amazon.* New York: Simon and Schuster.

Haviland, William A. 1993. *Cultural Anthropology.* New York: Harcourt Brace Jovanovich.

Hecht, Susanna B., and Alexander Cockburn. 1989. *The Fate of the Forest: Developers, Destroyers, and Defenders of the Amazon.* London: Verso.

Landon, Mark, and Brian Kelly. 1983. *Amazon.* San Diego: Harcourt Brace Jovanivich.

Margolis, Mac. 1992. *The Last New World: The Conquest of the Amazon Frontier.* New York: W. W. Norton.

Morrison, Marion. 1988. *Brazil.* New Jersey: Silver Burdett.
    Factual information about Brazil in a young people's book.

———. 1989. *Indians of the Amazon*. Vero Beach, Fla.: Rourke Publications.
    A young person's book of facts about Amazon Indians.
Osborne, Harold. 1986. *South American Mythology*. London: Peter Bedrick.
Ricciardi, Mirella. 1991. *Vanishing Amazon*. New York: Harry N. Abrams.
Shuttlesworth, Dorothy. 1974. *The Wildlife of South America*. New York:
    Hastings House.
Singer, Andre, and Leslie Woodhead. 1988. *Disappearing World*. London: Boxtree.
Smith, Anthony. 1990. *Explorers of the Amazon*. London: Viking.
Van Over, Raymond. 1980. *Sun Songs: Creation Myths from around the World*.
    New York: The New American Library.
World Book. 1991. *Christmas in Brazil*. Albuquerque, N.M.: World Book.

# *Egypt*

## Videocassettes

*Ancient Egypt*. 1988. A/V International. 30 mins.
    Egyptian civilization to 332 B.C.E.
*Egypt*. 1986. Republic Pictures Home Video. 50 mins.
    Travel guides and descriptions of the pyramids and Tutankhamen tomb.
*Egypt: Cairo and the Pyramids*. 1991. Chip Taylor. 16 mins.
    Exploring the World series.
*Egypt: 5000 Years Fascination*. 1991. VPI/AC Video. 60 mins.
    From the Artful Journeys series. Travel and civilization.
*Egypt: Land of Ancient Wonders*. 1993. International Video Network. 58 mins.
    Travel and description.
*Egypt 2: Temples of Luxor and Aswan*. 1991. Chip Taylor Communications. 22 mins.
    Exploring the World series.

## Audiocassettes

du Nil, Musiciens. 1989. *Luxor to Ishna*. Realworld.
    Folk songs and dance music of Egypt. Traditional instrumental music from Upper Egypt
    including some of Egypt's finest ethnic musicians: masters of the Egyptian oboes, rababah
    (two-stringed violin), and double-reed clarinet.
Jorgensen, Aurora. Records, 1975. *The Egypt Game*. Newberry Award Records.
Lamranie, Cherif, and Dissidenten Shanachie. 1988. *Sahara Electric*.
    Egyptian jazz.
*Music of the Nile Valley*. 1990. Lyrichord.
    Egyptian folk music.
*The Music of Upper and Lower Egypt*. 1978.
    Various artists recorded by Mickey Hart during the Grateful Dead's 1978 Egyptian tour are
    featured on this recording.

Racy, Ali Jihad. 1980. *Ancient Egypt.* Lyrichord.
Music composed for the Tutankhamen Exhibit at the Seattle Art Museum. Impressionistic in style, the recording uses traditional Egyptian ney flute, lutelike oud and buzuq, the Egyptian oboe and clarinet, finger cymbals, frame drum, the tar and some vocals. The music is composed using scales believed to exist in ancient Egyptian music.

# Books

## Juvenile

Abels, Harriette. 1987. *The Pyramids.* Mankato, Minn.: Crestwood House.

Aliki. 1989. *Mummies Made in Egypt.* New York: Franklin Watts.

Bendick, Jeanne. 1989. *Egyptian Tombs.* New York: Franklin Watts.

Caseli, Giovanni. 1986. *An Egyptian Craftsman.* New York: Peter Bedrick.

Diamond, Arthur. 1992. *Egypt: Gift of the Nile.* New York: Dillon Press.

Donnelly, Judy. 1988. *Tut's Mummy Lost . . . and Found.* New York: Random House.

Feinstein, Stephen C. 1988. *Egypt in Pictures.* Minneapolis, Minn.: Lerner Publications.

Flint, David. 1994. *Egypt.* Madison, N.J.: Raintree Steck-Vaughn.

Froman, Nan, and C. Reeves. 1992. *Into the Mummy's Tomb.* New York: Scholastic, Madison Press.

Hart, George. 1990. *Ancient Egypt.* New York: Alfred A. Knopf.

*The How and Why Library: Holidays and Birthdays.* 1982. Chicago: World Book-Childcraft.

*The How and Why Library: Stories and Fables.* 1982. Chicago: World Book-Childcraft.

Jacobsen, Karen. 1990. *Egypt.* Chicago: Childrens Press.

Knight, Joan, and Dick Dudley. 1986. *Journey to Egypt.* New York: Kestrel.
This is a UNICEF pop-up book.

Lye, Keith, and Henry Arthur Pluckrose. 1983. *Take a Trip to Egypt.* New York: Franklin Watts.

Millard, Anne. 1987. *The Egyptians. People of the Past* series. Englewood Cliffs, N.J.: Silver Burdett.

Mirepoix, Camille. 1988. *Egypt in Pictures.* Minneapolis: Lerner.

Morrison, Ian A. 1991. *Egypt.* Madison, N.J.: Raintree Steck-Vaughn.

Parker, Lewis K. 1994. *Dropping in on Egypt.* Vero Beach, Fla.: Rourke.

Pateman, Robert. 1993. *Egypt.* North Bellmore, N.Y.: Marshall Cavenish.

Payne, Elizabeth. 1964. *The Pharoahs of Ancient Egypt.* New York: Random House.
Details the life and history of pharaohs from ancient times through Rameses II.

Pitkanen, Matti A., and Harkonen Reijo. 1991. *The Children of Egypt.* Minneapolis, Minn.: Carolrhoda Books.

Robinson, Charles Alexander, and Lorna Greenberg. 1984. *Ancient Egypt.* New York: Franklin Watts.

Swinbourne, Irene, and Laurence Swinbourne. 1977. *Behind the Sealed Door*. New York: Sniffen Court.

Van Haag, Michael. 1992. *Egypt*. rev. ed. Englewood Cliffs, N.J.: Silver Burdett.

## Teacher

Abercrombie, Thomas J. 1977. *Egypt*. Washington, D.C.: National Geographic Society.

Grosvenor, Melville, ed. 1985. *Mysteries of the Ancient World*. Washington, D.C.: National Geographic Society.

Stead, Miriam. 1985. *Ancient Egypt*. New York: Gloucester Press.

Stuart, Gena S. 1979. *Secrets from the Past: Books for World Explorers*. Washington, D.C.: National Geographic Society.

# *Haiti*

## Videocassettes

Cousteau, Jacques-Yves, and the Cousteau Society. 1991. *Haiti, Waters of Sorrow*. Turner Home Entertainment. 48 mins.

Davis, Wade. 1988. *The Serpent and the Rainbow*. MCA Home Video. 98 mins.

*Josephine's Imagination: A Tale of Haiti*. 1991. Fireworks Films. 15 mins.
    An animated story.

## Audiocassettes

Casseus, Frantz, and Marc Ribot. 1987. *Haitian Suite*. Music of the World.
    Casseus is an important contemporary Haitian guitarist and composer. His music draws inspiration from the Haitian African-derived musical tradition. This recording contains a collection of his solo classical guitar music.

Deren, Maya. 1970. *Folk Music from Haiti*. Lyrichord.
    Merengues and ballads.

## Books

### Juvenile

Anthony, Suzanne. 1989. *Haiti*. New York: Chelsea House.

des Pres, Turenne. 1994. *Children of Yayoute: Folk Tales of Haiti*. Englewood Cliffs, N.J.: Universe Books.
    Fiction.

Eitzen, Ruth, and Allen Eitzen. 1972. *T. Jacques: A Story of Haiti*. New York: Crowell.
    Fiction.

Griffiths, John. 1989. *Take a Trip to Haiti.* New York: Franklin Watts.

Hanmer, Trudy J. 1988. *Haiti.* New York: Franklin Watts.

Mason, Antony. 1989. *The Caribbean.* Englewood Cliffs, N.J.: Silver Burdett.

Moriseau-Leroy, Felix. 1991. *Natif-Natal.* Miami: Pantaleon Guilbaud.

Nardo, Don. 1991. *Voodoo: Opposing Viewpoints.* San Diego, Calif.: Greenhaven Press.

Rouse, Irving. 1992. *The Tainos: Rise and Decline of the People Who Greeted Columbus.* New Haven, Conn.: Yale University Press.

Temple, Frances. 1992. *A Taste of Salt: A Story of Modern Haiti.* New York: Orchard Books.
   Fiction.

Weddle, Ken. 1987. *Haiti in Pictures.* Minneapolis, Minn.: Lerner.

## Teacher

Christensen, Barbara. 1977. *The Magic and Meaning of Voodoo.* Milwaukee, Wis.: Raintree.

Davis, Wade. 1985. *The Serpent and the Rainbow.* New York: Simon and Schuster.

Enloe, Walter, and Ken Simon. 1993. *Linking through Diversity: Practical Classroom Methods for Experiencing and Understanding Culture.* Tucson, Ariz.: Zephyr Press.

Fowler, Virginia. 1981. *Folk Art around the World.* Englewood Cliffs, N.J.: Prentice Hall.

Gold, Herbert. 1991. *Best Nightmare Earth: A Life In Haiti.* New York: Prentice Hall.

Haviland, William A. 1993. *Cultural Anthropology.* New York: Harcourt Brace Jovanovich.

*Lands and Peoples.* 1991. vol. 5. Danbury, Conn.: Grolier.

Lessac, Frane. 1989. *Caribbean Canvas.* New York: JB Lippincott.

Lieberman, Laurence. 1990. *The Creole Mephistopheles.* San Francisco: Collier Books.
   Poetry.

Thomson, Ian. 1992. *"Bonjour Blanc": A Journey through Haiti.* Chicago: Hutchinson.

# *Hawai'i*

## Video

*Hawaii: Paradise Found.* 1992. International Video Network. 54 mins.
   Description and travel.

Johnson, J. Mitchel. 1991. *Discovering Hawaii.* J. Mitchel Johnson Productions and International Video Network. 70 mins.
   Travel guide.

Van Arsdale, Bill. 1990. *The Best of Hawaii.* Van Video. 2 videocassettes, 90 mins. each.
> Travel guide.

## Audio

Burdick, Betty, and David Mataya. 1985. *Kaahumanu.* Dog Days Records.
> The story of Queen Kaahumanu.

*Hawaiian Steel Guitar Classics.* 1984. Arhoolie Productions.

Kamehameha Schools. 1967. *The Kamehameha Schools Choir Sings Folk Songs.* Scholastic Records.

Kamokila. *Legends of Hawai'i.* 2 vols. Kamolkila Record Company.
> Spell-binding legends told by a master storyteller.

Kiona, Kaulaheaonamiku. 1962. *Hawai'ian Chant, Hula, and Music.* Folkways.
> A variety of ancient Hawaiian instruments and chants.

McGuire-Turcotte, Casey. 1991. *How Honu the Turtle Got His Shell.* Clippers.

The New Hawaiian Band. 1980. *Hawaii's Greatest Hits.* MCA.
> Great classics about Hawaii played by some of the most famous Hawaiian performers such as Ohta San, Sonny Kamehele, and Benny Saks. "Blue Hawaii," "Lovely Hula Hands," "The Hawaiian Wedding Song," and "Aloha Oe" are among the favorites.

Stordahl, Alex, and the Hawaiian Village Serenaders. 1973. *Aloha, Apaka!* MCA.
> Hawaiian folk songs and popular music.

## Books

### Juvenile

Bates, Gale. 1992. *Tales of Tutu Nene and Nele.* Aiea, Hawaii: Island Heritage.
> Fiction.

Buffet, Guy. 1972. *Adventures of Kama Pua'a.* Aiea, Hawaii: Island Heritage.

Casey, Barbara. 1992. *Leilani Zan.* Nashville, Tenn.: Winston-Derek.

Daws, Gavan, and Oswald A. Bushnell. 1980. *The Illustrated Atlas of Hawaii.* Aiea, Hawaii: Island Heritage.

Feeney, Stephanie, and Hammid Hella. 1980. *A is for Aloha.* Honolulu, Hawaii: University Press of Hawaii.

Fradin, Dennis B., and Len W. Meents. 1994. *Hawaii: From Sea to Shining Sea.* Chicago: Childrens Press.

Howell, Dean. 1990. *The Story of Chinaman's Hat.* Aiea, Hawaii: Island Heritage.
> Folklore.

Jenkins, Bruce, and the Society for the Study of Native Arts and Crafts. 1990. *North Shore Chronicles: Big-Wave Surfing in Hawaii.* Berkeley, Calif.: North Atlantic Books.

Johnston, Joyce. 1994. *Hawaii.* Minneapolis, Minn.: Lerner.

Kane, Herb Kawainui. 1987. *Pele: Goddess of Hawaii's Volcanoes.* Captain Cook, Hawaii: Kawainui.

Land-Nellist, Cassandra. 1987. *A Child's First Book about Hawaii*. Kailua, Hawaii: Press Pacifica.

McNair, Sylvia. 1993. *America the Beautiful: Hawai'i*. 3rd ed. Chicago: Childrens Press.

Russell, William. 1994. Hawaii. Vero Beach, Fla.: Rourke.

Stanley, Fay, and Diane Stanley. 1994. *The Last Princess:* The Story of Princess Ka'iulani of Hawai'i . Palmer, Ark.: Aladdin Books.
Biography.

Thompson, Kathleen. 1991. *Hawaii: Portrait of America*. Madison, N.J.: Raintree Steck-Vaughn.

Von Tempski, Armine, and Paul Brown. 1993. *Pam's Paradise Ranch: A Story of Hawaii*. Woodbridge, Conn.: Ox Bow.
Fiction.

## Teacher

The University of Hawai'i Press publishes many excellent books on Hawai'i, Asian studies, and other areas of interest. You may want to write for their current catalogs: University of Hawai'i Press, 2840 Kolowalu St, Honolulu, Hawai'i 96822.

Daws, Gavan. 1968. *Shoal of Time: A History of the Hawai'ian Islands*. Honolulu, Hawai'i: University of Hawai'i Press.

Frierson, Pamela. 1991. *The Burning Island: A Journey through Myth and History in the Volcano Country, Hawaii*. San Francisco: Sierra Club.

Hansen-Young, Diana. 1990. *Aloha Mele (A Song of Aloha): A Collector's Book of Hawaiian Art and Poetry in English and Hawaiian*. Hawai'i: Kahaluu Press.

Kamakau, Samuel Manaiakalani, and Dorothy B. Barrere. 1991. *Tales and Traditions of the People of Old*. Honolulu, Hawaii: Bishop Museum Press.

Mrantz, Maxine. 1975. *Women of Old Hawaii*. Honolulu, Hawaii: Aloha Graphics.
Biography.

Thompson, Vivian Laubach. 1988. *Hawaiian Myths of Earth, Sea, and Sky*. Honolulu, Hawaii: University of Hawaii Press.

Trask, Huanani-Kay. 1994. *Light in the Crevice Never Seen*. Corvalis, Ore.: Calyx Books.
Poetry.

## Additional Resources

Hawai'iana Resource Units, Mitchell, Kamehameha Schools, Bishop Museum Education Dept., PO Box 6037, Honolulu, Hawaii 96818. Write for a list of available items including books, recordings and a variety of materials. Hula Supply Center, 2346 S. King Street, Honolulu, Hawaii 96822.
For hula instruments.

# *Lakota*

## Video

Burton, Levar. 1983. *The Gift of the Sacred Dog.* Great Plains National Instructional Television Library. 30 mins.

Reading Rainbow Series, no. 10. Includes reading of *The Gift of the Sacred Dog* by Paul Goble.

Video recording for the hearing impaired.

Ehanamani (Dr. A. C. Ross). *Mitakuye Oyasin (We Are All Related)*

Lecture on the American Indian point of view about the original North American inhabitants. From the book *Mitakuye Oyasin* by A.C. Ross.

Locke, Kevin. 1990. *The Seven Directions.* South Dakota Public Television. 120 mins.

Lakota music, dance, and folklore.

Smith, Henry. 1987. *Live and Remember.* The Project. 29 mins.

Discussions with Lakota elders, traditional dancers, and medicine men. Focuses on sacred traditions as portrayed through song and dance, oral traditions, life today, and traditional medicine.

Solaris. 1992. *Fulfilling the Vision.* 30 mins.

Contemporary issues of Lakota identity, ceremony, and tradition.

Stekler, Paul. 1993. *Last Stand at Little Big Horn.* Public Broadcasting Service. 60 mins.

A review of the Battle of Little Big Horn focusing on the views of the Lakota, Cheyenne, and Crow.

*The Yankton Sioux (Ihanktonwon Dakota).* 1993. Schlessinger Video Productions. 30 mins.

## Audio Recordings

Akipa, Brian. 1993. *The Flute Player.* Meyers Sound Studios.

Both traditional and contemporary Dakota flute songs. Includes nature sounds.

*American Indian Ceremonial and War Dances*

A collection of dances from a variety of tribes including the "Chief's Honoring Song" and a contemporary song entitled "Korea Memorial Song."

Bird, Gordon. *Music of the Plains.* Featherstone.

Traditional and modern flute songs.

Bullhead, Earl. 1993. *Walking the Red Road.* The Soar Coroporation.

Lakota songs.

Cikala, Wanbil Glaska (Gilly Running). *I'm Sending a Voice* vols. 1–3.

Three tapes and booklets of Lakota ceremonial song. Includes Lakota words, English translations, and spoken dictionary for pronunciations.

Darnell, Dik. *Following the Circle.*

Rooted in the music of the Sioux, this recording uses wooden flutes, voice, drums and rattles blended with environemtnal sounds.

The Elk Nation Singers. 1992. *Spirit Drum.* Etherean Native Spirit.

Twelve Lakota powwow songs by singers from the Pine Ridge Reservation.

Horne, Paula. *Heart Songs of Black Hills Woman.*
> A collection of prose and songs by this Dakota Sioux woman with the intention of "a vision created for all people who are of the Sacred Hoop of life. . .an inspirational journey that will touch the ancient one within you." DIR1

Inajin, Tokeya. *Dream Catcher.*
> Traditional Native American flute songs performed by a Lakota from the Standing Rock Reservation in South Dakota. A portion of the proceeds from *Dream Catcher* supports traditional arts projects serving Lakota youth on South Dakota reservations.

Locke, Kevin. 1990. *Lakota Love Songs and Stories.* Meyers Sound Studios.
> Stories about the flute, flute melodies, and vocal songs.

Pellowski. 1965. *American Indian Tales for Children,* vols. 1 and 11. CMS.

Rainer, John. *Songs of the Indian Flute*, vol. 1.
> Solo Native American flute by Rainer on his own handmade instruments, from the Crow, Sioux, and his own Pueblo tribe.

Thompson, Dovie. *Wopila: A Giveaway.*
> A storyteller and cultural educator who has been sharing the stories of her Lakota and Kiowa Apache background for years at schools, libraries and powwows. Lakota stories are intended to teach proper behavior. For ages 7 to adult. YM44

# Books

## Juvenile

Arden, Harvey, and Steve Wall. 1990. *Wisdomkeepers: Meetings with Native American Spiritual Elders.* Hillsboro, Ore.: Beyond Words.
> This book is an excellent guide to some elements of American Indian philosophy. The authors spoke to elders in many tribes, including two from the Lakota.

Bleeker, Sonia. 1962. *The Sioux Indians: Hunters and Warriors of the Plains.* Toronto: George J. McLeod.

Bonvillain, Nancy. 1994. *The Teton Sioux.* New York: Chelsea House.

Dolan, Terrance. 1995. *The Teton Sioux Indians.* New York: Chelsea Juniors.

Eisenberg, Lisa, and David Rickman. 1991. *The Story of Sitting Bull: A Great Sioux Chief.* New York: Dell.
> Biography.

Erdoes, Richard, and Alfonso Ortiz. 1984. *American Indian Myths and Legends.* New York: Pantheon.

Goble, Paul. 1987. *Gift of the Sacred Dog.* Palmer, Ark.: Aladdin.
> Folklore.

Guttmacher, Peter. 1994. *Crazy Horse, Sioux War Chief.* New York: Chelsea House.

Hicks, Peter. 1994. *The Sioux.* New York: Thomson Learning.

Hoover, Herbert T. 1988. *The Yankton Sioux.* New York: Chelsea House.
> Describes the past and present of the Yankton Sioux.

Kopper, Philip. 1986. *North American Indians.* Washington, D.C.: Smithsonian.

Lakota: *Seeking the Great Spirit.* 1994. San Francisco: Chronicle.

Landau, Elaine. 1991. *The Sioux.* New York: Franklin Watts.

McGovern, Ann. 1992. *If You Lived with the Sioux Indians*. New York: Scholastic.

Martini, Terry. 1982. Indians. Chicago: Childrens Press.
> Photos and text describing the five American Indian groups.

Nesbit, Jeffrey Asher. 1992. *The Sioux Society*. Wheaton, Ill.: Harold Shaw.
> Fiction.

Nicolson, Robert. 1993. *The Sioux*. New York: Scholastic.

Osinski, Alice. 1984. *The Sioux*. rep. Chicago: Childrens Press.

Sams, Jamie, and David Carson. 1988. *Medicine Cards*. Santa Fe, N.M.: Bear.

Sanford, William. 1994. Crazy Horse: *Sioux Warrior*. Hillside, N.J.: Enslow.

Sneve, Virginia Driving Hawk. 1993. *The Sioux*. New York: Holiday House.

Spencer, Robert F. 1977. *The Native Americans*. New York: Harper and Row Publishers.

Steptal, John. 1984. *The Story of Jumping Mouse*. New York: Lothrop, Lee and Shepard.
> Kindergarten and Primary. A Great Plains legend.

Tomkins, William. 1969. *Indian Sign Language*. New York: Dover.

Wolfson, Evelyn. 1992. *The Teton Sioux: People of the Plains*. Brookfield, Conn.: Millbrook.

## Teacher

Brigham Young University. *Bibliography of Nonprint Instructional Materials on the American Indian*. 1972. Provo, Utah: Brigham Young University Printing Service.
> A more recent edition of this book may exist, but it is invaluable in its guide to videocassettes, audiocassetes, and other nonbook media.

Brokenleg, Marti, and Herbert T. Hoover. 1993. *Yanktona Sioux Water Colors: Cultural Remembrances of John Saul*. Center for Western Studies.
> Watercolor painting of Yanktonai John Saul.

Eagle Walking Turtle and Black Elk. 1987. *Keepers of the Fire*. Santa Fe: Bear.
> Paintings interpret the visions of Black Elk, an Oglala Sioux.

Jacobson, Clair. 1991. *Whitestone Hill*. Augusta, Ga.: Pine Tree.
> Depicts the Whitestone Hill Battle of 1863.

Lame Deer, Archie Fire. 1994. *The Lakota Sweat Lodge Cards: Spiritual Teachings of the Sioux*. Rochester, Vt.: Destiny Books.

Utley, Robert M. 1993. *The Lance and the Shield: The Life and Times of Sitting Bull*. New York: Henry Holt.

## Additional Resources

Inter–Tribal Indian Ceremonial Association
PO Box 1
Church Rock, New Mexico 87311
(505) 863-3865

Canyon Records and Indian Arts
4143 North 16th Street
Phoenix, Arizona 85016
(602) 266-4823

# *Poland*

## Video

*Poland*. 1993. International Video Network. 30 mins.
> Description and travel.

*Poland: A Proud Heritage*. 1989. International Video Network. 55 mins.
> Description and travel.

## Audio Recordings

Ashkenazy, Vladimir. 1987. *Mazurkas*. Decca.
> Double cassette. Chopin's piano music.

Entremont, Philippe, and the New York Philharmonic. 1984. *Chopin: Greatest Hits*. CBS Masterworks.
> Orchestral arrangements of Chopin's piano music.

Polonia Instrumental Ensemble. 1990. *Memories of Poland*. Monitor.
> Folk songs and dance music.

Sowow, Rodzinna Kapela. *Polish Folk Music*. 1979. Polski Nagrania Warszawa.

To'stoki Ensemble and the Krosno Song and Dance Ensemble. 1976. *Polish Folk Songs and Dances*. Folkways.

## Books

### Juvenile

Angel, Ann, and Mary Craig. 1992. *Lech Walesa: A Champion of Freedom for Poland*. Milwaukee, Wis.: Gareth Stevens Children's Books.

Bachrach, Susan D., and the U.S. Holocaust Memorial Museum. 1994. *Tell Them We Remember the Story of the Holocaust*. Boston: Little Brown.
> An excellent resource for upper elementary that includes numerous references to Poland.

Bailey, Donna. 1990. *Poland*. Madison, N.J.: Raintree Steck-Vaughn.

*Eastern Europe*. 1969. New York: Time Life Books. 176 pages.

Green, Carol. 1983. *Poland: Enchantment of the World*. Chicago: Childrens Press.

Haviland, Virginia. 1995. *Favorite Fairy Tales Told in Poland*. Fairfield, N.J.: Beech Tree Books.

Heale, Jay. 1994. *Poland*. North Bellmore, N.Y.: Marshall Cavendish.

Holland, Gini. 1993. *Poland Is My Home*. Milwaukee, Wis.: Gareth Stevens Childrens Books.

Holz, Loretta. 1980. *The Christmas Spider: A Puppet Play from Poland and Other Traditional Games, Crafts, and Activities*. New York: Philomel Books in Cooperation with the U.S. Committee for UNICEF.

Lye, Keith. 1984. *Take a Trip to Poland*. New York: Franklin Watts.

Mark, Michael. 1984. *Toba*. Minneapolis, Minn.: Bradbury.
> Fiction

———. 1985. *Toba at the Hands of a Thief*. Minneapolis, Minn.: Bradbury.
> Fiction.

Michener, James A. 1990. *Pilgrimage: A Memoir or Poland and Rome*. Emmaus, Penn.: Rodale.
> Michener tells of his trip to Poland and Rome and his visits with Lech Walesa and the Pople. Valuable insights into the country and her people. Appropriate for upper elementary.

Obojski, Robert. 1969. *Poland in Pictures*. New York: Sterling.
> Good basic information about Poland with many black-and-white photographs.

Pellowski, Anne, and Charles Mikolaycak. 1980. *The Nine Crying Dolls: A Story from Poland*. New York: Philomel Books, U.S. Committee for UNICEF.

Pfeiffer, Christine. 1991. *Poland, Land of Freedom Fighters*. New York: Dillon Press.

Sandak, Case R. 1986. *Poland*. New York: Franklin Watts.

Saunders, Alan. 1984. *The Invasion of Poland*. New York: Franklin Watts.

Singer, Isaac Bashevis, and Margot Zemach. 1994. *Shrewd Todie and Lyzer the Miser and Other Chilrdren's Stories*. San Francisco: Barefoot Books.
> Short stories.

Skipper, G. C. 1983. *Invasion of Poland*. Chicago: Childrens Press.

Szambelean-Strevinsky, Christine. 1982. *Dark Hour of Noon*. Philadelphia: Lippincott.
> Fictional story about the war and the underground movements from 1939–1945.

Vnenchak, Dennis. 1993. *Lech Walesa and Poland*. New York: Franklin Watts.

*Christmas in Poland*. 1989. Albuquerque, N.M.: World Book.

## Teacher

Holz, Loretta. 1980. *The Christams Spider: A Puppet Play from Poland and Other Traditional Games, Crafts, adn Activities*. New York: Philomel, UNICEF.
> An excellent resource for Polish activities that you can do in the classroom.

Radlowski, Roger Jan, and John Kirvan. 1980. *The Spirit of Poland*. Akron, Oh.: Winston Press.
> Pictorial work.

Sharman, Tim. 1990. *Poland: a Picture Memory*. Avenal, N.J.: Crescent Books.

# Additional Resources

Polish National Tourist Office Information Center
333 North Michigan Avenue. Chicago, Ill. 60601
(312) 236-9013 or (312) 236-9123

# *Sweden*

## Video Recordings

*Faces of Sweden.* 1985. Polonius Films and the International Film Bureau. 26 mins.
Travel video.

*Sweden.* 1991. Chip Taylor Communicatons. 28 mins.
Description and travel.

*Sweden: Nordic Treasure.* 1991. International Video Network. 53 mins.
Description and travel.

## Audio Recordings

Persen, Mari Boine. 1990. *Gula Gula.* Realworld.
Mari Boine is a Sa'mi who has dedicated herself to preserving her people's culture. Gula gula means "hear the voices of the foremothers." The words to her songs are sung in Sa'mi and have English translations. Many of her songs express the cultural struggle of her people, especially the women.

Sjoberg, Saya, and Kai Soderman. 1970. *Best Loved Songs of Sweden.* Monitor.
Folk music of Sweden.

## Books

### Juvenile

Bailey, Donna. 1992. *Sweden: We Live in Sweden.* Madison, N.J.: Raintree Steck-Vaughn.

Bjerner, Tamiko, and MaryLee Knowlton. 1987. *Sweden.* Milwaukee, Wis.: Gareth Stevens.

Dickmeyer, Lowell A. 1993. *Lyndsey Sees the Midnight Sun.* Thornville, Ohio: Gemstone Books.
A fictional soccer adventure.

Fun, Delice Gan Cheng. 1992. *Sweden.* North Bellmore, N.Y.: Marshall Cavendish.

Haviland, Virginia. 1994. *Favorite Fairy Tales Told in Sweden.* Fairfield, N.J.: Beech Tree.

Hintz, Martin. 1985. *Sweden.* Chicago: Childrens Press.

James, Alan. 1989. *Lapps: Reindeer Herders of Lapland.* Vero Beach, Fla.: Rourke.

Langton, Jane. 1994. *The String of Pearls: A Story from Sweden.* New York: Hyperion Books for Children.
Fiction.

Larsson, Carl, and Lennart Rudstrom. 1980. *A Family.* New York: Putnam.

Lindgren, Astrid, and Harald Wiberg. 1989. *The Tomten and the Fox.* New York: Coward-McCann.
Fiction.

Lye, Keith. 1982. *Take a Trip to Sweden*. New York: Franklin Watts.

McDonald, Jo. 1990. *Sweden in Pictures*. Minneapolis, Minn.: The Company and Lerner.

Munson, Sammye. 1994. *Goodbye Sweden, Hello Texas*. Austin, Tex.: Eakin Press.
    Ficton. A story about Swedish immigration to the United States.

Olsson, Kari. 1983. *Sweden: A Good Life for All*. Minneapolis: Dillon.

Price, Susan. 1994. *Ghost Dance*. New York: Farrar, Straus and Giroux.
    Fictional story about the Sami people.

Zickgraf, Ralph. 1988. *Sweden*. New York: Chelsea House.

## Teacher

Beach, Hugh. 1988. *The Sami of Lapland*. New York: Minority Rights Group.

Brask, Per K. 1992. *Aboriginal Voices: Amerindian, Inuit, and Sami Theater*. Baltimore, Md.: Johns Hopkins University Press.

Ehlers, Chad, and Lars Nordstrom. 1990. *Sweden*. Portland, Ore.: Graphic Arts Center.
    Pictorial work about social life and customs.

Madej, Hans. 1985. *Lappland*. Ellert and Richter.

Valkeapaa, Nils-Aslak. 1983. *Greetings from Lappland: the Sami, Europe's Forgotten People*. UK: Zed Press.

*Sweden*. 1985. New York: Time-Life Books.

## Additional Resources

Swedish Consulates in the U.S.
Embassy of Sweden
One Dag Hammarskjold Plaza
New York, N.Y. 10017-2201
(212) 751-5900

Swedish Institute
Box 7474
S–103–91 Stockholm, Sweden
Swedish Institute. "Fact Sheets" Stockholm, Sweden
To order fact sheets in the US. write to:
The Swedish Information Service
One Dag Hammerskjold Plaza
New York, N.Y. 10017-2201

Embassy of Sweden
150 North Michigan Avenue, Suite 1250
Chicago, Ill. 60601
(312) 781-6262

Embassy of Sweden
120 Montgomery Street, Suite 2175
San Francisco, Calif. 94104
(415) 788-2631

Embassy of Sweden
Watergate 600, Suite 1200
600 New Hampshire Avenue NW
Washington, D.C. 20037
(202) 944-5600

# *Tibet*

## Video Recordings

*Discovering China and Tibet*. 1988. Centre Productions and International Video Network.
> Travel video.

*Tibet*. 1988. Paramount.
> Description and travel.

*Tibet: The Lost Nation*. 1989. Jeffrey Iverson and the BBC.
> Documentary.

## Audio Recordings

Gray, Randall. *One Hand Clapping*.
> This recording includes Tibetan Bells with environmental sounds added including: thunder and rain, birds, wind, stream and surf and occasional chanting.

The Gyuto Monks. 1987. *Freedom Chants from the Roof of the World and Tibetan Tantric Choir*. Windham Hill.
> An authentic example of Tibetan chant. The Gyuto Monks are exiled in India.

The Gyuto Monks. *Tibet: Buddhist Chant*. 1990. JVC World Sounds.

*Heart Dance, River Flow*. 1983. Dorje Ling Publishers.
> Tibetan folk music that uses the lingbu, dramiyan, peewan, and yangchin instruments as well as voice.

Moffett, Karma. *Tibetan Soft Bowls*.
> Softly struck Tibetan bowls are featured in this recording.

Wolff, Henry. *Tibetan Bells*. 1973. Antilles.

## Books

### Juvenile

Dorje, Rinjing. 1975. *Tales of Uncle Tompa, the Legendary Rascal of Tibet*.
> Available from the author: Dorje Ling, P.O. Box 1410, San Rafael, Calif. 94902.

Govinda, Li Gotami. 1976. *Tibetan Fantasies: Paintings, Poems, and Music.* Berkeley, Calif.: Dharma.
  Children's poetry and songs.
Halpern, Gina. 1991. *Where Is Tibet?* Ithaca, N.Y.: Snow Lion.
  In Tibetan and English. Available by writing P.O. Box 6483, Ithaca, N.Y. 14850.
Kalman, Bobbie. 1993. *Tibet.* Federal Way, Wash.: Crabtree.
Kendra, Judith. 1994. *Tibetans.* New York: Thomson Learning.
Pilarski, Laura. 1974. *Tibet: Heart of Asia.* New York: Bobbs-Merrill.

## Teacher

Ash, Niema. 1992. *Flight of the Wind Horse: a Journey into Tibet.* North Pomfret, Vt.: Rider.
Barber, Noel. 1960. *The Flight of the Dalai Lama.* North Pomfret, Vt.: Hodder and Stoughton.
Buckley, Michael, and Robert Strauss. 1986. *Tibet: A Travel Survival Kit.* Berkeley, Calif.: Lonely Planet.
David-Neel, Alexandra. 1971. *Magic and Mystery in Tibet.* New York: Dover.
  Description of female explorer's journey into Tibet.
Farwell, Edie, and Anne Hubbell Maiden. 1992. "The Wisdom of Tibetan Childbirth." *In Context: A Quarterly of Humane Sustainable Culture,* 31 (Spring): 26–31.
Gerstein, Mordicai. 1987. *The Mountains of Tibet.* New York: Harper Trophy.
Guise, Anthony. 1988. *The Potala of Tibet.* New York: Stacey.
  Describes the art and structure of the potala in Lhasa.
Gyatso, Tenzin. 1984. *Kindness, Clarity, and Insight: The Fourteenth Dalai Lama.* Trans., ed. by Jeffrey Hopkins. Ithaca, N.Y.: Snow Lion.
*"Icy Hike to School."* 1993. World, March: 30–33.
Iyer, Pico. 1989. "The Tibetan Spirit: Jolly and Rainbowed and Welcoming." *Utne Reader,* March/April: 44–46.
Jensen, Bernard. 1989. *In Search of Shangri-La: A Personal Journey to Tibet.* Garden City Park, N.Y.: Avery.
Ma, Li-hua. 1991. *Glimpses of Northern Tibet.* San Diego, Calif.: Panda.
Majupuria, Indra. 1990. *Tibetan Women, Then and Now.* Mandir Martinez, Calif.: M. Devi.
Rawson, Philip S. 1991. *Sacred Tibet.* New York: Thames and Hudson.
Rowell, Galen, and the Newark Museum. 1990. *My Tibet.* Los Angelas: University of California Press.
  Excellent pictorial with quotations from the Dalai Lama.
Sakya, Jamyang, and Julie Emery. 1990. *Princess in the Land of Snows: The Life of Jamyang Sakya in Tibet.* Boston: Shambhala.
Schaller, George R. 1993. "In a High and Sacred Realm." *National Geographic,* vol. 184, no. 2 (August): 62–87.
Wilby, Sorrel. 1988. *Journey across Tibet.* Chicago: Contemporary Books.

# *Vietnam*

## Video Recordings

*Vietnam: Land of the Ascending Dragon.* 1993. International Video Network.
*Vietnam: Picking up the Pieces.* 1980. Downtown Community TV Center.
*Vietnam: The War that Divided America.* 1987. Center for Humanities.
*Vietnam Revisited.* 1988. T and T Productions.
> Travel guide.

## Audio Recordings

Hai, Tran Quang. *Vietnamese Zither.* 1993. Playa Sound.
> The Vietnamese zither is similar to the Japanese koto, except the zither has metal strings. The music is performed by Tran Quang Hai, who is known worldwide as a musician, performer, and lecturer in universities.

Nguyen, Phong Thuyet. *Traditional Music of Vietnam.* 1980. Lyrichord.

## Books

### Juvenile

Forney, Inor, and E. H. Forney. 1970. *Our Friends in Viet-Nam.* Boston: Charles E. Tuttle.
> A coloring book about the history and life of Vietnamese.

Garland, Sherry. 1990. *Vietnam, Rebuilding a Nation.* New York: Dillon Press.
———. 1992. *Song of the Buffalo Boy.* San Diego, Calif.: Harcourt Brace Jovanovich.
> Fiction.

———. 1993. *The Lotus Seed.* San Diego, Calif.: Harcourt Brace Jovanovich.
> Fiction.

Gibbons, Alan. 1994. *The Jaws of the Dragon.* Chicago: Lerner.
Graham, Gail B. 1970. *The Beggar in the Blanket and Other Vietnamese Tales.* Dial Press.
———. 1972. Cross-Fire: a Vietnam Novel. New York: Pantheon Books.
> Fiction.

Jacobsen, Karen. 1992. *Vietnam.* Chicago: Childrens Press.
Keller, Holly. 1994. *Grandfather's Dream.* New York: Greenwillow.
> Fiction.

Lee, Jeanne M. 1987. *Ba Nam.* Henry Hold.
> Fiction.

MacMillan, Dianne, and Dorothy Freeman. 1987. *My Best Friend, Duc Tran: Meeting a Vietnamese-American family.* New York: Julian Messner.
Norland, Patricia. 1991. *Vietnam.* Milwaukee, Wis.: Gareth Stevens Children's Books.

Nuyen, Chi. 1985. *Cooking the Vietnamese Way.* Chicago: Lerner.

Parker, Lewis K. 1994. *Vietnam.* Vero Beach, Fla. Rourke Book.

Roland, Donna. 1985. *Grandfather's Stories from Viet Nam.* San Diego, Calif.: Open My World Publishing.
    Includes activities.

Ruttledge, Paul. 1987. *The Vietnamese in America.* Chicago: Lerner.

Seah, Audrey. 1994. *Vietnam.* North Bellmore, N.Y.: Marshall Cavendish.

Stanck, Muriel. 1985. *We Came From Vietnam.* New York: Albert Whitman.

Surat, Michele Marid. 1983. *Angel Child, Dragon Child.* New York: Scholastic.

Tr'an, Van Di'en. 1983. *A Shadow on the Wall and Other Stories.* Lincolnwood, Ill.: National Textbook.

———. 1985. *The Bridge of Reunion and Other Stories.* Lincolnwood, Ill.: National Textbook.

———. 1987. *Magic Cross Bow and Other Stories.* Lincolnwood, Ill.: National Textbook.
    Van Di'en's books comprise a series of bilingual books of Vietnamese folktales.

Tran-Kranh-Tuyet. 1987. *The Little Weaver of Thai-Yen Village.* Chicago: Childrens Book Press.
    The cruelty of war is depicted in this bilingual book for young children.

*Vietnam in Pictures.* 1994. Milwaukee, Wis.: The Company and Lerner Publications.

Wormser, Richard. 1993. *Three Faces of Vietnam.* New York: Franklin Watts.

Wright, David K. 1989a. *The Story of the Vietnam Memorial.* Chicago: Childrens Press.

———. 1989b. *The Story of the Vietnam Veterans Memorial.* Chicago: Childrens Press.

———. 1989c. *Vietnam.* Chicago: Childrens Press.

———. 1989d. *The War in Vietnam.* Chicago: Childrens Press.

———. 1989e. *A Wider War.* Chicago: Childrens Press.

———. 1993. *Vietnam Is My Home.* Chicago: Childrens Press.

## Teacher

Balaban, John. 1974. *Vietnamese Folk Poetry.* Petaluma, Calif.: Unicorn Press.

Dane, Barbara, ed. 1969. *The Vietnam Songbook.* Brentway, Tex.: The Guardian.

Nielsen, Jon. 1969. *Artist in South Vietnam.* New York: Julian Messner.
    Vietnam in art.

Robertson, Dorothy Lewis. 1968. *Fairy Tales From Vietnam.* New York: Dodd, Mead.

Shalant, Phyllis. 1988. *Look What We've Brought You From Vietnam: Crafts, Games, Recipes, Stories, and Other Cultural Activities from New Americans.* New York: Simon and Schuster.

Stuart, Anh Thu. 1986. *Vietnamese Cooking: Recipes My Mother Taught Me.* New York: Angus and Robertson.

Tran, Paula. 1990. *Living and Cooking Vietnamese.* San Antonio, Tex.: Corona.

*Vietnam Heroes: The Long Ascending Cry: Memories and Recollections in Story and Poem.* 1985. New Castle, Del.: American Poetry and Literature Press.

# Two more excellent resources by Chris Brewer

Listen to the heartbeat of your students
## RHYTHMS OF LEARNING
### *Creative Tools for Developing Lifelong Skills*
by Don G. Campbell and Chris Boyd Brewer
Grades K–12

Here are more than 75 classroom activities to boost learning and provide opportunities for personal growth.

Learn about physical and emotional highs and lows to promote a learning environment that is nonstressful and focused. Specific activities for teachers precede and complement the student activities.

- ◆ Discover the best learning modes of your students
- ◆ Learn to use music, art, movement, and drama to promote optimal learning
- ◆ Use effective rhythms of presentation in your teaching
- ◆ Learn to use the methods of Lozanov and Tomatis and the techniques of accelerated learning

317 pages, 7" x 9", softbound.
**ZB21-W . . . $24.95**

Enhance self-concept and reduce discipline problems
## FREEDOM TO FLY
### *101 Activities for Building Self-Worth*
by Chris Brewer
Grades 3–8

Stimulate students' self-esteem and encourage creativity. Promote student feelings of self-worth with 101 activities you can use in all subjects. Students will learn how to set goals, to solve problems, and to manage their energy levels. You can select from a wide variety of activities that support these concepts—

- ◆ The emotional body, energy cycles and circles, identity
- ◆ Listening, expressing, communicating, balancing
- ◆ Life processes, life experiences, life visions
- ◆ Teaching rhythm, sound environment, bonding, learning space

224 pages, 8 1/2" x 11", softbound.
**ZB46-W . . . $29**

## CALL, WRITE, OR FAX FOR YOUR FREE CATALOG!